MW01625627

Beverly Hallam

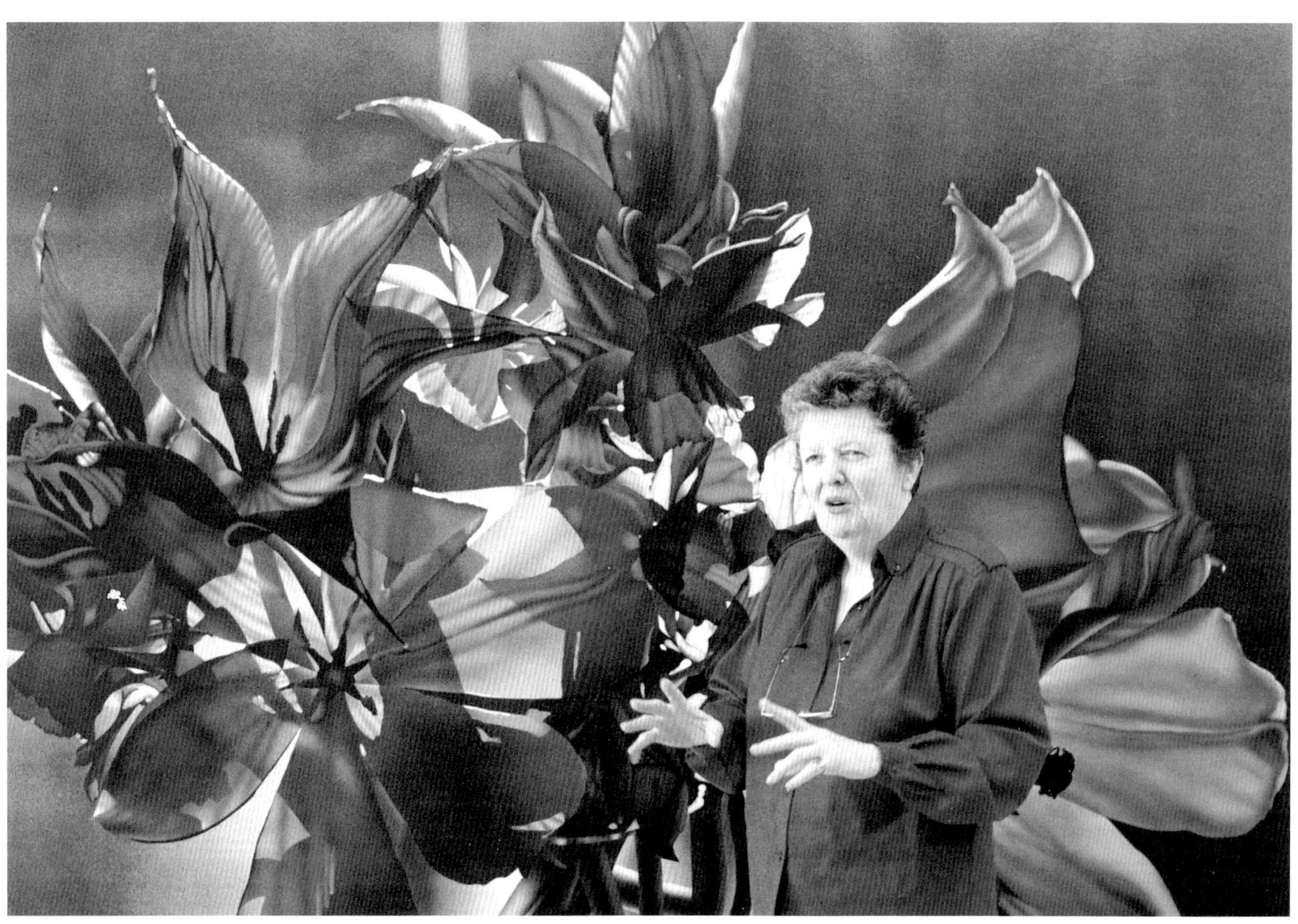

Photo by Edward F. Dana

Beverly Hallam
An Odyssey in Art

by Carl Little

Whalesback Books
Washington, D.C.

Whalesback Books is an imprint of Howells House
Box 9546 Washington, D.C. 20016

Edited by Mellen Candage

Produced by
Chameleon Books, Inc.
31 Smith Road
Chesterfield, MA 01012

Book and cover design: Arnold Skolnick
Editorial Assistant: Laura J. MacKay
Copy Editor: Jamie Nan Thaman
Indexer: Nancy Crompton
Printed (alk paper) in Hong Kong by
O. G. Printing Productions Ltd.

Library of Congress Cataloging-in-Publication Data

Little, Carl.
Beverly Hallam : an odyssey in art / by Carl Little.
p. cm.
Includes bibliographical references and index.
ISBN 0-929590-18-X (alk paper)
1. Hallam, Beverly, 1923– . 2. Artists—United States–
–Biography. I. Title
N6537.H3358L58 1998
709′.2—dc21 97–39962
CIP

Acknowledgements

I thank Beverly Hallam and Mary-Leigh Call Smart for their gracious hospitality during several visits to their marvelous home in York. I am indebted to W. Dean Howells for his constant belief in this book and this amazing artist. I also salute Arnold Skolnick and Laura MacKay for their invaluable work in producing this book.

I make a special dedication to my father, John W. Little, poet, writer, and master of the asparagus; and to Peggy, Emily, and James, one awesome threesome.

C. L.

Photo credits

All photography by Beverly Hallam except as follows: Douglas Armsden: pages 55 (left, left middle), 65, 70 (right, lower left), 75, 76, 77, 79 (left), 80, 81, 84, 89, 91, 92, 93, 94, 96, 97, 98, 102, 104, 106, 111, 112, 114, 116, 118, 119, 121. Christopher Ayres: 2, 3, 4. Betsey Baybut: 62. Jon Bonjour: 98. Barney Burnstein: 30 (top). George M. Cushing: 34 (top), 66. Edward Hipple: 29, 31, 34 (bottom), 37 (bottom), 45, 46, 71. Ernestine Mosman Lyman: 58. Alessandro Macone, Inc.: 40 (left). Joshua Nefsky: 123. Nathan Rabin: 102. Gary Samson: 81. Arnold Skolnick: 5 (left). Philip A. Stack: 55 (top).

Contents

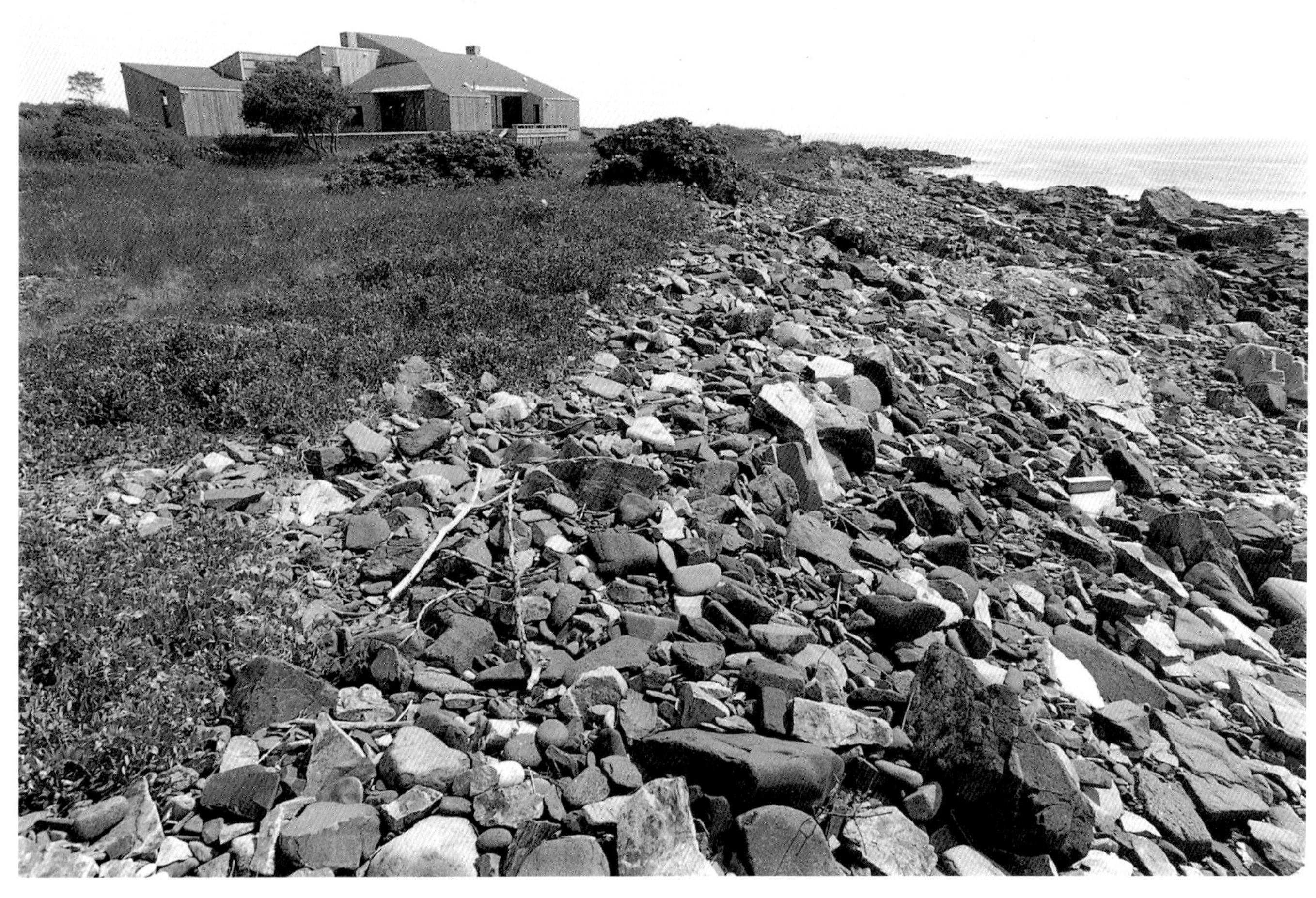

Surf Point, York, Maine, June 1988

Introduction

When we consider the art of Beverly Hallam, we find more than half a century of work. From a meticulous tempera rendering of a grasshopper, which she painted as a student at the Massachusetts School (now College) of Art in 1942, to the magnificent acrylic flower paintings of the past 15 years, Hallam has pursued her art with vigor and passion.

We also find an artist of exceptional inventiveness and creative range. Hallam is a brilliant collagist who also happens to be a master of the airbrush. Her work can be as representational as a well-composed Maine landscape, as abstract as a Kandinsky-esque study of electronic circuitry. There is profound beauty in her large-scale still lifes of flowers and wicked humor in her surreal lobster-and-shell assemblages. And reviewers have more than once noted that Hallam's photography can stand on its own as a significant artistic achievement.

A partial list of the materials Hallam has used in her art makes a fascinating and unusual inventory. Over the years, these have included black oil, encaustic, gray brick, mica talc, gold leaf, mirrors, mylar, automotive spray paint, cast stone, sand, lobster shells, and cigarette butts. She has also worked in oil, pastel, conté crayon, and pen and ink, frequently mixing one or more of them to come up with decidedly unorthodox effects.

A pioneer and an inventor, Hallam has explored mediums and techniques as diverse as polyvinyl acetate—better known as acrylic—monotype, and stencils. For this artist, "exploration" involves a meticulous, almost scientific, approach to technique, with experiments carried out over time with care and concentration. Writing in *The Boston Globe*, Robert Taylor invoked the work of Man Ray, one of the most innovative artists of this century, in describing Hallam's art.

Hallam had visited Maine since childhood and has lived on the southern coast of Maine for 35 years, since 1974 at Surf Point in York. The natural surroundings of her home are what first strike the visitor. The landscape one encounters at the end of a spruce-shaded winding road is wide open to the elements. It is almost a plain, an illusion that is strengthened as one drives up the long driveway to the contemporary, gray, cedar-sided house. Beyond lies the Atlantic, with just a glimpse of the Isles of Shoals to the south.

In her book *A House By the Sea* (1977), May Sarton wrote of the origins of Hallam's home in this idyllic setting:

> ...My friends Mary-Leigh Smart and Beverly Hallam came over [and] were full of excitement as they had just bought an old estate on the coast near York and were in the midst of making plans to

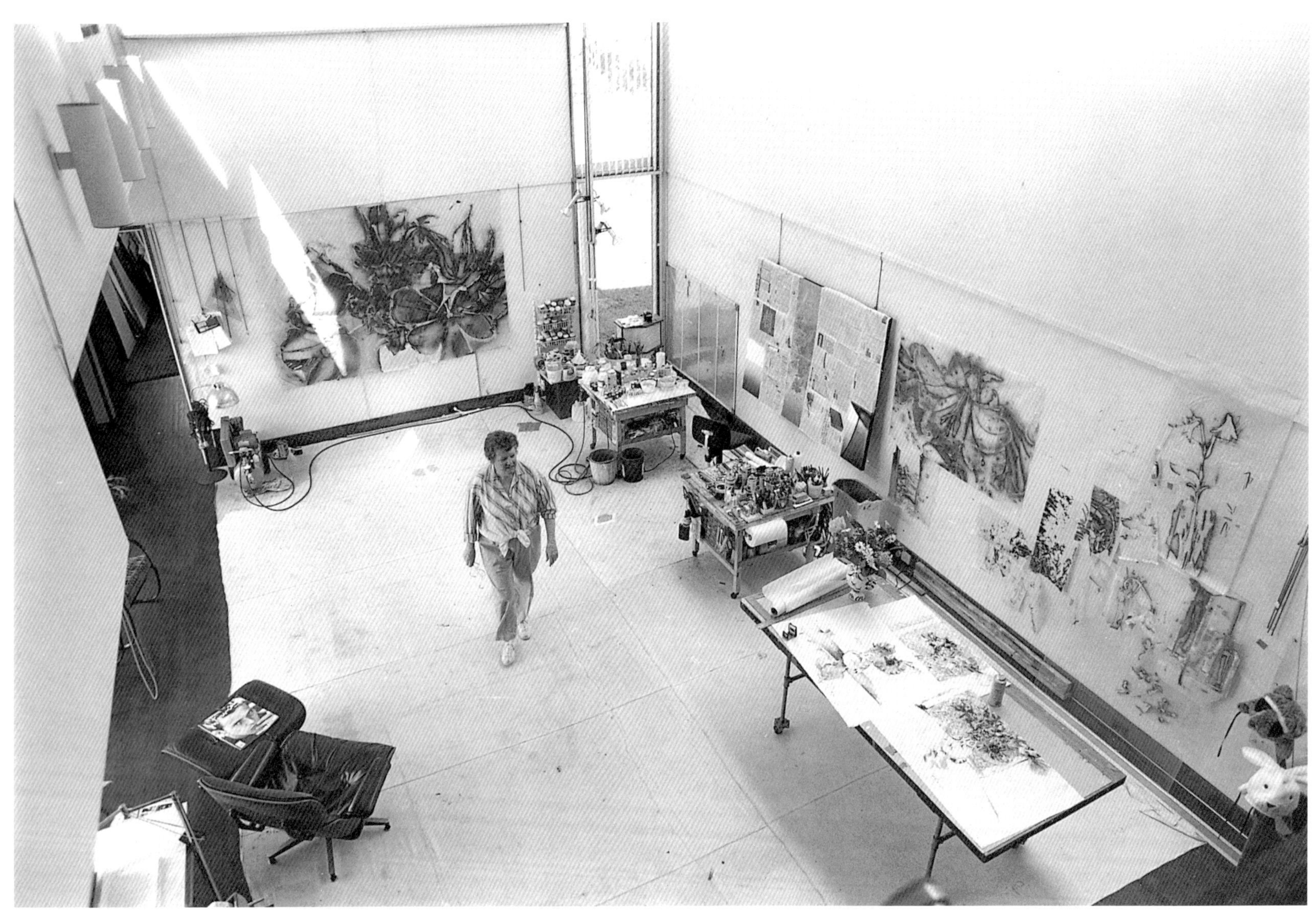

Hallam in her studio
at Surf Point, York, Maine, June 1988
Behind her: used stencil from *Thalia with Tulips*
Side wall: used stencil from *Golden Splendor*

build a modern house right on the rocks. They described vividly the combination of open fields, rocky beaches, ponds, a swamp, and the big woods at the back, and showed me photographs, and I listened.

Hallam built this house with her longtime friend and companion, Mary-Leigh Smart, an art consultant and patron who, with her late husband, the actor and radio personality J. Scott Smart, helped found the Barn Gallery in Ogunquit. Hallam and Smart designed the layout for the house, dividing it into two sections, creating a horizontal duplex of sorts, with common areas in the middle and an indoor pool on the ocean side.

It doesn't take long to realize that this is a house of art. The walls of the entrance hallway serve as a gallery, for both Hallam and Smart are avid collectors, and there is a guest book awaiting the signatures of visitors—artists, curators, writers, friends, and family. The glowing remarks alongside the signatures of those who have visited Surf Point speak of a warm and welcoming place.

Entering Hallam's half of the house on a sunny day is like stepping into

Surf Point Studio, 1992
End wall: *Thalia with Tulips*; on table: *Amaryllis*
Side wall: *Orange Prince*, *Canada Lilies*, *Bouquet Shadow*

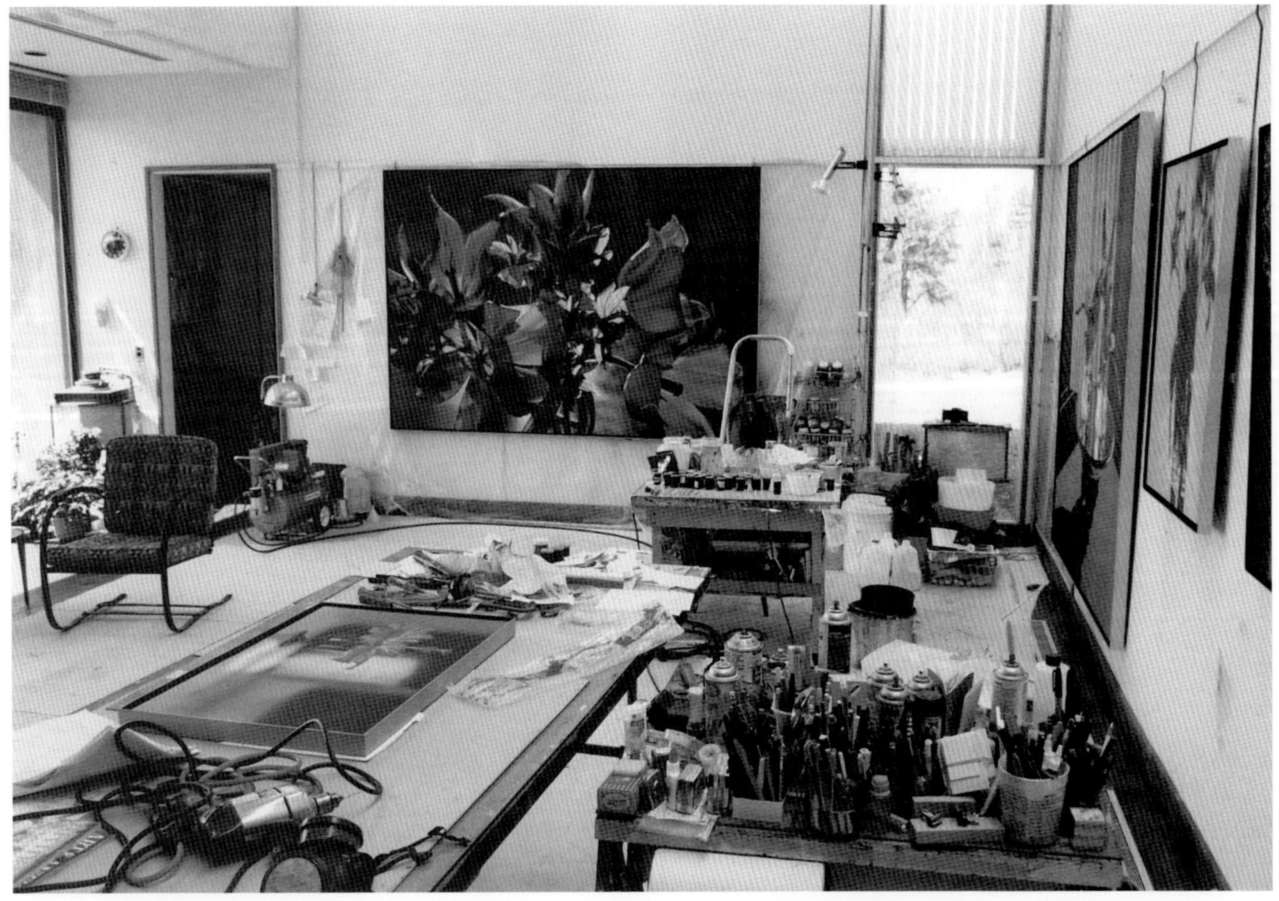

one of her paintings. There is the round dining table that has served as the setting for many of her flower canvases. Around the table are other elements from her paintings—the vertical blinds she adjusts to create the right light for her still lifes, a vase holding a single flower or simple bouquet, and the shadows that so intrigue her.

A few steps further is the studio, a large, light-filled space broken up by work tables, easels, and art supplies. The compressor for the airbrush sits in the corner at the ready; postcards and amusing quotations are pinned to the wall; pictures lean here and there; and magazines form a small pile on a stool. In an adjoining room, art books fill a wall from floor to ceiling. Here, an assortment of different-sized gelatin rollers, which Hallam uses in her monotype work, hang at eye level. This is also where mats are dropped in and frames are fitted.

Hallam's studio is a working artist's space, comfortably informal yet tidy. The room measures 22 by 28 feet, with the high ceiling sloping from 18 to 13 feet. The main light is south, controlled by narrow, horizontal blinds. Having worked in studios with north light for far too long, Hallam

Work table with air compressor (far right) in studio.

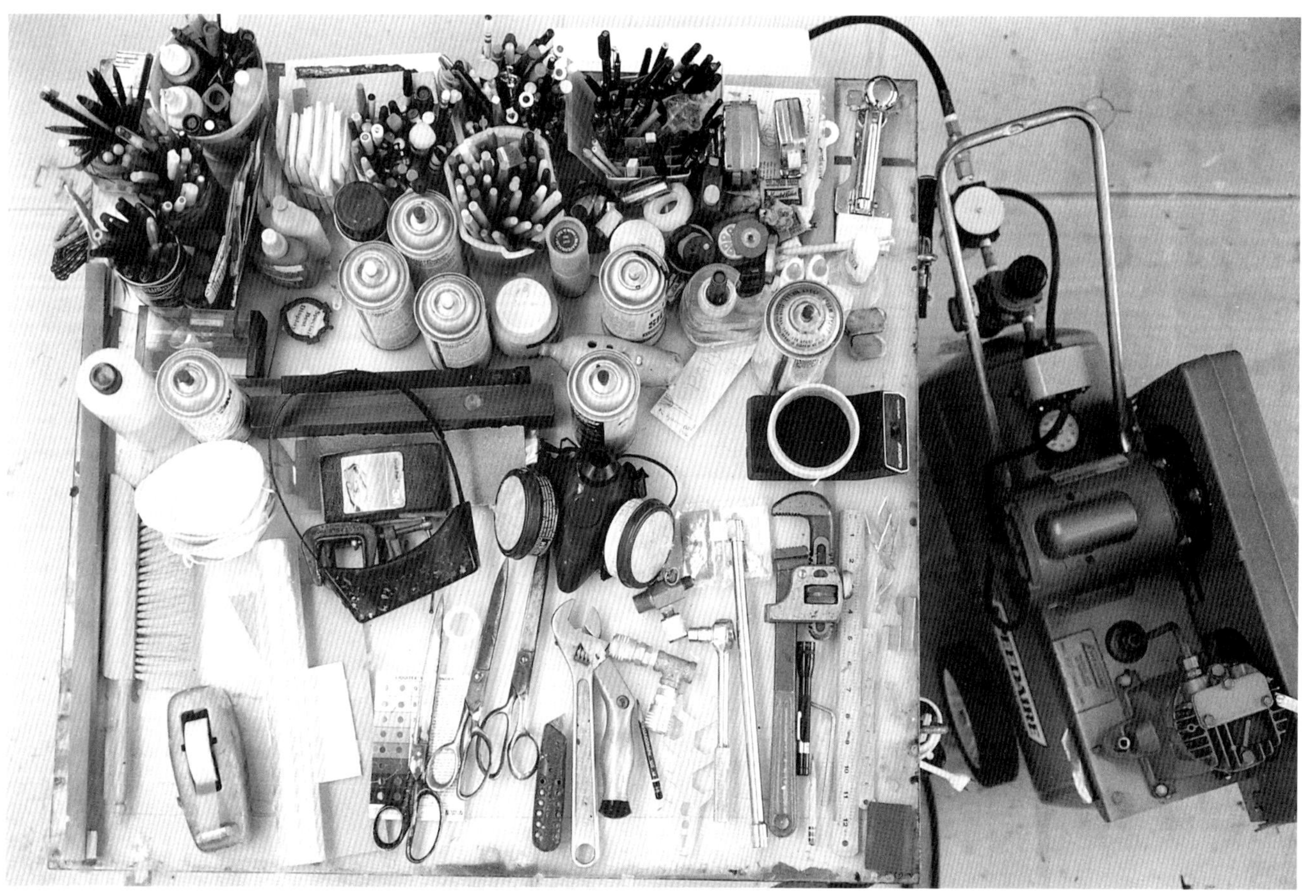

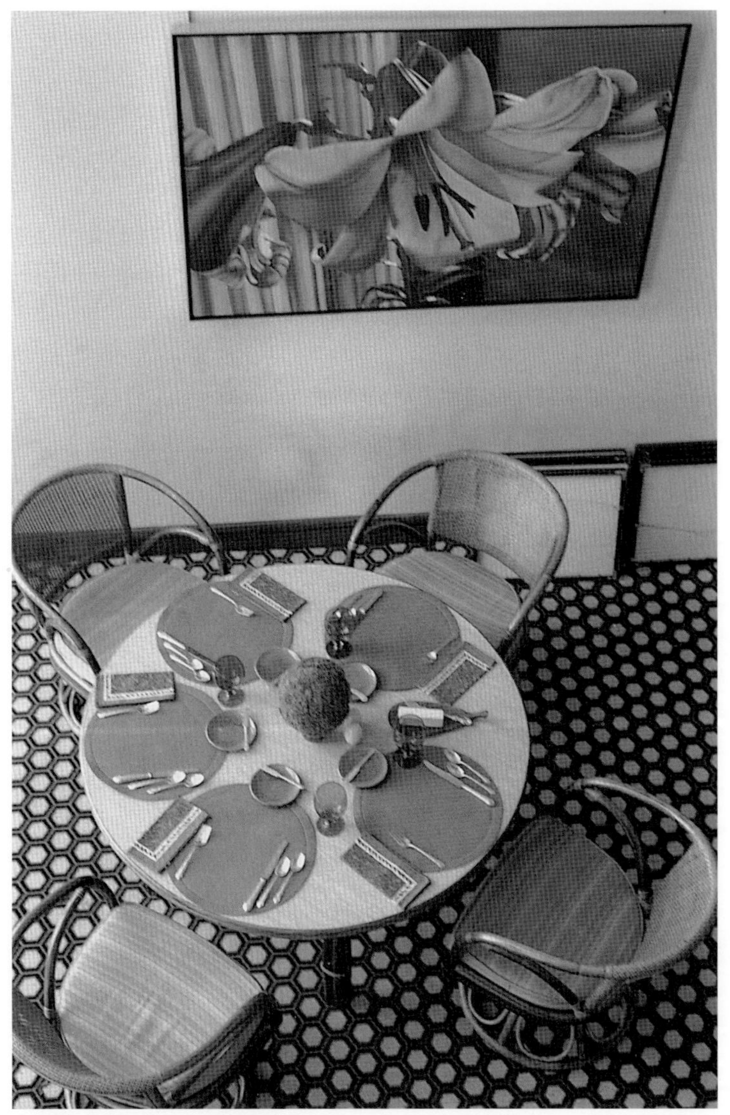

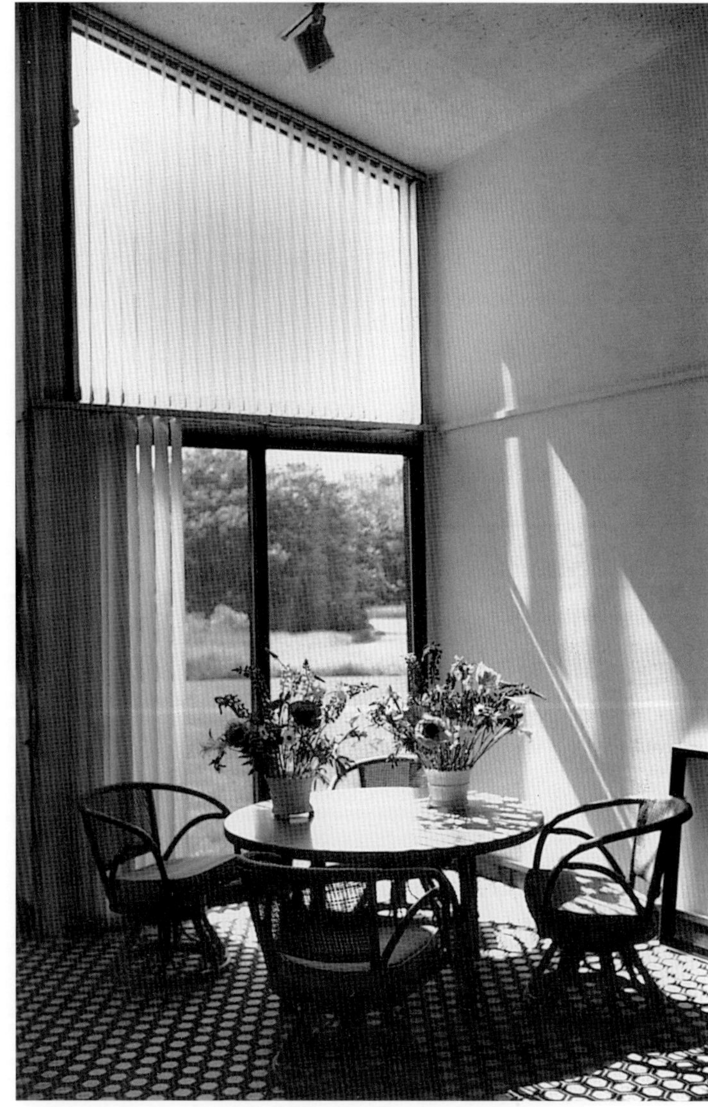

Left: Hallam dining room

Right: Dining room table

had determined that if she ever built her own space she would have the south light enjoyed by one of her favorite painters, Georges Braque. She has never regretted that decision, noting that if she has to mix a color and make a true match, she simply goes into the next room, which features north light.

A long ceiling skylight slants north and a long narrow window faces west. The wall facing the Atlantic consists of four large sliding glass doors. Hallam's design called for all the interior doors to be placed at the far end of walls, leaving large uninterrupted spaces for displaying paintings. To avoid pounding nails into the wall, she had a narrow, flat-faced molding installed to which moveable Lynch hangers are hooked.

Hallam is exacting in her specifications; she researches everything, from art supplies to cuisine. She will tell you the fluorescent banks of lights in the ceiling are Criticolor Verd-A-Ray F40 tubes used in cosmetic schools. Other lights are 150-watt floods, and there are spots mounted on tracks. The floor, which is dark hardwood over sleepers, is covered with stretched heavy white painter's dropcloth. The cloth is wonderful, says Hallam, for reflecting light, and it protects the floor when she gessoes her canvases. The walls are painted an off-white, with a cool, slightly green tint.

Hallam has had several studios in the course of her career and each has been intimately associated with her work of the period. Her first space was just off the Lasell Junior College campus in Auburndale, Massachusetts, at the home of her friend Inez Atwater. Some of Hallam's earliest work in polyvinyl acetate was done there.

When she needed more room, Hallam rented a space in the Fenway Studios on Ipswich Street in Boston. Upon moving to Maine, she used the studio of J. Scott Smart, who was also a painter and sculptor, and another named "Stonecrop," both in Ogunquit. From these spaces, Hallam made exploratory excursions along the Maine coast, discovering motifs such as the mussel shell and Bald Head Cliff near Ogunquit, subjects of some of her best-known paintings.

Yet it is the studio she built in York that has most delighted her. Here, Hallam has continued to forge new visual languages, and gained ingenuity and authority in her aesthetic pursuits. Technically expert—and a teacher and lecturer of the first order—she is above all an artist, ever seeking new visions even as she lets her curiosity and talent carry her into heretofore unknown territories.

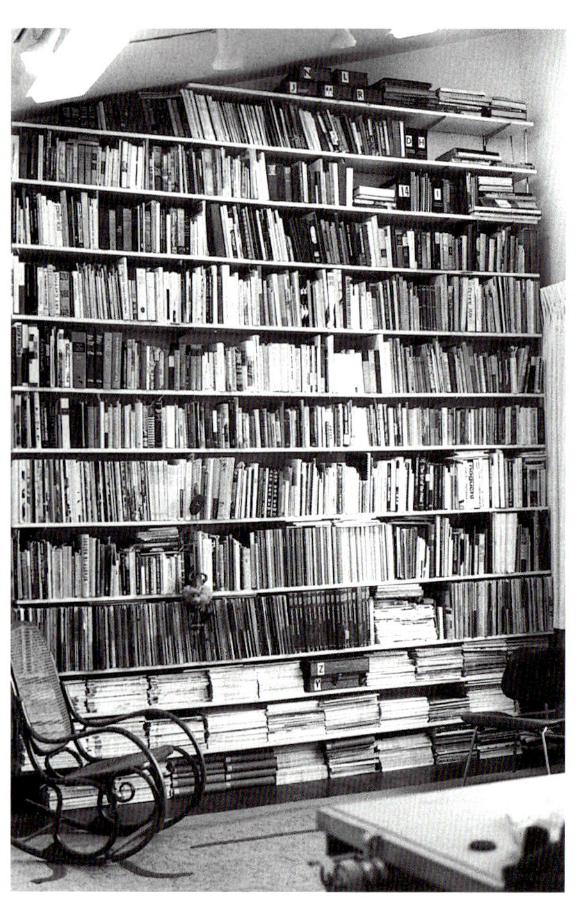

Part of Hallam's library

2

Origins

The course of an artist's life is rarely predictable. The happenstance of birthplace, parentage, education, and travel; of studio space and location; of friends and patronage—all these elements and more shape the individual and his or her sensibility.

When Beverly Hallam speaks of her ancestors, one senses the connections, the threads of influence and inspiration stretching across the years. On her father's side, Hallam comes from a line of inventors and craftsmen. Her English-born great-grandfather devised a staging contrivance used to build church steeples. Her grandfather, Thomas J. Hallam, was born in Massachusetts and worked as a machinist for United Shoe, where he invented an apparatus that made eyelets for footwear. Her paternal grandmother, Sarah Johnson, came to America from Nottingham, England, renowned for its lacemakers. The legacy of this last art can be found in the elaborate stencil friskets that play a crucial role in the making of Hallam's extraordinary flower paintings.

Hallam's father, Edwin Francis Hallam (1900-1990), was an engineer. As a youth he built his own short-wave radio and at one point was the youngest licensed radio operator in the United States. His license was signed by Guglielmo Marconi. A graduate of the Massachusetts Institute of Technology, during World War I he served as a wireless operator in the Navy and illustrated artillery manuals. In World War II, he designed turbines for General Electric, which was busy outfitting aircraft and submarines. Hallam thinks back on her father's engineering skills when she does anything mechanical, such as taking apart the compressor for her airbrush.

Hallam's mother, Alice Linney, was born in Lewiston, Maine, in 1901. She studied to be a pianist and took lessons in aesthetic dancing, but gave up music when she married Beverly's father. During the Depression she mastered the skills of hairstyling, eventually setting up a successful salon.

Alice Hallam relates meeting Leonard Bernstein's father, Sam, who sold hairdressing supplies. One day they got talking about their kids. "You can't imagine what my son Lennie wants to be," said Mr. Bernstein. "He wants to be a composer...of music...a musician! Can you believe it? I can't stand it." He then asked Alice what her daughter wanted to do. "She's going to be an artist," Beverly's mother proudly answered. "Oh my God," Bernstein replied, "they're both going to starve to death!"

When she retired from hairdressing, Alice became an inspector of gyroscopes for General Electric during World War II. Later, Alice bought a kiln and taught herself enameling on copper, making jewelry and decorative dishes. According to Beverly Hallam, her mother was one of the first people to melt Venetian glass gold beads and glass chunks into enamel. Alice's mother, Nettie Frazier Farnum, did beautiful weaving and needlework; she was also mechanically inclined and could repair anything around the house. Clearly, Alice and Nettie were ideal models for a budding artist.

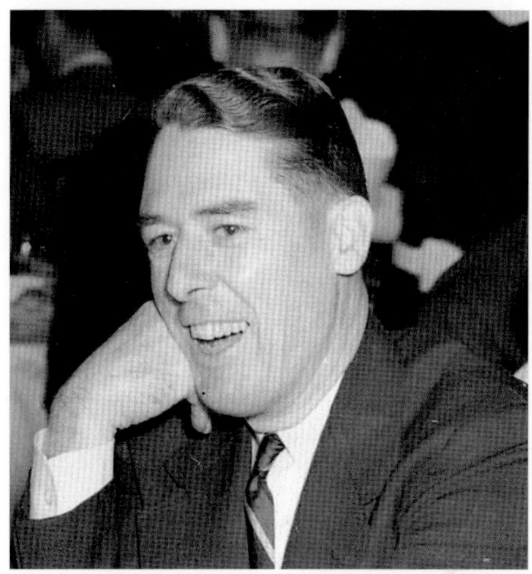

Edwin Francis Hallam

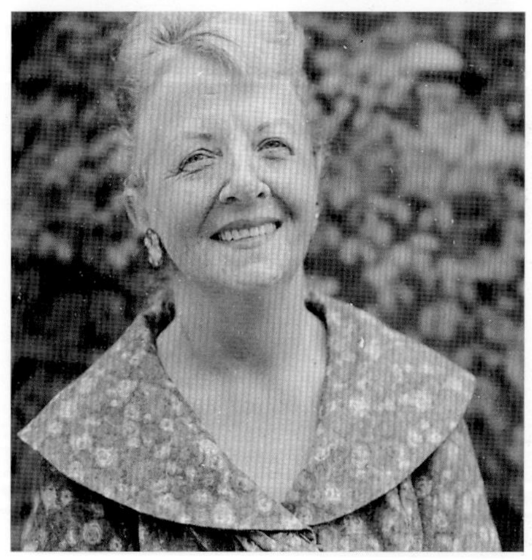

Alice Linney Murphy

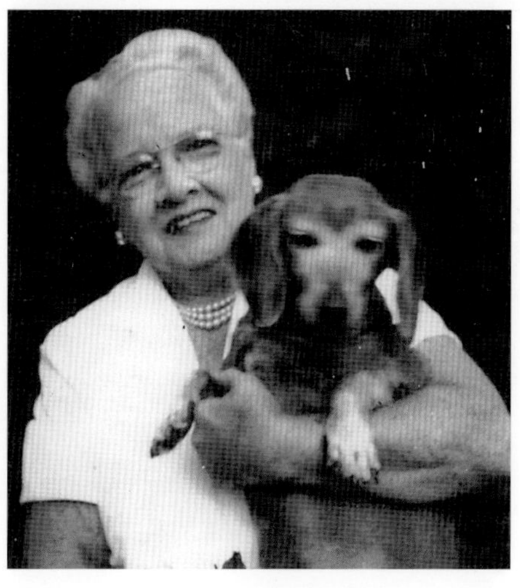

Nettie Frazier Farnum

3

First Impressions

Beverly Hallam was born in Lynn, Massachusetts, in 1923. A shy child, she remembers playing with an erector set and tinker toys, and owning a chemistry set whose contents she loved looking at so much she never used it. She also recalls buying magic tricks at Howe's Rubber Store in Lynn.

On her way to school, Hallam walked through a cemetery where she often found new graves and new flowers. She studied the bouquets and looked up the different floral varieties in the library. It was in this cemetery, Hallam believes, that her love of flowers was born.

Another early inspiration for her lifelong love of flowers was viewing the Ware Collection of glass flowers in the Botanical Museum of Harvard University. These marvelous glass models, created by Leopold and Rudolph Blaschka, artist-naturalists from northern Bohemia, left an indelible impression on Hallam.

At age six, while in first grade at the Lynn Woods School, Beverly decided that she wanted to be a doctor. So serious was her ambition, she accompanied a physician, who lived across the street, on his rounds. He outfitted her with a black bag, stethoscope, bottles of tapioca, bandages, and a thermometer that Hallam recalls was 10 inches long. She even had printed pads on which to write her prescriptions. This career came to an abrupt end when she saw blood for the first time.

As a child, Hallam was musically inclined. She played piano by ear and mastered the clarinet and saxophone. Today she has lost none of her love of music and has an enormous record collection—matched only by her extensive art library.

Hallam the artist began to emerge early. She recalls discovering her mother's rouge as a toddler. Starting with a mural on her bedroom wall, she went on to paint her arms and face. The precocious artist also made "earthworks," using ashes from the fireplace to create patterns on the carpet.

Some of Hallam's earliest drawings were imitations of the shapes of animals in Howard Garis's *Uncle Wiggily* books. A rabbit dressed as a gentleman in black top hat and tails, Uncle Wiggily was very inventive, building devices to outsmart the bad guys—to discourage them, not to hurt them. Hallam saw Uncle Wiggily as "clever, very logical, and also a prankster, full of fun"—a good description of herself as the creator of surreal and witty assemblages.

Crayon drawings of cowboys and, later, comic figures captured Hallam's fancy, with Dick Tracy her favorite. At the age of 10, she reports, she graduated to movie stars, "...always men like Warner Baxter and Spencer Tracy. I did big heads in charcoal." Hallam would do little portraiture later in her life, although, like Arthur Dove, she did some remarkable evocations of individuals using assemblage; both artists depicted "The

Critic" in this manner.

Box camera photography caught Hallam's interest early on, and she took her first serious photograph with an Argus C-3 camera in 1937 at the age of 14. Her mother had bought her a developing and contact-printing kit; a small closet was appropriated for processing, while the family bathtub served for washing the prints. The Argus C-3 was replaced by a Kodak Monitor camera with a flash attached when Hallam attended Lynn English High School. She photographed school activities and sports and was also humor editor of the school magazine.

Hallam's first job was with Sanborn Studios in Lynn, which specialized in portraits and had a large processing laboratory. She gathered wet prints from the washer and placed them on the canvas of a huge drum ferrotype dryer.

One early photograph, a black-and-white study of gladiolas, has stamped on the back "Sep 17, 1938." Hallam was 15 years old. A significant accomplishment for a teenager, the photograph has sharp focus, capturing the shadow play of the bright blossoms that have been set against a dark background. Already Hallam shows herself enamored of flowers, and how they can be arranged to maximize their beauty and mystery.

At the same time, working with the camera helped train Hallam's eye to compose and capture the essence of a scene. She once told an interviewer that upon graduating from high school her dream was "to go to New York and be [the photographer] Margaret Bourke-White"—a very glamorous aspiration for the young artist.

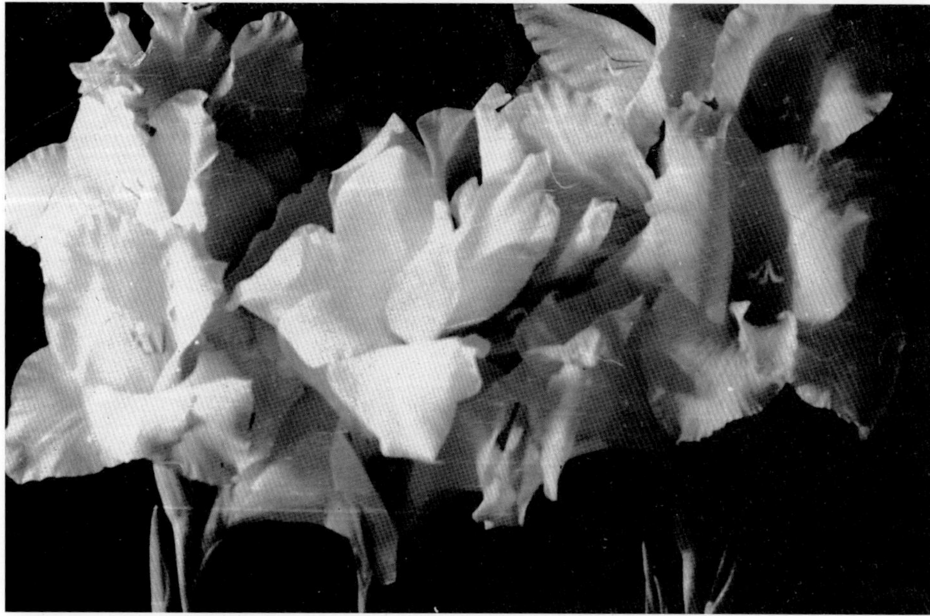

Gladiolas, 1938, PHOTOGRAPH

4

Education

Some artists cultivate a "self-taught" image, but Beverly Hallam openly pays homage to the teachers who encouraged her, from grade school on, to pursue art. By her own account, she was blessed with an excellent art education.

Hallam recalls first taking drawing seriously in fourth grade. Her account of how this came about speaks volumes about the importance of exposure to art in one's youth, even to simplistic exercises led, in this case, by an "art supervisor" at the once-a-week art lesson. Armed with brown crayon and an 8-by-10-inch sheet of manila paper, Hallam and her classmates followed the teacher as she "grew a tree" on the blackboard. At that moment she felt as if she were on her way to becoming an artist.

Later, Hallam recognized that the art supervisor's method of teaching stymied creativity: the children were merely copying and making identical trees. At the time, however, this cursory lesson led to her drawing at home and taking all the art classes available in junior high school, where, under the direction of Stephen Thornton, she learned the rudiments of composition through designing posters.

Hallam's first significant teacher was Anne Wainwright Carleton (1878-1968), who taught art at Lynn English High School. A student of Charles Woodbury, the famed Boston-Ogunquit artist, Carleton had studied at the Art Students League in New York City and at the Ecole d'Art in Paris, where the great Russian artist Archipenko taught her sculpture.

Carleton favored an impressionist approach to painting. At Ogunquit she was close to painters Mabel May Woodward and Gertrude Fiske, among others. When Hallam knew her, she was pursuing what the authors of *A Century of Color: Ogunquit, Maine's Art Colony 1886-1986* called "new trends in the art world."

In a tribute written on the occasion of Carleton's memorial service in 1968, Hallam remembered her mentor's special appeal to students:

> She attracted the sensitive mind and spent her life encouraging people...to find their own expression and the expression of the times....She never praised unless she felt it was worth it, and then it was without end. Her attack was matter-of-fact, with both barrels quietly aimed and a smile. She knew you.

In addition to being a very imaginative instructor (Hallam recalls that she brought a live goat to class one day for the students to draw), Carleton was well known for successfully advising hundreds of students in the preparation of their portfolios for entrance to art school. Many of her protégés, including Hallam, went on to become teachers, supervisors, art directors and executives, designers, painters, and sculptors.

Carleton did not realize that Hallam had decided on an art career, and that she had quietly procured the application forms for the Massachusetts School of Art. Upon learning this, she immediately arranged to stay after school for several days to coach her pupil, training Beverly to draw everything she predicted would be on the entrance exam.

Among the setups was a wastebasket placed on its side on a table, which Carleton instructed Beverly to draw from a series of different angles. Hallam recalls "the big day":

> I arrived at the Massachusetts School of Art with about fifty other scared kids. A committee interviewed me and looked at my portfolio. Then we were all taken to a huge studio. There in the center of drawing easels was a complicated still life, including a butter firkin similar to the wastebasket that I had learned to draw in perspective. I whizzed around that room and positioned myself in front of the firkin at the angle I knew I could draw. Here was everything that Miss Carleton had drilled into me. I passed with eleven points out of a possible fifteen.

Carleton was thrilled with her student's success; in Hallam's words, "I saved her reputation and she started my career." The two became close friends and often corresponded. Carleton invited Beverly to visit her in Ogunquit, the well-known artist colony on the southern coast of Maine that in its heyday featured two summer art schools. Carleton rented a renovated fish shack from the Riverside Hotel, overlooking picturesque Perkins Cove and next to Charles Woodbury's studio.

On her one-day visit to Ogunquit, Hallam remembers seeing Woodbury give a critique on the rocks outside his large studio. The ladies wore wide-brimmed hats. Carleton introduced her guest to Woodbury, whom Hallam recalls as being "very dapper, with a goatee and knickers." That Woodbury (1864-1940) had also been born in Lynn and had attended Lynn English High School must have been reassuring to the young painter. Surely this initial impression of the artistic milieu in Maine played a part in Hallam's move to Ogunquit when she became a full-time artist.

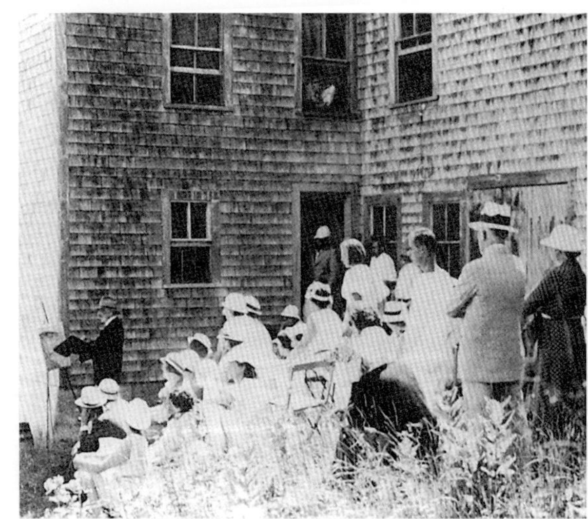

Charles Woodbury giving a Saturday critique

5

Art School

Hallam's decision to go to the Massachusetts School of Art in Boston came about through a chance meeting. One day, she spied a young man pouring plaster of Paris molds in the yard next door to her home in Lynn. He turned out to be Allison Macomber, a sculptor, who designed patterns on coins, medals, and flatware for Towle and other silver companies to supplement his income.

Introducing herself, Hallam mentioned that she was interested in photography and wanted to study in New York City, but that her mother felt she was too young to go off alone. Macomber recommended the Massachusetts School of Art, his alma mater. There, he said, Hallam could learn the basics of design.

Macomber not only encouraged Hallam to head for Boston but also took her under his wing. Together, they went on art-seeing trips to the Isabella Stewart Gardner Museum in Boston to study Anders Zorn's etchings. Macomber taught Hallam how to etch and expanded her knowledge of printmaking.

Hallam also recalls stunt flying with Macomber, who had his pilot's license. Every Sunday, the two of them would take to the skies in the cockpit of an open 65-horsepower biplane. Macomber, a skilled airman, became a bombardier in World War II. After the war, he taught sculpture at Boston College and also fashioned architectural works in bronze throughout the United States and Europe. He is perhaps best known for his bronze busts of Knute Rockne and Babe Ruth in the Football and Baseball Halls of Fame.

Hallam formally enrolled at the Massachusetts School of Art in the fall of 1941, at the outset of World War II. The school's curriculum was intense; all courses were required with no electives. "We all spent long hours working very hard and nobody complained. I feel that this diversified training has stood me in good stead throughout my life," she has noted.

Grasshopper, 1942
Tempera on illustration board, 3 3/4 x 10 in.
Collection of the artist

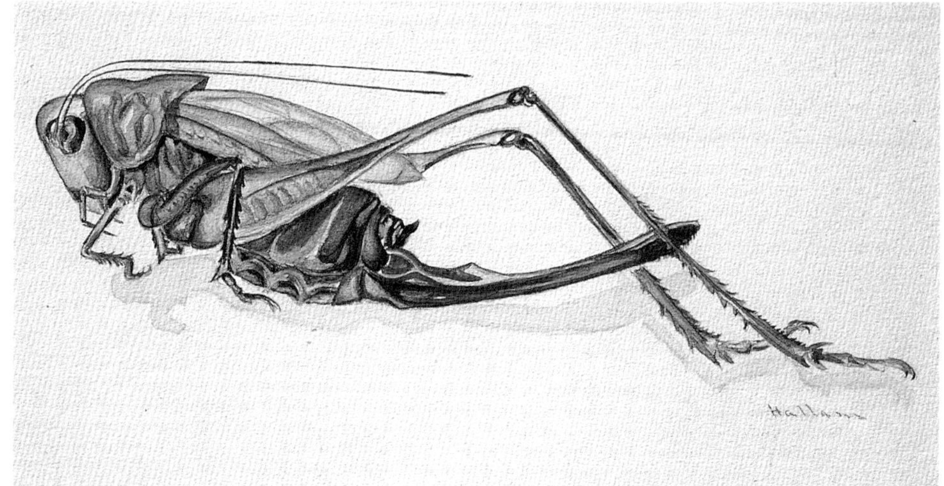

Freshman year, 1941-1942, included courses in art history, Munsell color theory, design, drawing, mechanical drawing, music, sculpture, painting, perspective, and watercolor, as well as English composition and sociology. Courses during sophomore year were the same, only more advanced, with the addition of ceramics, life drawing, structural design, and psychology. "This was the most difficult year," Hallam says. "Time seemed to run thin."

The mechanical drawing course at Mass Art, as the school has come to be known, was thorough enough to enable Hallam to land a summer job drafting at General Electric during the war. As she tells it, she took five little exercises she had made using a ruling pen and compass, and marched herself into the employment office. They were so surprised and amused that they sent her to the company's drafting school for a month. Hallam ended up in the supercharger section, where her father worked.

A typical day at Mass Art consisted of one class in the morning, usually academic, three-quarters of an hour for lunch, and one studio class in the afternoon. The students and faculty were expected to leave at 3 P.M. By the time Hallam got home to Lynn, it was dark and she could do only the academic part of the homework; color theory and painting had to wait until the weekends when there was daylight in which to mix colors.

In addition to her courses, Hallam was treasurer of her class and then president of the student government. These years were something of a trial, but through hard work and with her family's support, the young student kept up with the course work.

Among the few pieces that Hallam has held on to from her years at Mass Art are two tempera studies executed for a design class she took in 1942. One is a design for glazed chintz adapted from a Persian pattern, the other, a close rendering of a grasshopper. The former demonstrates Hallam's innate sense of the decorative; the latter testifies to her exacting eye for detail, one that would do a naturalist proud.

Hallam has some wonderful memories of teachers she admired at Mass Art, including Emma Lennon, who taught color theory and design. Lennon's presentation was dramatic; it made an impression. She worked long hours after class to help those who were having trouble matching color or understanding basic design principles.

Edwin Hoadley emphasized design in nature and drew fantastic white chalk drawings of animals and plants on an enormous blackboard. Painting instructor Otis Philbrook punctuated his sessions with his marvelous philosophy. And Hallam remembers how Lawrence Kupferman awakened the freshmen to contemporary art by lugging tons of illustrated books to his painting class, introducing his students to the work of Cézanne, Braque, Nolde,

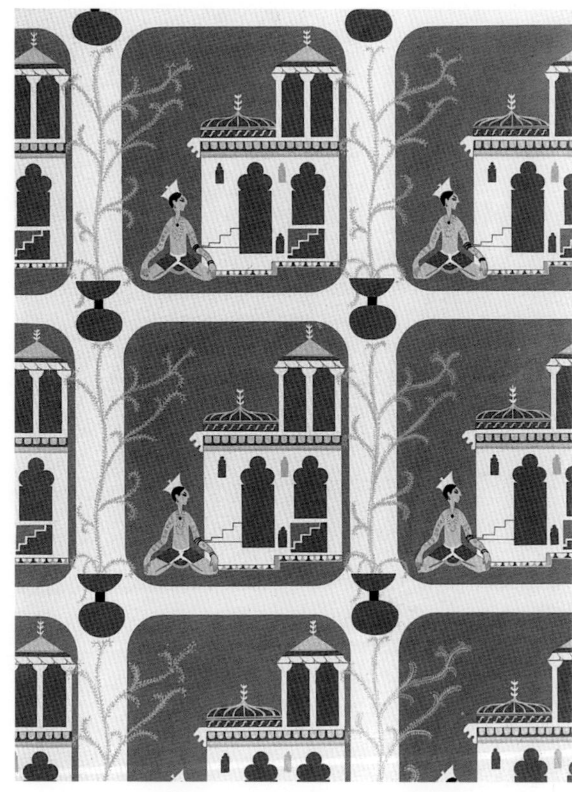

Historic adaptation for glazed chintz, design class
Massachusetts School of Art, 1942
Tempera on illustration board, 24 x 18 in.
Collection of the artist

Klee, Kandinsky, Picasso, Miró, Dufy, and others. His enthusiasm was infectious, and long after Hallam graduated he encouraged her to push on.

"I learned from these teachers what the word 'dedication' meant," says Hallam. She found it inspirational to witness the superior results they were able to get from their students. "Their methods of teaching most likely led to my wanting to be a teacher myself."

Hallam also learned about research and how to look at works of art, thanks to another strong personality, Ella Munsterberg, who taught the history of art at the college. In her four-year course, Munsterberg started in ancient Egypt and ended up in Boston.

Bull Fight, 1944
Silk screen, 10 x 13 1/2 in.
Collection of the artist

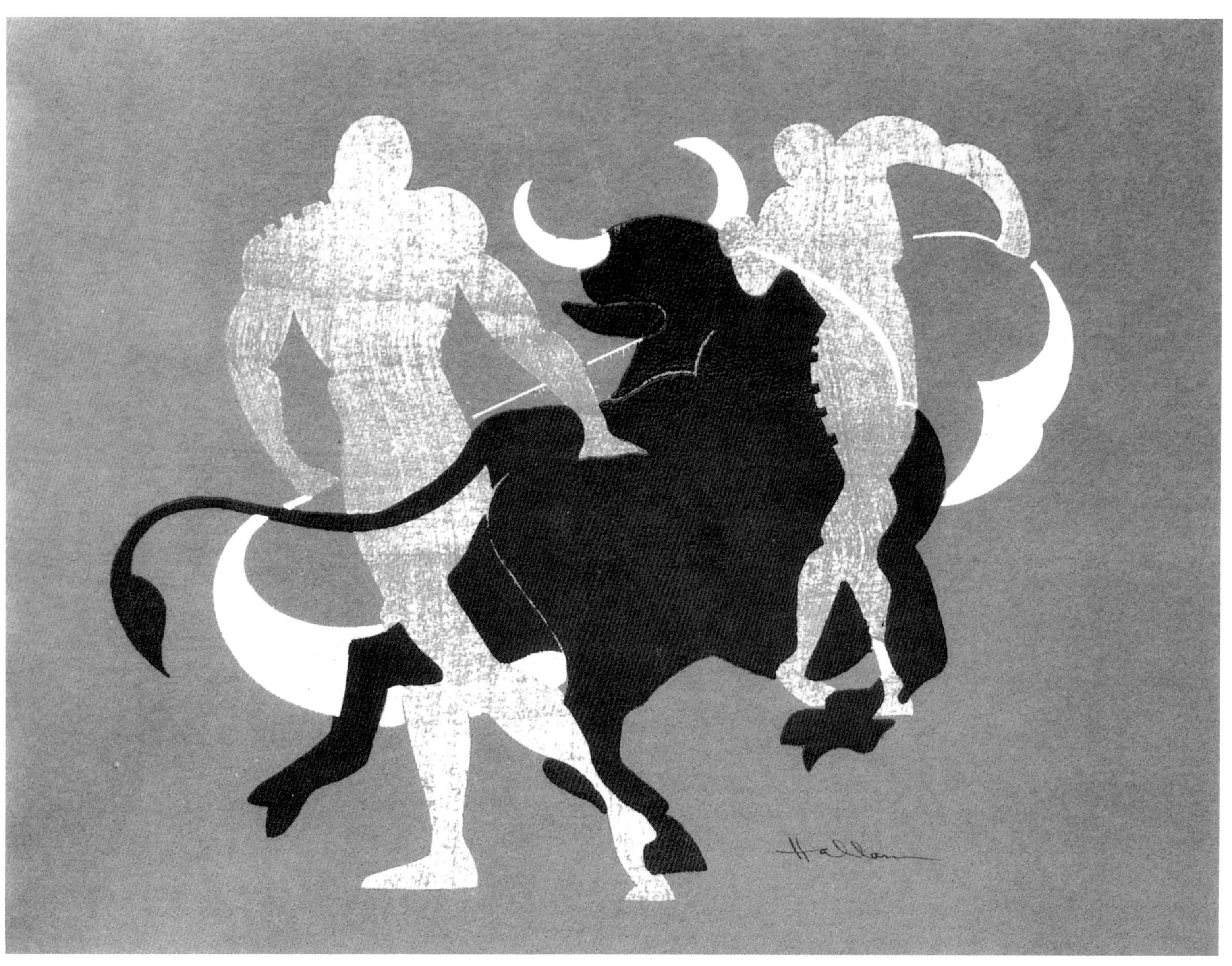

Once a week, Munsterberg's students visited all the art galleries on Newbury Street. Pretending they were critics, they made thumbnail sketches in pen and ink and wash of works on display and jotted down comments about specific pictures. For one final exam, Munsterberg had the students make floor plans of the Museum of Fine Arts and label the various exhibitions on all three floors!

"Because of this exposure I felt at ease in galleries," Hallam reflects, "not intimidated the way a lot of people were. I became very familiar with the gallery scene." In 1944, while in her junior year, she finished a picture called *Bull Fight* in a silk screen class and entered it in a group exhibition at the Institute of Contemporary Art in Boston. The piece was accepted. "I was overcome!" Hallam says. "This experience whetted my appetite for showing work, so I began painting on my own during the summer."

In a diary entry from October 13, 1944, Hallam describes a typical art-filled day as a Mass Art student. She visits the Boston Public Library to do research on ancient Greek education, then moves on to Hatfield's color shop, then to the nearby Stuart Art Gallery, where she makes notes on specific pieces by several artists. (A year later, Hallam herself would have a painting shown at the Stuart, an oil on gesso titled *Red Coat*.) She then proceeds to the Institute of Contemporary Art, where, for a fee of 30 cents, she views a show of French paintings. Later, she visits the Boston gallery Doll and Richards, and the Guild of Boston Artists, where again she takes notes on paintings. She finishes the day by buying some art supplies at Peases' and heading home.

Hallam remembers walking everywhere in Boston, for miles without a thought of distance or weather. She'd walk from the Museum of Fine Arts to Cornhill to the old bookstores. She and fellow art students would sketch at the old Howard Burlesque Theater. "We'd take our lunch with us," Hallam recalls. "Lots of the bums did."

There was no real Cedar Bar-type experience for Hallam in these days, no hobnobbing with fellow artists as the Abstract Expressionists had done in that famous New York hangout. She lived a sheltered life, content with music, books, photography, and painting. She went to the Boston Symphony Orchestra concerts every Tuesday night, where she heard Koussevitzky conduct the likes of Wanda Landowska, Rubinstein, Rachmaninoff, and the von Trapp Family. Occasionally, she took in a play.

Hallam was also exposed to contemporary European artists, many of whom had emigrated to the United States during the war. As a student she recalls having lunch at Longwood Towers with the Hungarian constructivist László Moholy-Nagy. She had designed the exhibition installation at Mass Art when he lectured there. "We could hardly understand his talk,"

These paintings were done on the spot. Collage was added to the bridge using snippets from Architectural Digest.

Brunswick—Topsham Bridge, 1959
Acrylic and collage on paper, 22 x 30 in.
Collection of Drummond, Woodsum, Plimpton and McMahon, Portland, Maine

she recalls, "but then at lunch his heavy accent disappeared." Lecturing, the artist confessed to his listeners, made him nervous.

Around the same time Hallam met another Hungarian, Gyorgy Kepes, who became a professor of visual design at M.I.T. in 1946. Kepes had a work space at the Fenway Studios where Hallam painted. She was fascinated by the encrusted surfaces of Kepes's canvases, which one critic likened to "volcanic formations or earth before the coming of man."

When Hallam asked Kepes one day what he used to achieve his surfaces, he quickly changed the subject. On another occasion, during a tour of Kepes's studio, someone asked him the same question and he wouldn't

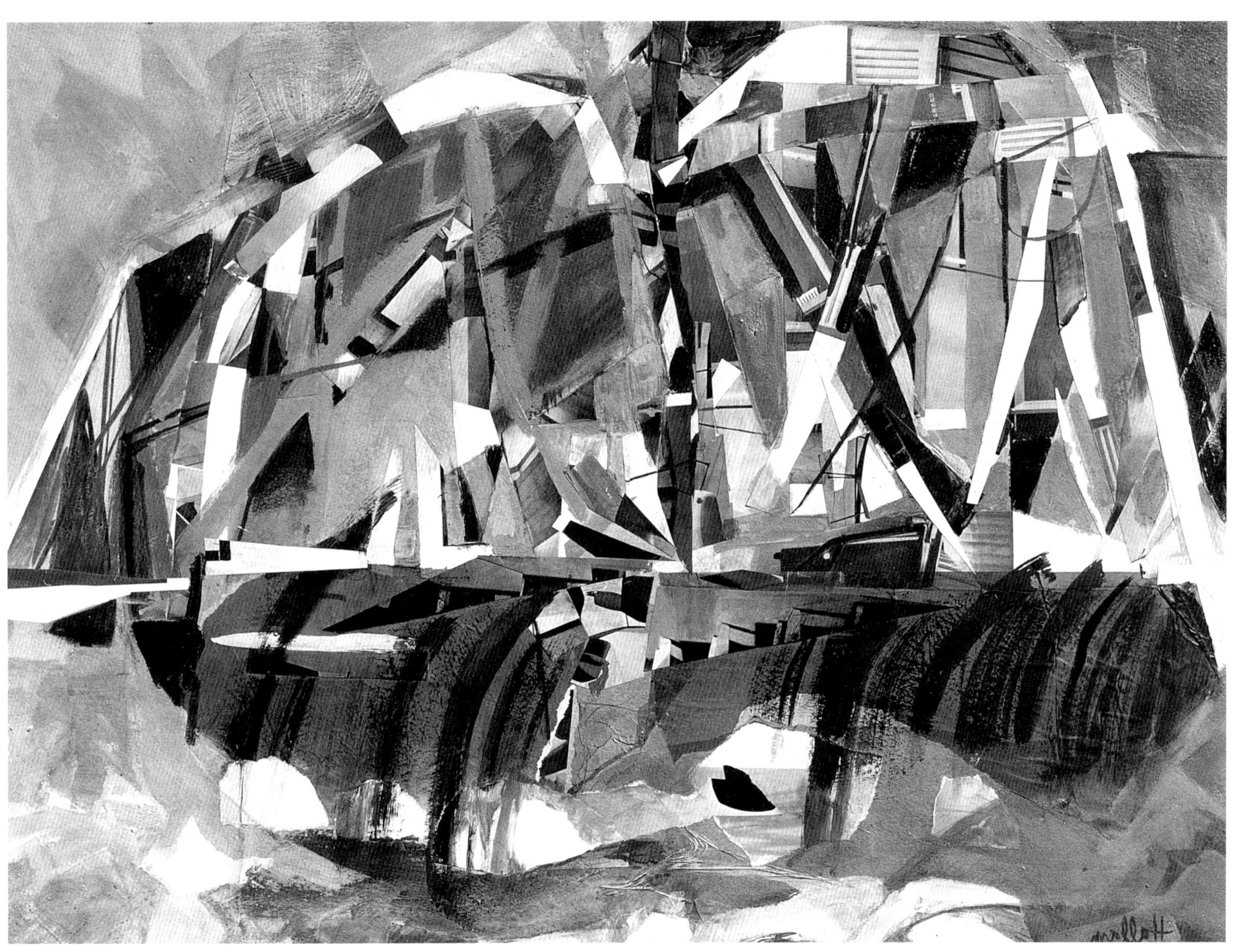

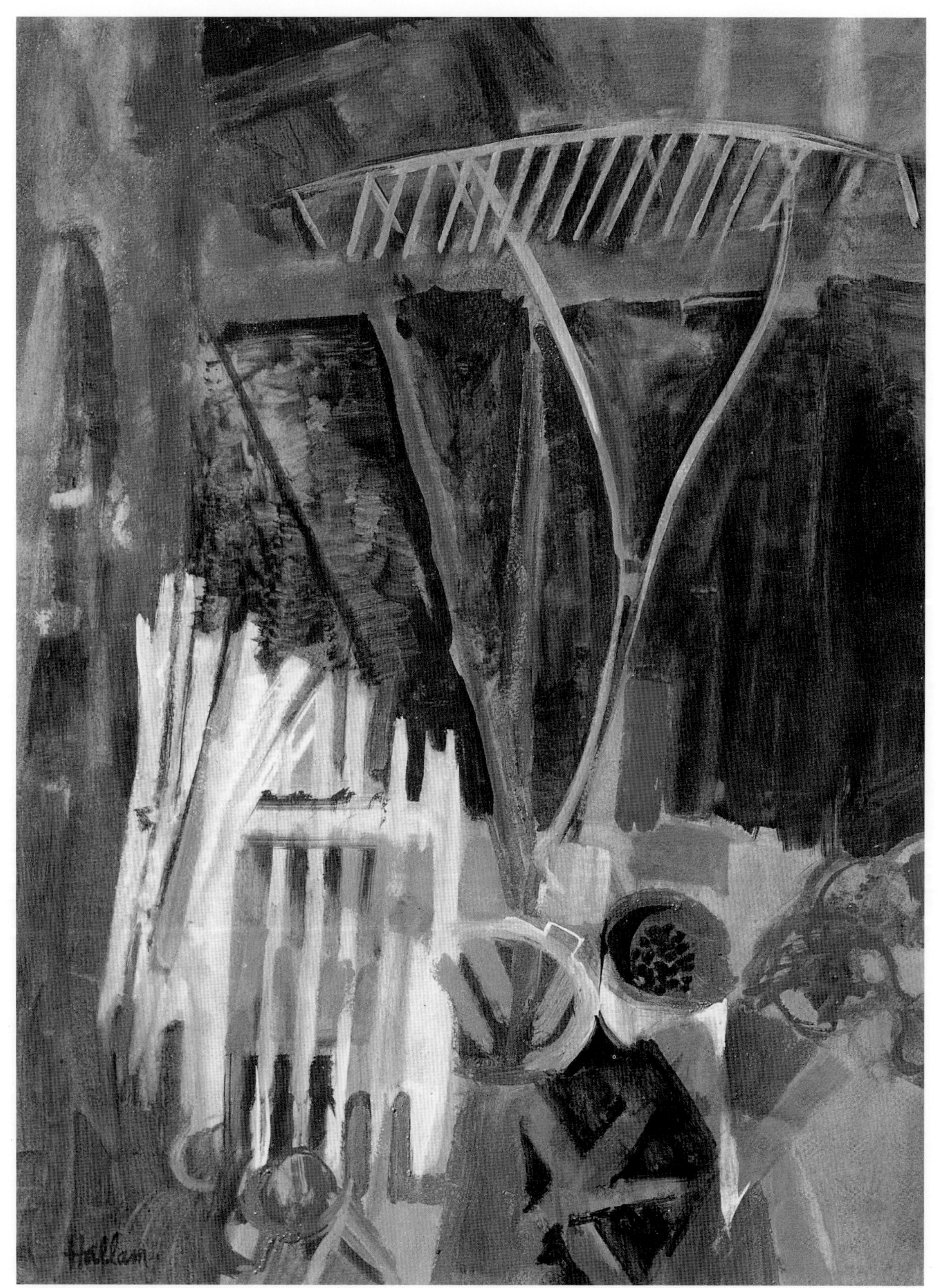

Mr. Barnes's Drag Rake (Priscilla Nye's barn, Topsham, Maine), 1959
Acrylic on Cox paper,
22 1/2 x 30 1/2 in.
Collection of the artist

say. Finally, Hallam asked the question of one of Kepes's friends, who replied, "He uses ground coffee!" Hallam thought the friend was putting her on.

After two years of rigorous training, a Mass Art student could choose any one of several different fields—teacher education, drawing and painting, design, sculpture, ceramics, or fashion design—as a focus for the remaining two years of study. Hallam opted for teacher education, with the thought that she could get a job teaching and have summers off to paint.

The teacher education program boasted several top-notch professors, including Priscilla Nye, chair of the department. When not teaching, Nye dedicated much of her energy to placing her students in teaching positions. She herself often arranged interviews and, in Hallam's words, "spent her whole life, practically every hour of every day, trying to upgrade the quality of art education in the Boston area and throughout the country."

Hallam remained a close friend of Nye's after graduation, visiting her at her 1850's summer home in Topsham, Maine. Three acrylic paintings—*Feldspar Mill, Topsham, Maine*; a Cubist collage of the Brunswick-Topsham bridge; and an acrylic, *Mr. Barnes's Drag Rake*—are among the pieces that resulted from a stay with her mentor in 1959.

The Teacher Education Department was, in Hallam's day, the strongest in the school, and it graduated the most students each year. One day a week the students were sent out into the field to various schools where they "practice taught" classes at a variety of levels, from first grade to college.

Hallam also volunteered as a teacher for the Cambridge Public Schools' Department of Art Education, leading Saturday morning classes at the Peabody Museum and at the Kinghooper Mansion in Marblehead. She taught nights at the Boston Center for Adult Education and at the YWCA with painter Carl Nelson.

Hallam graduated from Massachusetts College of Art in 1945 with a Bachelor of Science degree in education. As she has stated, the curriculum was so well designed to prepare the graduate "for the cold world" that students wishing to pursue a master's degree had little trouble gaining admission to the college or university of their choice.

Hallam herself was admitted to Harvard, but decided against it as the university offered little in the way of studio courses. She also turned down Yale when she learned that they were interested in painting in egg tempera with tiny pointed brushes. Instead, she chose to attend Cranbrook Academy of Art in the summer of 1948 and then went on to Syracuse University, where she earned her Master of Fine Arts degree in 1953.

6

Teaching and Painting

In 1945, after she graduated from the Massachusetts College of Art, Hallam began what would be a four-year teaching stint at Lasell Junior College in Auburndale, Massachusetts. Appointed chair of the art department, she taught painting, drawing and design, art appreciation, and crafts. As Hallam noted in a 1977 interview, Lasell gave her "$1,500 a year, plus room and board and not a worry." She did many figure paintings there and is now sorry that she destroyed all but a couple of them.

In her formative years, Hallam worked in a realistic mode, favoring landscape and figural subjects, painting primarily in oils and gouache. A small portrait of a boy and his dog, *Francis Twohey and Heidi*, painted in 1945 during her senior year in art school, stands out among her earliest works in oil. It was the first of the artist's paintings to be selected by a jury, on the occasion of a members' exhibition at the Institute of Contemporary Art in Boston. Although not exactly surreal, there is something Dali-esque about this portrayal of a child holding a dachshund in his arms. Perhaps this impression derives from the eerie landscape behind the figure, empty but for the shadows of the boy and the trunk of a tree we cannot see.

Among her landscapes of this period are *Rockport Low Tide* (Rockport, Massachusetts), 1945, and *Turbot Creek* (Kennebunkport), 1948. Both pictures are the work of an accomplished young oil painter working in the realist tradition of artists like Leon Kroll and Peggy Bacon. The lobstermen's shacks and beached dories are rendered with a sure hand, and Hallam proves herself in tune with coastal weathers. A little more than a decade later, she painted Turbot Creek again, in a more abstract manner, evidence of a gradual shift away from realism.

Hallam showed in exhibitions at the Stuart Art Gallery in 1945, where fellow artists included Werner Drewes, Jean Charlot, Hyman Bloom, and Jacob Lawrence. Since 1947 she has been a member of the New England Watercolor Society (formerly called the Boston Society of Water Color Painters). In that same year she joined the Boston Society of Independent Artists, a group of contemporary painters and sculptors who for the most part avoided the conservative Newbury Street galleries. Hallam served on the society's board of directors for a number of years.

The summer of 1948 found Hallam attending the Cranbrook Academy of Art. Founded in 1932, the academy was, and continues to be, the only institution in America devoted solely to graduate education in the fine arts. Located in Bloomfield Hills, Michigan, Cranbrook and its associated schools are renowned for their achievements in education, art, architecture, science, and culture.

At Cranbrook, Hallam studied painting with Clifford West and sculpture with William McVey. During this period, Sepeshy, Grotel, Milles,

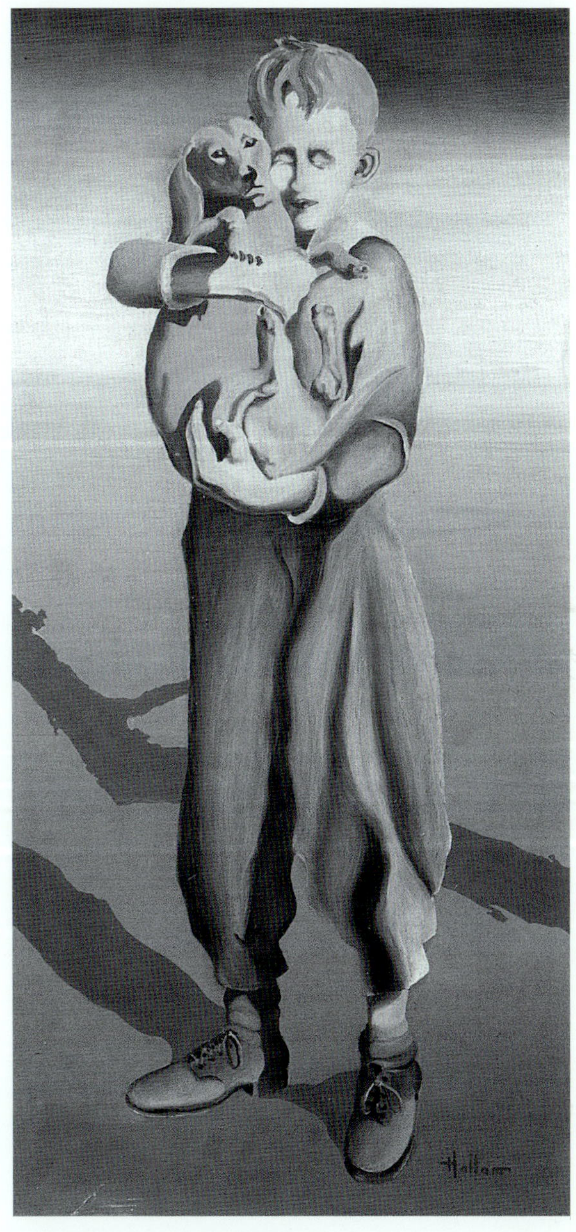

Francis Twohey and Heidi, 1945
Oil on masonite, 15 1/2 x 8 in.
Collection of the artist

Fifty years ago I used to buy frames from the Salvation Army. They had wide gesso and gold ornamentation. I whacked it off down to the bare wood and refinished them to suit the paintings. I think they might have been worth a lot of money now if I'd left them alone.

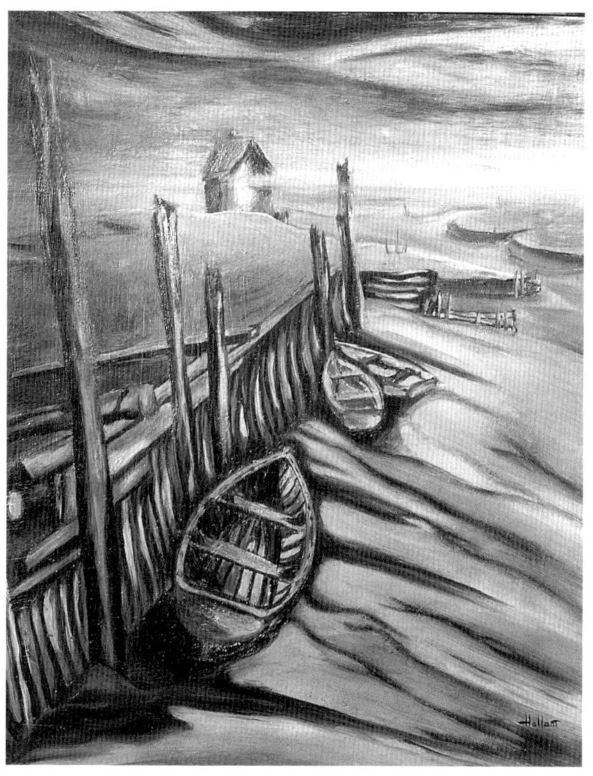

Turbot Creek (Kennebunkport), 1948
Oil on masonite, 17 1/2 x 14 1/2 in.
Collection of the artist

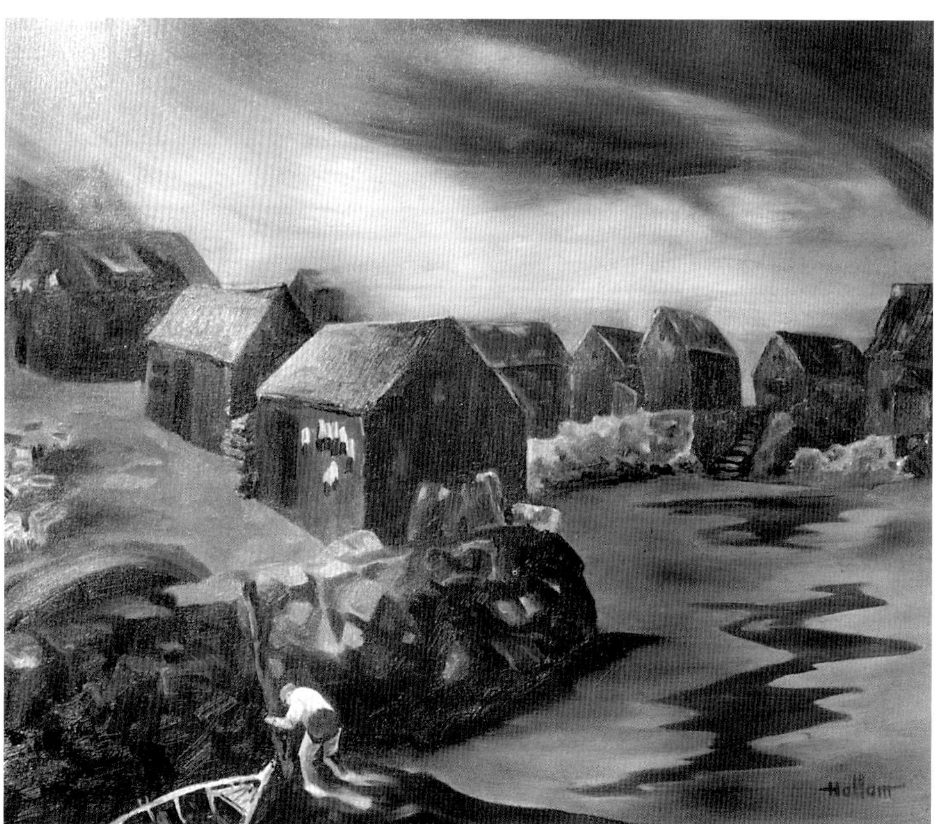

Low Tide (Rockport, Massachusetts), 1945
Oil on canvas, 20 x 24 in.
Collection of the artist

Saarinen, Eames, and other well-known artists, architects, and designers were in residence at the school. Hallam saved several pen-and-ink studies made that summer, quick sketches of the Cranbrook Lake boathouse and dam, as well as several views of the surrounding countryside, some of them with color notations.

Returning to Massachusetts at the end of the summer, Hallam drew a variety of subjects, including the Lynnfield railroad station. Over the following two summers she would also make drawings of the sand pits at Auburndale and execute a series of handsome ink-on-paper studies of Schoodic, Maine. Also of note is a drawing of a waiter at the Parker House in Boston.

In 1949, Hallam left Lasell to assume an associate professor position at the Massachusetts College of Art. The college had been founded in 1873 to train art teachers to teach industrial and mechanical drawing and design in the public schools of Massachusetts in order to supply designers for state industries. The school remains the only publicly assisted, free-standing college of visual art in the country.

To be made a professor at the college did not depend on one's ability and record alone: the state legislature had to approve the funds for teachers. Ironically, in Hallam's day, Mass Art teacher education graduates often ended up getting teaching jobs outside the state in schools and universities that paid higher salaries.

In a letter to Sinclair Hitchings, curator of prints and drawings at the Boston Public Library, Hallam describes Mass Art's distinct quality:

> The whole idea of the college was that it was very closely knit—*with individual teaching*. Everyone was loyal and everyone loved the place and fought to keep it alive, with no endowment and very little funds from the state.

The first year at the college, Hallam taught painting, drawing, and design. She also served on the college's board of directors and admissions, and was treasurer of the college's art store.

In 1950, Hallam introduced the first courses in theater arts, audiovisual aids (which she had minored in at Syracuse University), and photography, the last at the behest of Gordon Reynolds, the progressive president of the college. No other art school in Boston offered photography at that time. The course was compulsory for all sophomores.

Hallam had four divisions of photography to teach, with 35 to 40 students in each—and no budget. She converted two closets into darkrooms. The class worked with two 4-by-5-inch speed Graflexes, three 4-by-5-inch studio view cameras, and two Omega enlargers. A lab fee was charged each

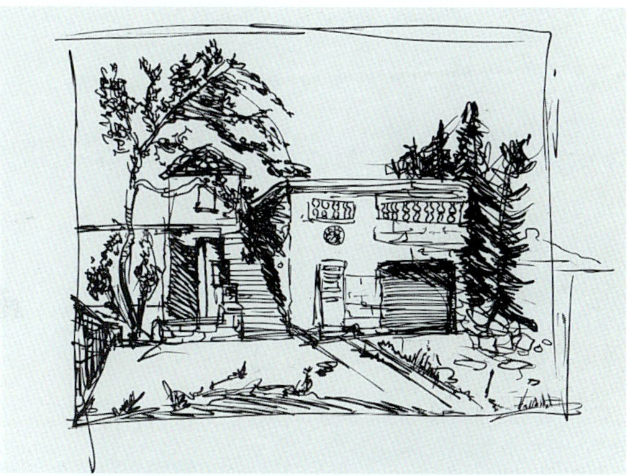

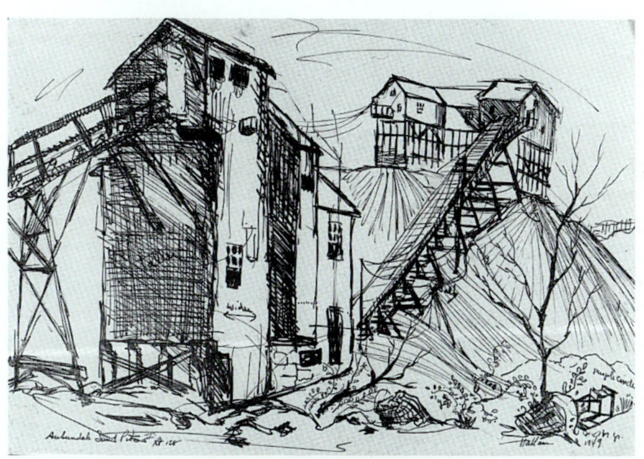

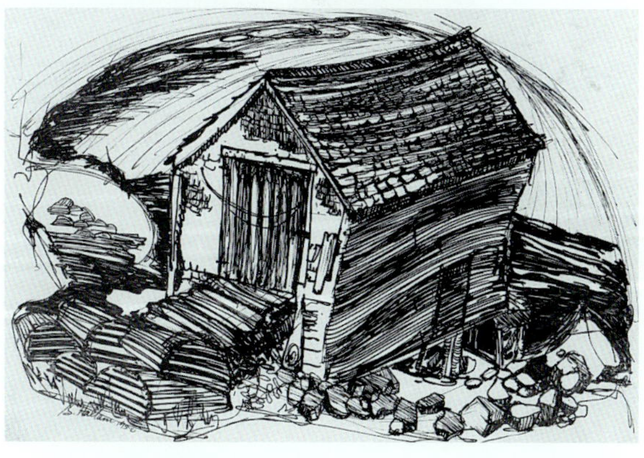

TOP: *CRANBROOK LAKE BOATHOUSE III* (MICHIGAN), 1948
INK ON CALENDERED PAPER, 9 X 11 IN. ON A 12 X 18 IN. SHEET
COLLECTION OF THE ARTIST

MIDDLE: *AUBURNDALE SAND PITS II* (ROUTE 128), 1949
INK ON CALENDERED PAPER, 12 X 18 IN.
COLLECTION OF THE ARTIST

BOTTOM: *SCHOODIC II MAINE, WINTER HARBOR*, 1950
INK ON CALENDERED PAPER, 12 X 18 IN.
COLLECTION OF THE ARTIST

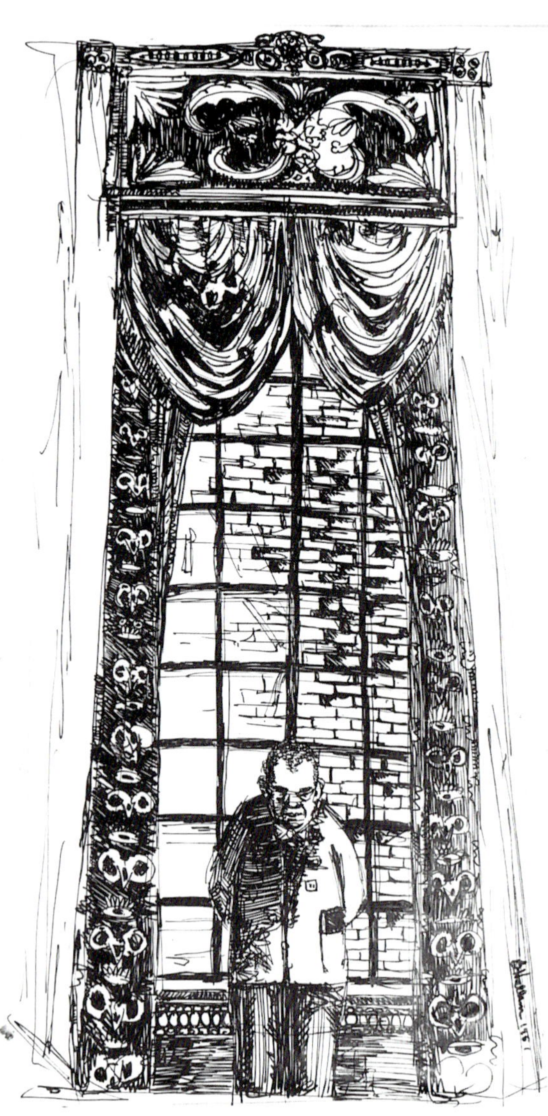

Waiter at the Parker House, Boston, 1951
Ink on calendered paper, 18 x 12 in.
Collection of the artist

student to pay for the chemicals. Hallam bought dry lots and did her own mixing in large quantities. "The air was white," she recalls. "It's a wonder I didn't develop lung problems." On a return visit to the college some years ago, she was amazed to see how enormous the photography department had become, with lots of space and equipment and even a giant 20-by-24-inch Polaroid camera.

The theater arts course began as a class called Art in a Democracy, which Hallam was assigned to teach to education students. Unsure as to what this course was about, she went to Priscilla Nye, the head of the department, for advice. Nye told her to teach the students how to work together in small and large groups on a project, with everyone sharing ideas and participating.

Hallam decided to meet the class on the stage in the college auditorium. She had bought a book on stagecraft, a subject of which she had little knowledge, and proceeded to lead her students in orchestrating a variety of multimedia events, like the "happenings" that would take place years later. They projected images on the stage and did contemporary productions using electronic sound and Stockhausen's music.

The class went on to adapt and produce such pieces as James Thurber's *13 Clocks*, Ludwig Bemelmans's *Madeline*, T. S. Eliot's *The Hollow Men*, and Walt Kelly's cartoon *Pogo*. They also made the sets and did the lighting and background music for the school's annual fashion show, an elaborate function put on by the fashion department.

Hallam's tenure at Mass Art lasted until 1962. During that time, in addition to her regular classes, she supervised junior and senior student teachers at the elementary, secondary, and college levels and directed the Saturday morning high school art classes at the college's laboratory school. This was challenging work. As Hallam once stated, "The most tricky thing to teach student teachers is how to evaluate their students' work. The idea is not to feed the students your own solutions, but to ask questions and try to offer them many suggestions so that the students arrive at their own solutions to satisfy their original vision."

In an interview in the *Maine Sunday Telegram*, Hallam noted that teaching "is an art, and good teaching is very difficult. It takes imagination and thoughtful preparation." The test of a good teacher, she said, is to make him or herself "progressively useless." At its best, Hallam found teaching to be creative and felt that it helped her in her own painting. "Teaching," she states, "keeps one immersed and propelled."

7

A Pioneer in Acrylic

In the early 1950s, Hallam began moving away from strictly representational art, following her own instincts to experiment, but also taking her cues from some of the modern art she was seeing. *Fish and Buoys*, 1951, is a case in point. Hallam painted this still life after visiting a Max Beckmann exhibition at the Germanic Museum in Cambridge. The approach to the subject matter is more direct and abstract than in her previous work, and the medium, black oil on Belgian linen, is quite out of the ordinary.

Hallam made eight paintings in black oil before switching to oil and encaustic. *Gourds*, painted in 1951, led the way to six more encaustic canvases interspersed with nine pieces using Hypalon. This new, sensational medium, used by many of the students at Mass Art, was a dammar-like clear varnish that produced brilliant colors when mixed with oil paints. The glazes gave a dazzling stained-glass-window effect. Hallam remembers Mass Art president Gordon L. Reynolds calling a special assembly at which he read to the students the special warning from the government regarding the deadly fumes emitted by Hypalon.

Hallam eventually abandoned Hypalon and latched onto another new medium—this time, a nontoxic one. In 1951, she tested a milk-like emulsion on many small Masonite panels. Called polyvinyl acetate, now commonly known as acrylic, the medium was virtually unknown to artists in the United States. Hallam conducted some of the earliest research on its use as a painting medium.

In 1951, Hallam had her first solo show. Sixteen oils were shown in the

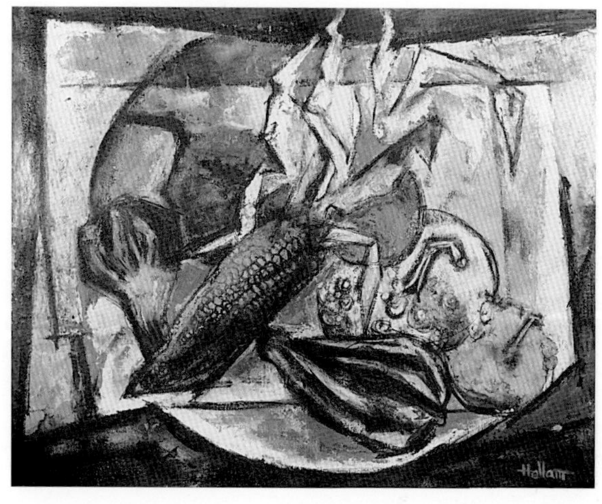

Gourds, 1951
Encaustic on Belgian linen, 20 x 26 in.
Collection of the artist

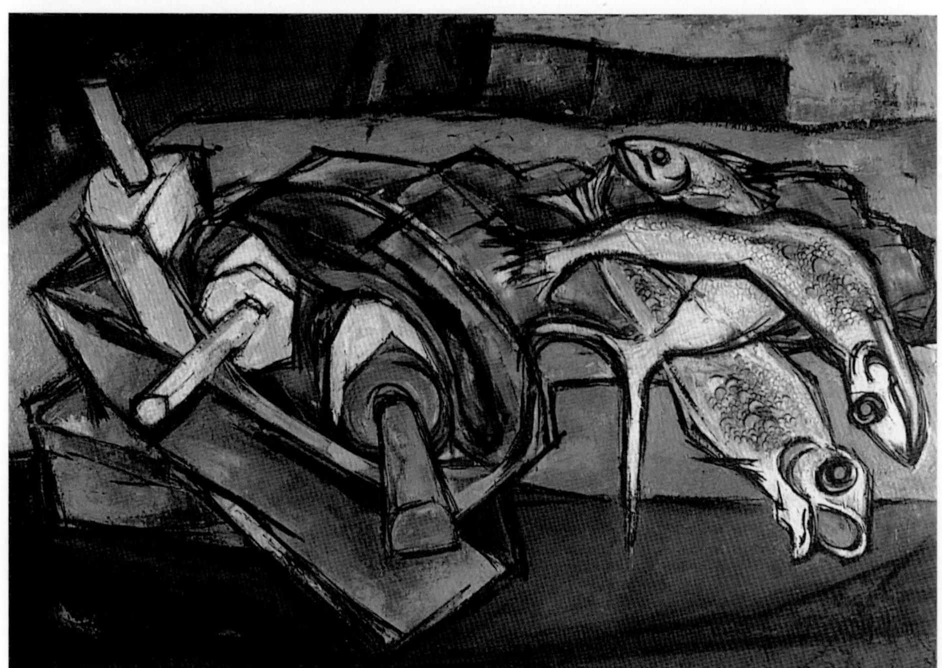

Fish and Buoys, 1951
Black oil on Belgian linen, 22 x 32 in.
Private collection

lobby of the Boston Dance Company on Hemenway Street during a Boston Dance Theater Associates production.

In the same year, Hallam enrolled in Syracuse University's graduate art program, which she attended for three summers running, having transferred credits from Cranbrook. She was asked to teach there, but declined the offer, preferring Boston's climate to that of Syracuse.

Hallam's experiments at the university led to a significant change in her art. Polyvinyl acetate had been used for highway pavement materials and by industry for, among other things, binding plywood together. Alfred Duca, a student at the School of the Museum of Fine Arts in Boston, has been credited with first applying this commercial binder to the field of fine arts, mixing it with dry color. A former teacher of Duca's, Carl Zerbe, started to use polymer tempera in the early 1950s, having discovered that he was highly allergic to encaustic, his favorite medium. *Art News* published an article on the medium, written by Frederick S. Wight, called "Zerbe Paints a Picture," in the February 1952 issue.

The Syracuse University Art Department had never seen anything like this medium, polyvinyl acetate. I was breaking new ground here. Later, a commercial firm put it on the market and called it acrylic.

Like Hallam, Zerbe found that acrylic, a synthetic resin, could provide a luminous palette and textural variety. What critic George Rivers wrote about Zerbe's Arctic series of the late 1950s could just as well be applied to Hallam's work of this time. These works, Rivers said, "managed, while remaining landscapes, to contain all the spontaneity, mystery and surface excitement of the by-now established school of abstract expressionists."

Hallam purchased her polyvinyl acetate from the Borden Milk Company in Leominster, Massachusetts. In exchange for her reports on how it performed as a medium in painting, the company gave Hallam gallon samples. Her painting students were using it at Mass Art. Those in Theater Arts dipped bed sheets into the binder in order to construct sturdy "stone" walls and other props.

Hallam created her first sizable canvas using this synthetic medium at

Dragonfly, 1953
Polyvinyl acetate on linen, 20 x 44 in.
Collection of the artist

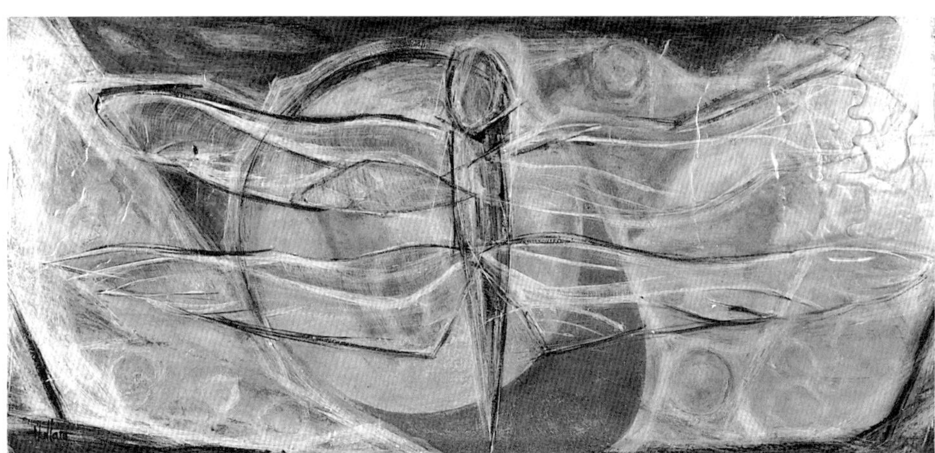

Syracuse in 1953. Titled *Dragonfly*, the piece was literally poured in transparent layers with a minimum of brush work. This 22-by-44-inch work, exhibited with the Boston Society of Independent Artists in an exhibition at the Boston Museum of Fine Arts, was selected from the show to tour New England museums for a year.

At times, Hallam's arrangements of greenery and flowers were presented in decidedly untraditional containers, such as *Rooted Vines in Bomb Sight* (the bomb sight came from an army surplus store) and *Bidet Bouquet*.

In 1954, Hallam showed with the Cambridge Art Association in a cellar on Church Street. One day, she relates, two members of the Ladies Committee of the Institute of Contemporary Art visited the cellar gallery, looking for new talent. They were taken with Hallam's work, which led to her having a mini-exhibition at the prestigious Institute of Contemporary Art on Newbury Street. Thirty years later, when Hallam met one of the Committee members again at a cocktail party in Maine, she remembered Hallam and informed the guests, "I found her in a cellar years ago!"

Hallam had one-person shows at several colleges, including Wellesley, Simmons, and Radcliffe, and her work was included in group exhibitions mounted by the Ogunquit Art Association and the Boston Arts Festival. Since those early days, her work has been included in more than 100 exhibitions and she has had more than 40 solo shows.

Frederick C. Walkey, director of the DeCordova Museum in Lincoln, Massachusetts, gave Hallam her first one-person museum show in 1954. The exhibition highlighted her paintings in polyvinyl acetate. Among the reviews was a favorable write-up by Dorothy Adlow, the well-known art critic for the *Christian Science Monitor*. "Miss Hallam displays a versatility in the variations of pictorial projects," Adlow wrote. She was especially keen on the pieces done in poly-vinyl acetate and devoted an ample bit of text to a description of the medium's qualities:

> This material lends itself to interesting and pleasing textural qualities that are waxen or enamellike. They are rich in decorative effect. Colors are luxuriant, and there is a gleaming luminosity.

Hallam gave her first lecture on polyvinyl acetate at Syracuse in 1953. She went on to give demonstrations throughout New England, to Sunday painters, art associations and guilds, high school and college students, and art supervisors, as well as to audiences in museums and galleries.

"Like a medicine man," Hallam describes herself, recalling how she traveled around with bottles full of polymer, wetting agents, plasticizers, dry color, and various supports and grounds, giving painting demonstrations.

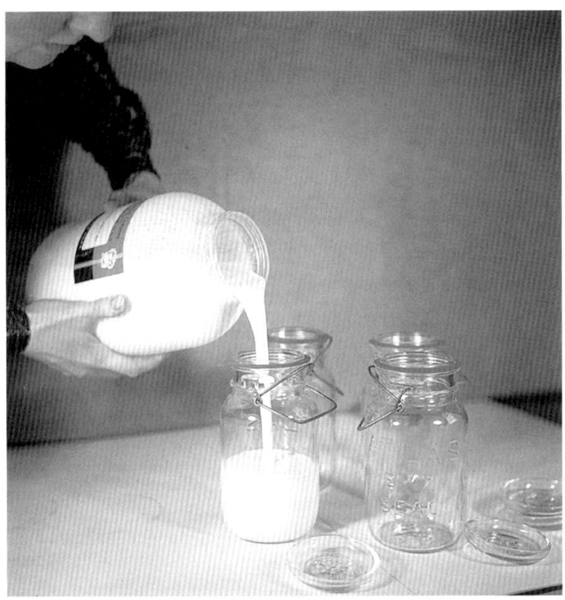

Hallam purchased her polyvinyl acetate from the Borden Milk Company.

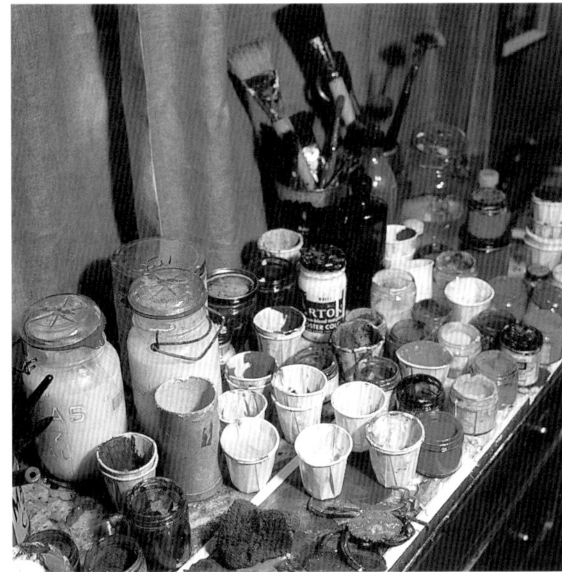

"Like a Medicine Man"
Before acrylic was known…Before Liquitex, colors were all dried powder

Because the medium was brand new, everyone was eager to learn about it, and Hallam's talks were well attended.

Weary of lugging all these materials around, Hallam eventually made slides, which showed in detail the various steps in the polymer process.

To make acrylic, dry color is mixed with Methocel, a wetting agent. This medium is then mixed with the binder, polyvinyl acetate, which is a liquid emulsion (like milk of magnesia or Elmer's glue in appearance). Over the years, Hallam would blend in a variety of aggregates.

Around 1956, Edward Betts, then professor of painting at the University of Illinois, was introduced to polyvinyl acetate at the Barn Gallery in Ogunquit, Maine. Years later, in 1971, he wrote of the experience on the occasion of a Beverly Hallam retrospective exhibition at the Addison Gallery of American Art in Andover, Massachusetts:

> [Hallam's] demonstration was something of an electrifying experience for me. She was introducing a new painting medium called polyvinyl-acetate, a name I suspected would never catch on. She was lavish in her use of it, pouring great milky pools of it over Masonite panels, funneling off excess polymer medium into enormous jars, playing freely with medium and paints, tossing off formulae and instructions and precautions, and sharing with the audience her own enthusiasm for a painting medium that was almost as new to her as it was to us. That enthusiasm was infectious, as it would be to many subsequent audiences, and I left the gallery determined to find out more for myself about the new polymer paints.

Polyvinyl acetate allows a great variety of painterly effects, and Hallam took full advantage of the medium's versatility. She could create multiple layers in a single picture, as in *Birthday Bouquet*, 1956.

It was in 1956 that Hallam's friend, the painter Ruth Cobb, introduced her to Robert B. Campbell and Donald F. Witherstine, directors of the Shore Galleries in Boston. They were very enthusiastic about her paintings in polyvinyl acetate and took several on consignment. A year later, Hallam was given her first solo commercial gallery exhibition and she continued to show with Shore Galleries for the next 22 years.

Visits to Ogunquit in the summer provided Hallam with various sea motifs. *Horseshoe Crab*, painted in the Ramsdell shack in Ogunquit, Maine, 1958, is a fine study in green acrylic and black ink of this denizen of coastal shallows. She turned to the same subject a year later, this time working in acrylic and silver leaf on gessoed Masonite to portray the upended crab. Likewise, Hallam captures the essence of a marine scene in her acrylic collage

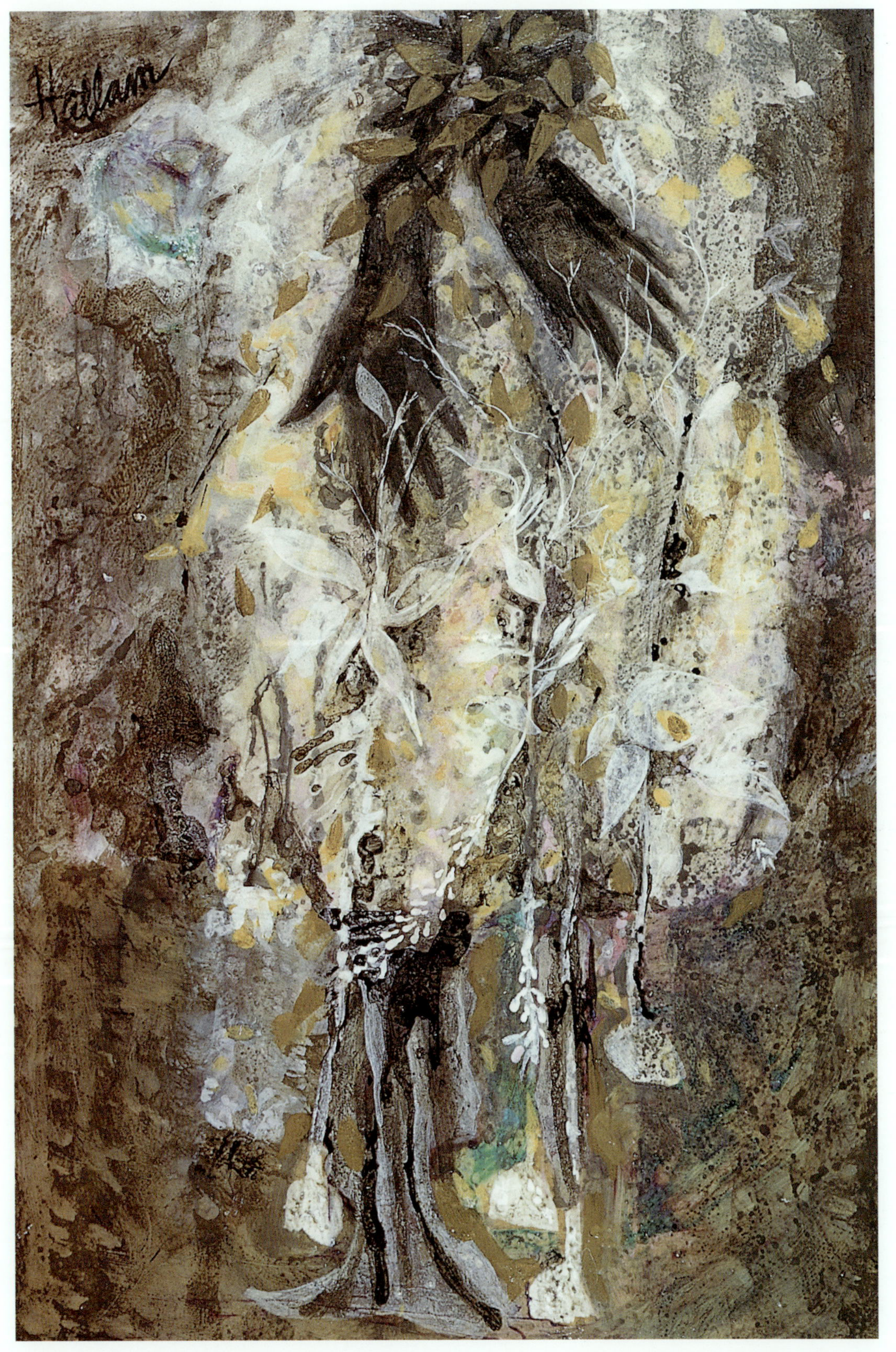

Birthday Bouquet *was my first museum-acquired painting. Curator Louisa Dresser of the Worcester Art Museum selected it for their permanent collection. The acquisition gave me a great boost.*

Birthday Bouquet, 1956
Polyvinyl acetate on masonite, 36 x 24 in.
Worcester Art Museum, Worcester, Massachusetts, Gift of the Boston Society of Independent Artists, Inc., 1956

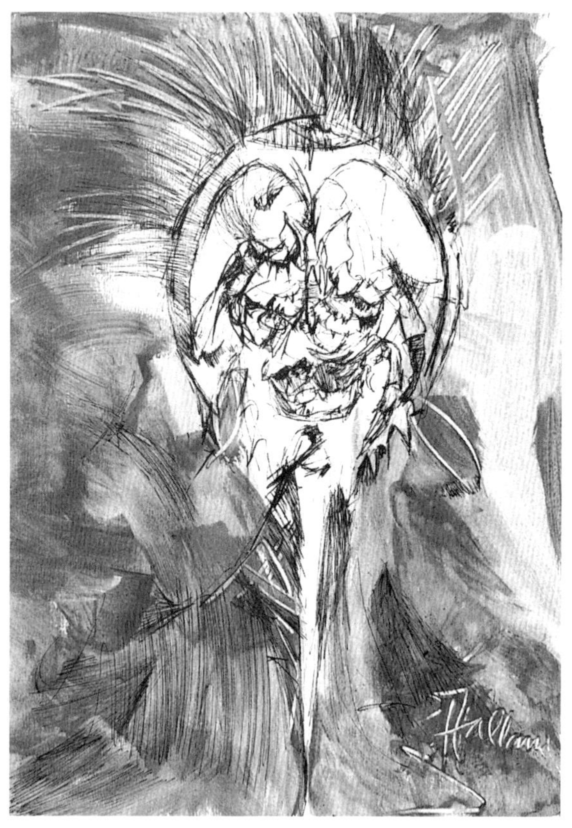

Horseshoe Crab
(Ramsdell shack, Perkins Cove, Ogunquit, Maine), 1958
Green acrylic and black ink on paper, 18 3/4 x 13 1/4 in.
Collection of the artist

on buff Cox paper. Hallam would return to the shoreline for inspiration in the following years, pushing the aesthetic envelope in ways new to the art of her time.

A full-time art professor, Hallam was hard-pressed to find time to do her own work, but she still managed to produce some notable pictures. She rented a space in the Fenway Studios, at 30 Ipswich Street in Boston. *The Fenway Studio Kitchen*, an acrylic on Belgian linen from 1960, provides a view of the studio's interior.

Two marvelous acrylic pieces from the same period, *Piano and Plants*, 1959, and *Violins*, 1960, demonstrate how Hallam's background in music influenced her painting over the years. Both paintings strive to capture the essence of the instruments. Loosely rendered interiors set off the distinct shapes of the piano and violin, giving them center stage. She also painted rock and ocean scenes with similar freedom, such as *Cliff, Sun, and Sea*, 1959.

The natural color and weave of the Belgian linen were left untouched to play an important role in the overall tonality of the painting. Hallam preserved the stretched linen by sizing it with equal parts polyvinyl acetate and water. When the linen was dry, she began work by quickly using 3-inch brushes to block in the composition with titanium white; after that, she worked with color from light to dark, leaving areas of white and patches of

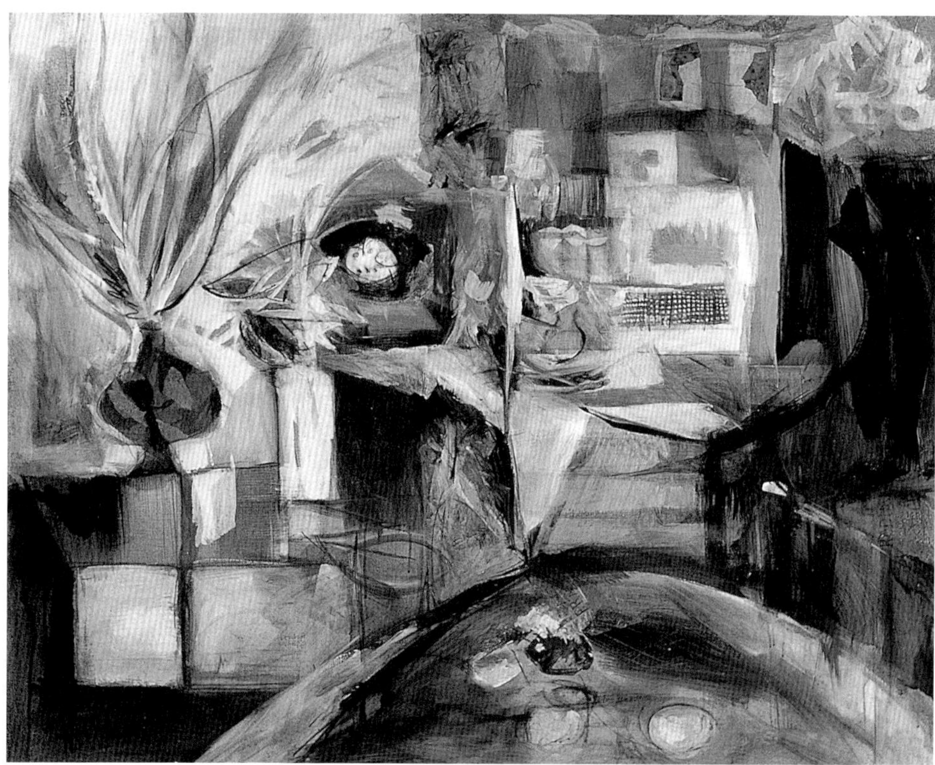

The Fenway Studio Kitchen
(at the Fenway Studios, Boston), 1960
Acrylic on Belgian linen, 45 x 50 in.
Private collection

the natural linen within the composition.

Hallam was groomed to be chairman of the Teacher Education Department at the Massachusetts College of Art, but she felt the administrative end of the position would detract from her teaching and would further cut into painting time. Winning the first Blanche E. Colman Art Foundation Award in 1960, a $5,000 grant for advanced study abroad, gave Hallam the impetus, encouragement, and wherewithal to stake her life on art. The sabbatical to paint full time in Europe proved to be a turning point in her life.

This old piano belonged to my friend Inez Atwater. We took the front off and I painted and decorated the hammers with sequins and diamonds. Everyone loved to watch the sparkle as we made music.

Piano and Plants, 1959
Acrylic on light brown paper, 18 1/2 x 24 1/2 in.
Collection of Mr. and Mrs. William Copithorne

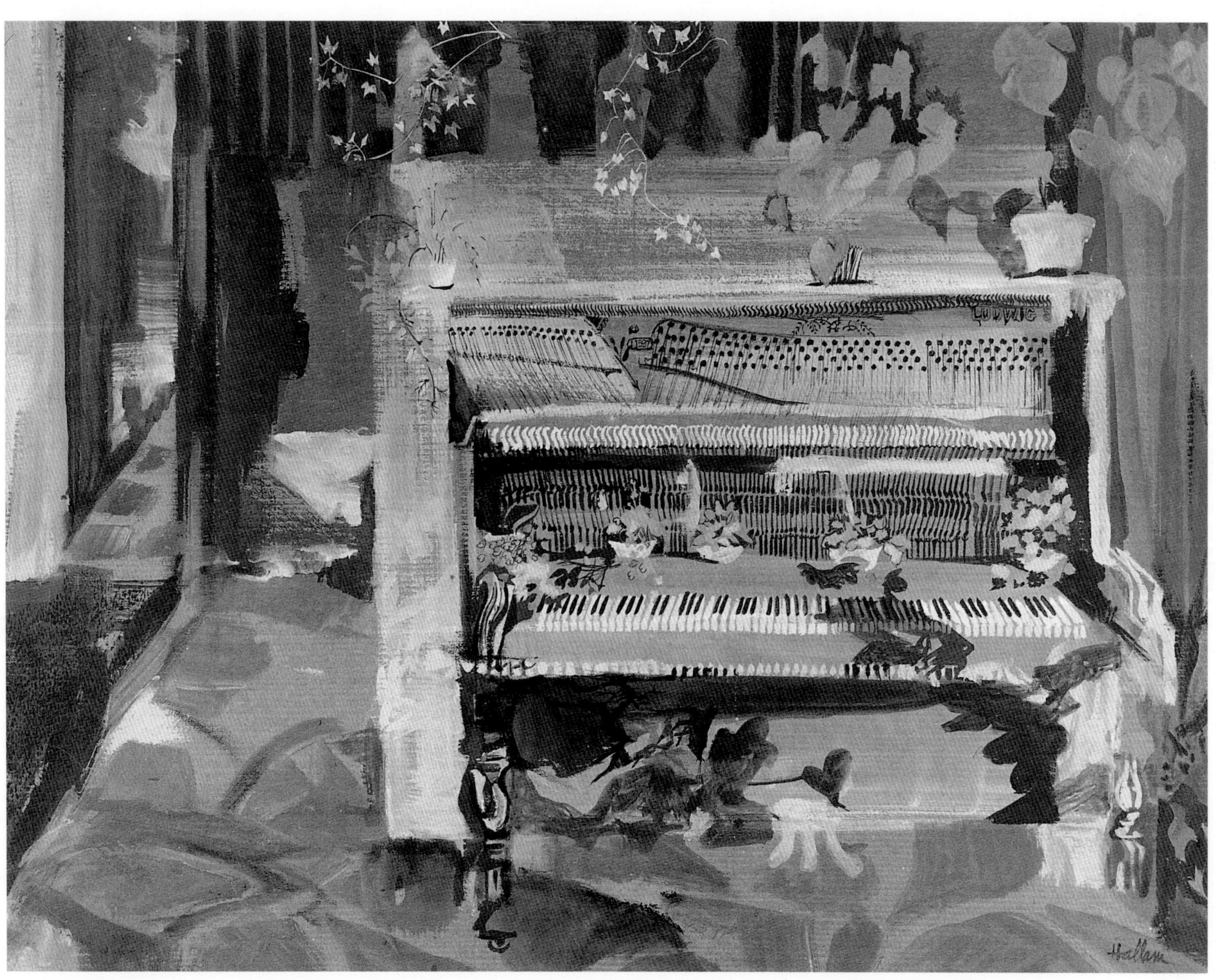

The local druggist's hobby was making violins. He was in my evening class and lent parts of his violins for our still life.

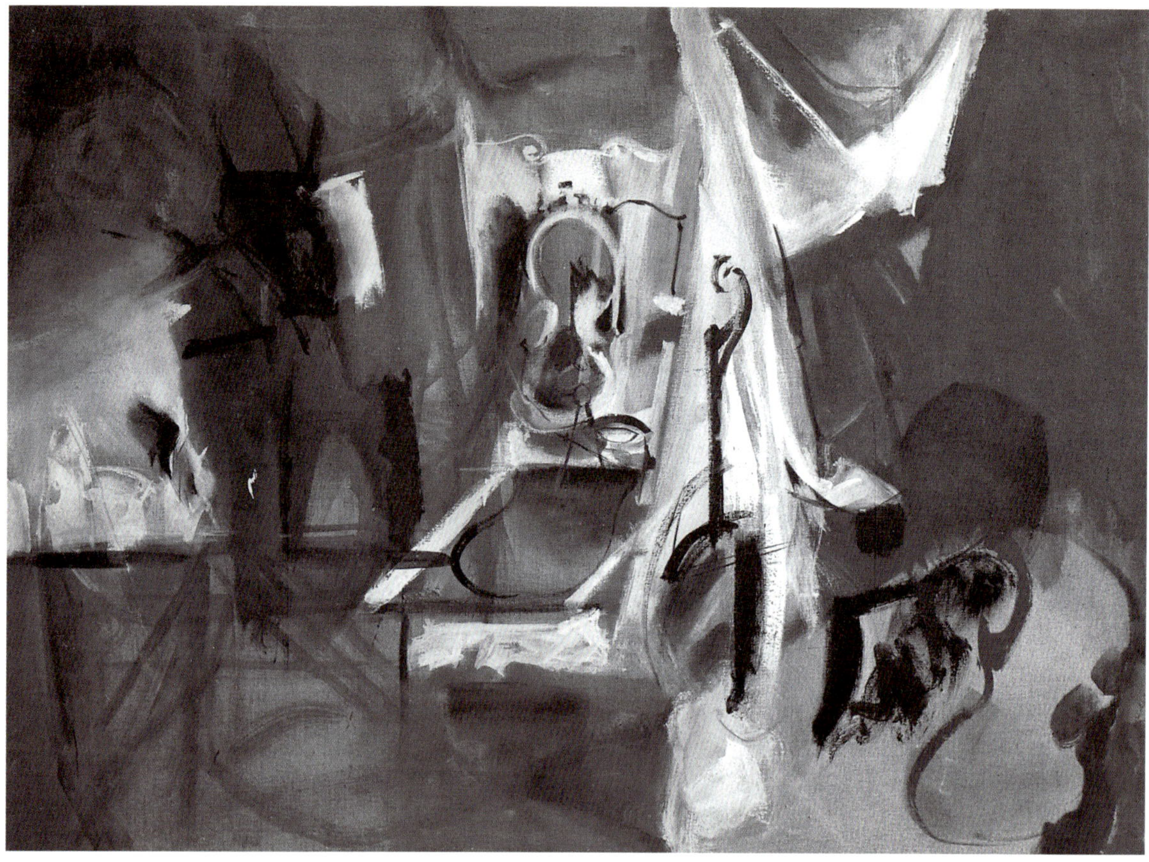

Violins, 1960
Acrylic on Belgian linen, 36 x 50 in.
Colby College Museum of Art
Waterville, Maine
Gift of Mary-Leigh Call Smart

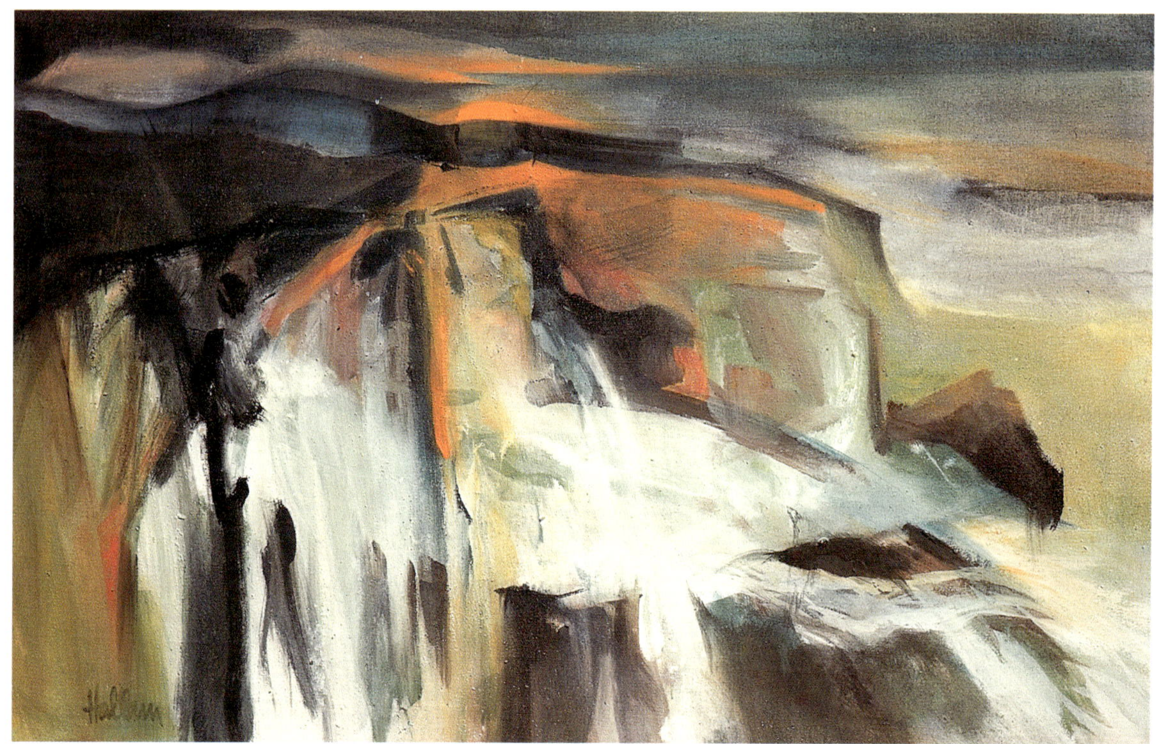

Cliff, Sun, and Sea, 1959
Acrylic on Belgian linen, 26 x 42 in.
Collection of Mr. and Mrs.
Edwin M. Talbott, Jr.

8

Europe and New Freedom

The will of Blanche E. Colman of Rockport, Massachusetts—an artist, feminist, interior decorator, and art teacher at Boston University who had died in 1959—provided for Hallam's grant. An eminent foursome served as judges for the prize: artist Gardner Cox; Bartlett H. Hayes, Jr., director of the Addison Gallery of American Art; Thomas Messer, director of the Institute of Contemporary Art; and Philip Hofer, curator of painting and graphic art at Harvard University.

With the Colman Art Foundation Award, Hallam headed for Europe to live and paint for four months. She sailed on the MV *Vulcania* for Venice, accompanied by her friends Mary-Leigh Smart, whose husband had died earlier in the year, and Floyd Covert, an artist and Mass Art colleague. One of their fellow passengers was the poet E. E. Cummings, with whom Hallam struck up an acquaintance. She had always admired his poetry and paintings. He and his wife, Marion Morehouse, left the ship at Taormina to visit their daughter in Sicily. Many years later, Hallam would recall with fondness the fact that her passport said "artist and professor." The Europeans, she recalled, thought she was "a god."

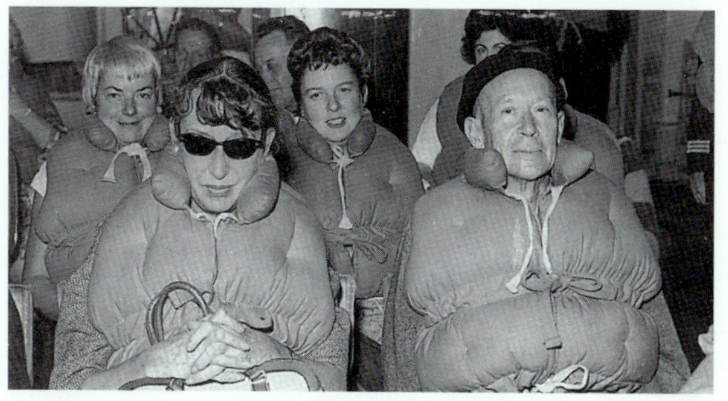

Life boat drill, MV *Vulcania*, September, 30, 1960
Front row: Marion Morehouse
(Mrs. E. E. Cummings), E. E. Cummings
Second row: Mary-Leigh Smart, Beverly Hallam

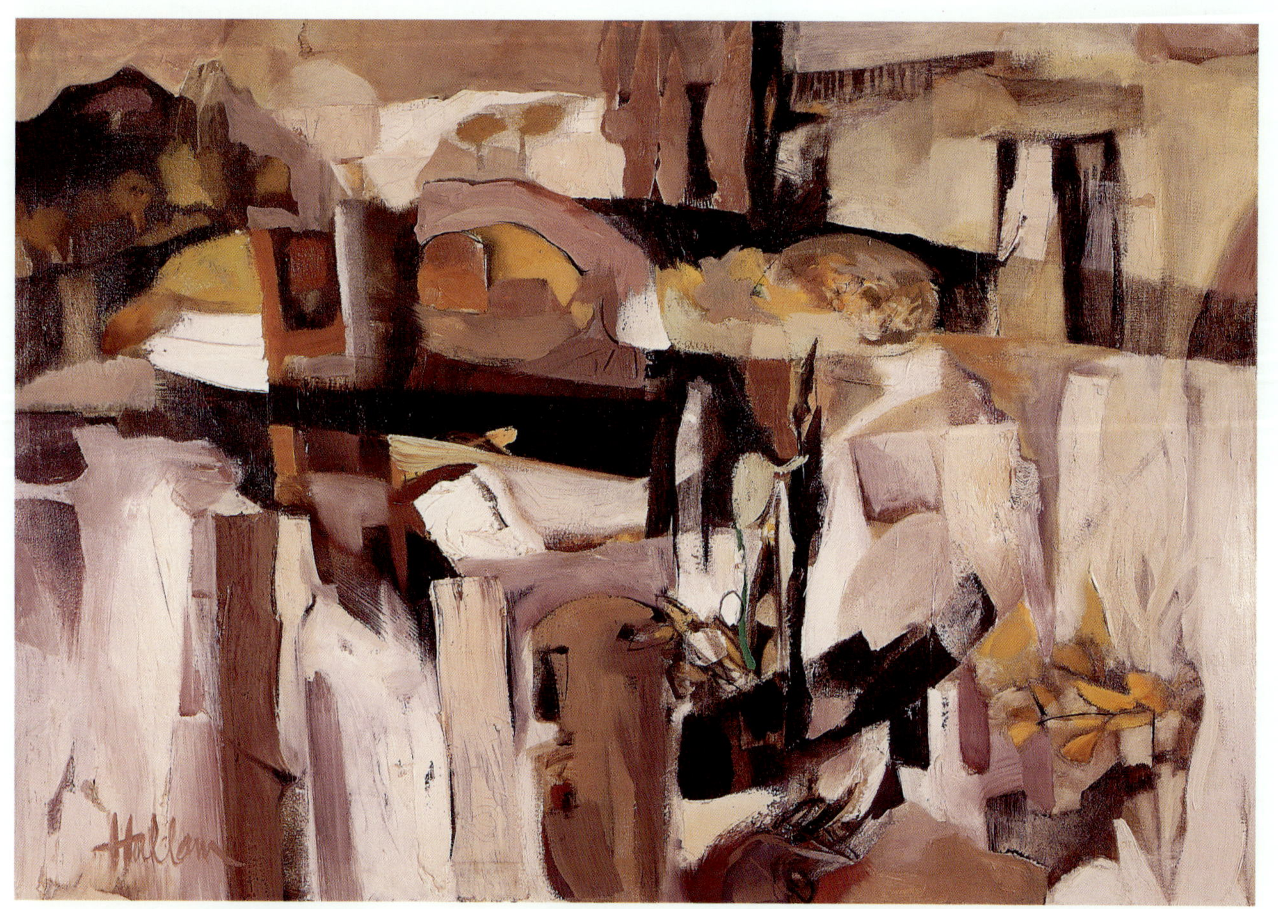

Hadrian's Villa, 1961
Oil on Belgian linen
42 x 50 in.
Private collection

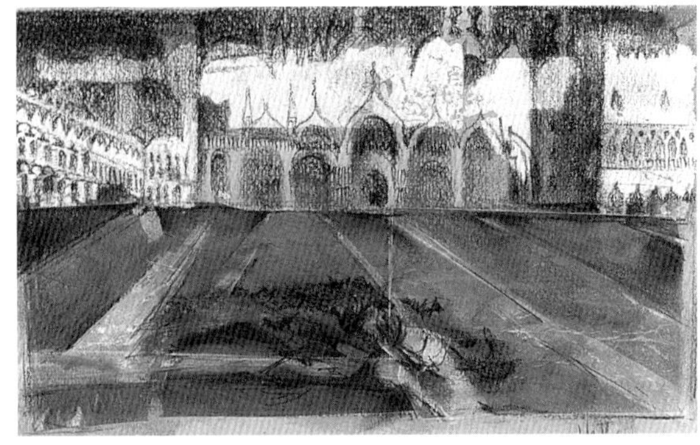

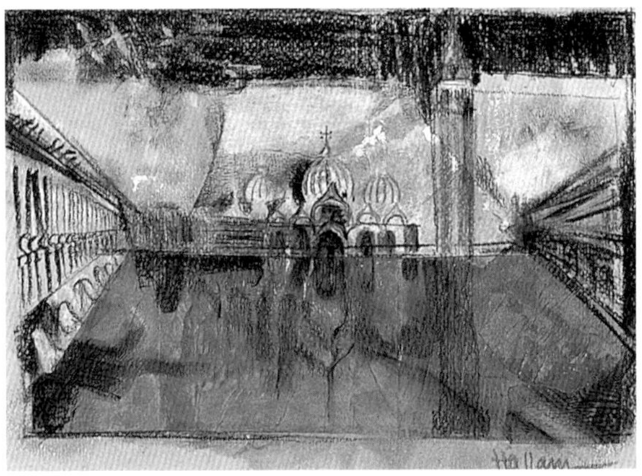

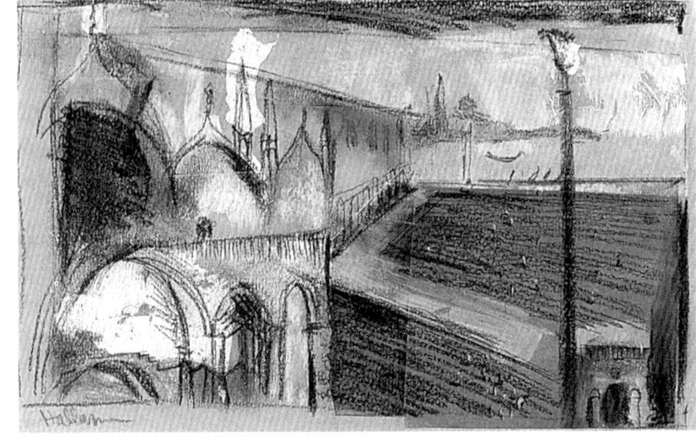

Top: *Piazza San Marco, Venice I*, 1961
Pastel collage with gold leaf on tan Canson Mi-Teintes paper, 10 x 13 in.
Collection of the artist

Middle: *Piazza San Marco, Venice II*, 1961
Pastel collage with gold leaf on tan Canson Mi-Teintes paper, 10 x 13 in.
Collection of the artist

Bottom: *Piazza San Marco, Venice III*, 1961
Pastel collage with gold leaf on tan Canson Mi-Teintes paper, 10 x 13 in.
Collection of the artist

Hallam spent seven days in Venice, then traveled through Italy by car, gathering material for painting. She made stops in Bologna, San Marino, Urbino, Gubbio, Tivoli, and Pisa and spent many weeks in Florence and Rome. The oil-on-linen depiction *Hadrian's Villa*, 1961, is a composite view based on a number of black-and-white snapshots Hallam made of this famous structure. Most unusual for her, Hallam also made a pastel of the subject after the painting was completed, but it scarcely resembles the oil.

After an extended stay in Italy, Hallam and her companions crossed over the Alps to southern France. In Mougins, a hill town near Cannes, Hallam, Smart, and Covert rented a house where they stayed for four months. "I was saturated with Italy," Hallam recalls, "and was fired up to paint my memory of several places I had just visited, especially Venice."

Hallam notes that when she travels she is never able to make elaborate paintings on the spot. For reference, she uses slides. In Mougins, she studied the slide images of Italy through a hand-held viewer, interested less in details than in the overall effect of the place.

Hallam began with two paintings of Pisa, then made several of Bologna. Following these, she made three small studies on paper, *Piazza San Marco, Venice I, II,* and *III*. For these pieces Hallam used what she calls her "traveling kit," comprising 8-by-10-inch colored sheets of Canson Mi-Teintes paper, a small bottle of polyvinyl acetate; a small, flat sable brush; a tiny book of gold leaf (separated by thin pieces of sepia paper); and sticks of black, white, and sepia conté crayon. With these materials she made quick impressions by establishing overlapping patterns using the white and sepia tissue with accents of gold leaf, after which she defined the images with conté crayon.

Two of the Piazza San Marco studies were developed into major paintings—*Pigeons, Piazza San Marco* and *Glass of Campari*. For these large canvases Hallam worked on unsized Belgian linen and built up layers of white tissue paper with polyvinyl acetate. She then added color by dipping her brush first into Methocel, a clear wetting agent, and then into finely ground dry pigment. Mixing this on a glass palette with polyvinyl acetate, she swept in color and, before it had dried, wiped it off with a wet sponge—a technique like that used in antiquing furniture.

For several of the Venetian paintings Hallam applied gold leaf over damp polyvinyl acetate and then sealed it in with more of the emulsion. According to the artist, the gold is still beautiful to this day. The gold leaf is particularly effective in views that incorporate the domes of St. Mark's, with a bit of decorative ironwork, a glass of Campari, and gondolas accenting the scene. Hallam worked in this fashion, with a brush in one hand and sponge in the other, for the next seven years, gradually replacing the tissue with the higher texture of mica talc.

In Mougins, Hallam also produced landscapes, interiors, and still lifes using conté crayon and pastel, often combined with acrylic. *Tilleul Tree in Mougins*, 1961, is a fine study of a linden tree pollarded in the manner that so appealed to van Gogh. With *Mediterranean Sardines*, 1961, and *Bovardia in Venice*, 1962, she incorporated French newspapers, decorative paper, and even admission tickets to the 1962 Venice Biennale, which she had visited and photographed (and later lectured on back in the United States). It is interesting to note that Robert Motherwell was pursuing a similar aesthetic at the time, as one sees in his *Pyrénéen Collage*, 1961.

Mougins was the perfect place for a flower painter. "The vases of flowers around the villa really got to me," Hallam remembers, "and I couldn't resist them." One of her paintings featured a long high wall of yellow jasmine that ran along the driveway. And she recalls with delight driving to Cannes one day and having a large ball of yellow fluff whiz by her. She couldn't believe her eyes: it was a Volkswagen completely covered with mimosa. The city of Nice seemed to Hallam to be the capital of carnations, and she used them often in her work.

Pastel has been a constant in Hallam's art, and is a medium she frequently uses in combination with others, as witness the two acrylic and pastels on rice paper, *Spanish Corral* and *Field of Flowers, Gerona*, 1962. The latter received first prize at the 73rd exhibition of the Boston Society of Water Color Painters, held at the Boston Museum of Fine Arts in May 1962. According to the prize committee, the Edwin S. Webster Award of Honor was given "to honor the superlative accomplishment of this annual exhibit."

Writing in *The Boston Sunday Globe*, critic Edgar J. Driscoll, Jr., noted that the prize-winning piece caused a certain quandary on account of its unusual medium, "opaque watercolor and pastel [used] in the manner of oil." As one of three judges—Anne Freedberg of the Museum of Fine Arts and artist Roger Cormier were the other two—Driscoll reported that there was some deliberation over whether the use of "pure" watercolor techniques was a requisite for the award. In the end, their unanimous decision was to present the prize to Hallam.

Venice is my favorite place outside of Maine. Water, for me, is to look at. . . not for getting into.

In the same column, Driscoll gave a rave review of a one-woman show of Hallam's work at the Shore Galleries on Newbury Street. The exhibition was composed, in the critic's words, of "a number of freely handled, wonderfully colored oils, gouaches and pastels reflecting [Hallam's] painting spree abroad." Driscoll mistakenly referred to the works as oils, not realizing they were done in polyvinyl acetate.

Driscoll found the approach in this new work to be "more abstract and

Pigeons, Piazza San Marco, 1961
Acrylic with tissue collage and gold leaf
on Belgian linen, 32 x 51 in.
Collection of Arnold W. Ginsburg

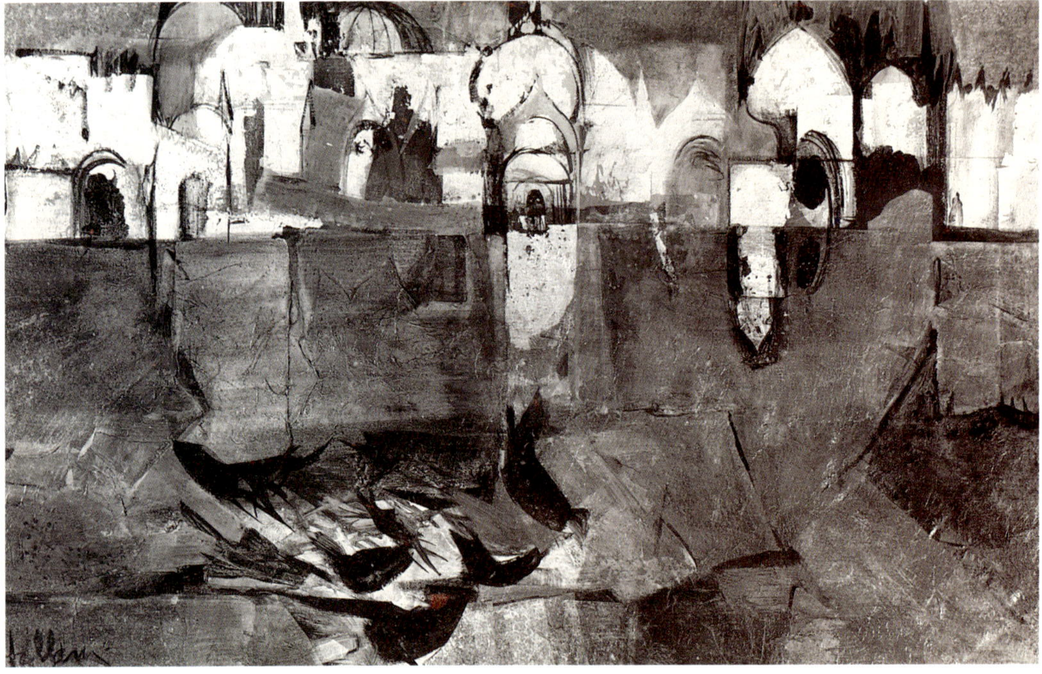

Glass of Compari, 1961
Acrylic with tissue collage and gold leaf
on Belgian linen, 38 x 50 in.
Private collection

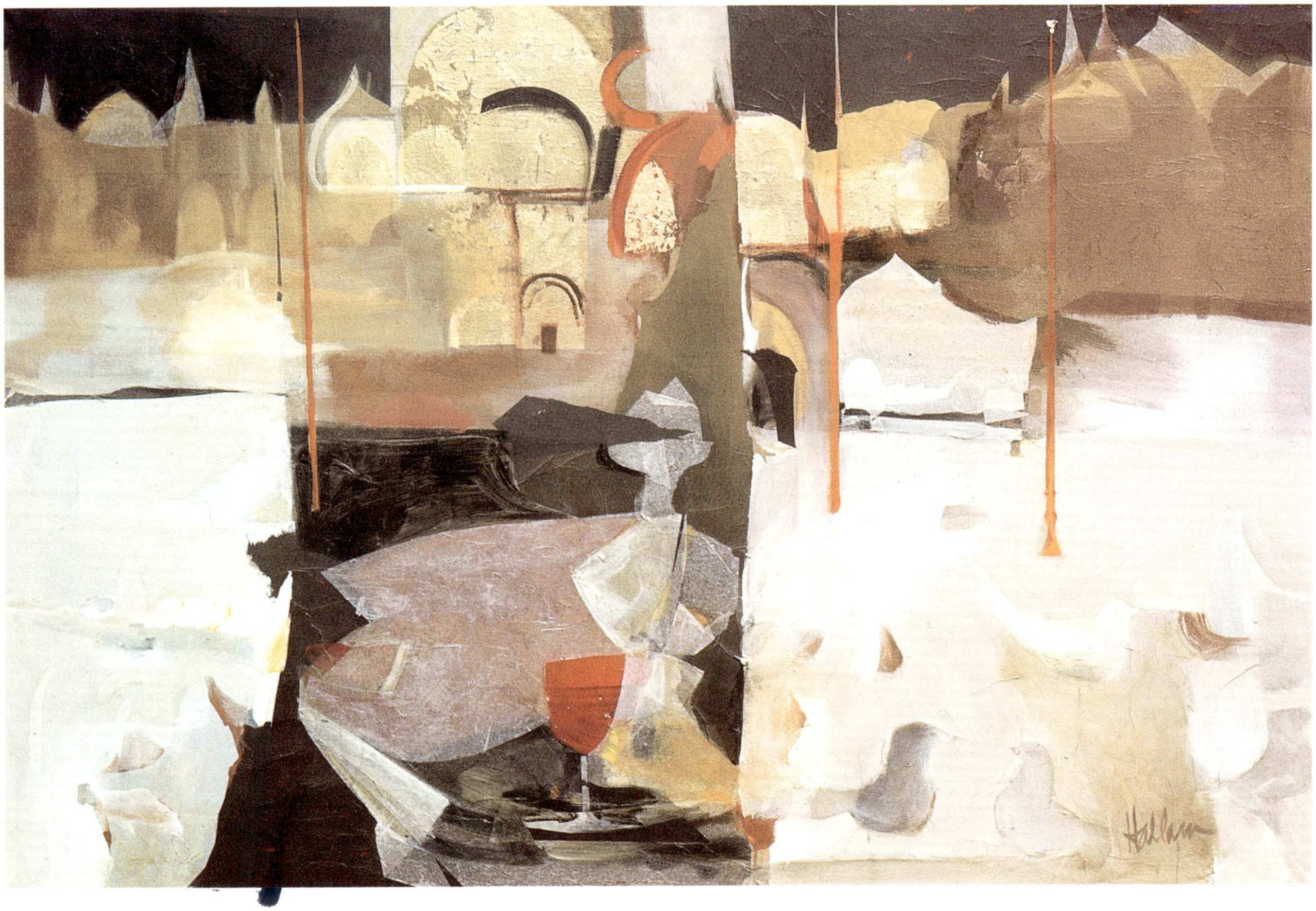

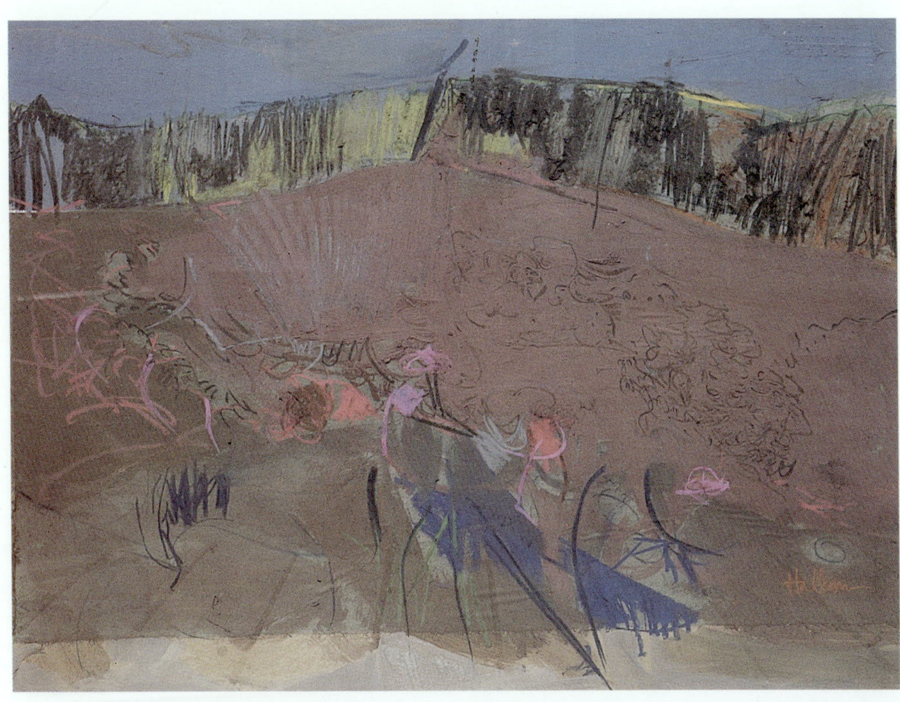

Field of Flowers, Gerona, 1962
Acrylic and pastel on mounted rice paper, 30 x 40 in.
Rose Art Museum, Brandeis University

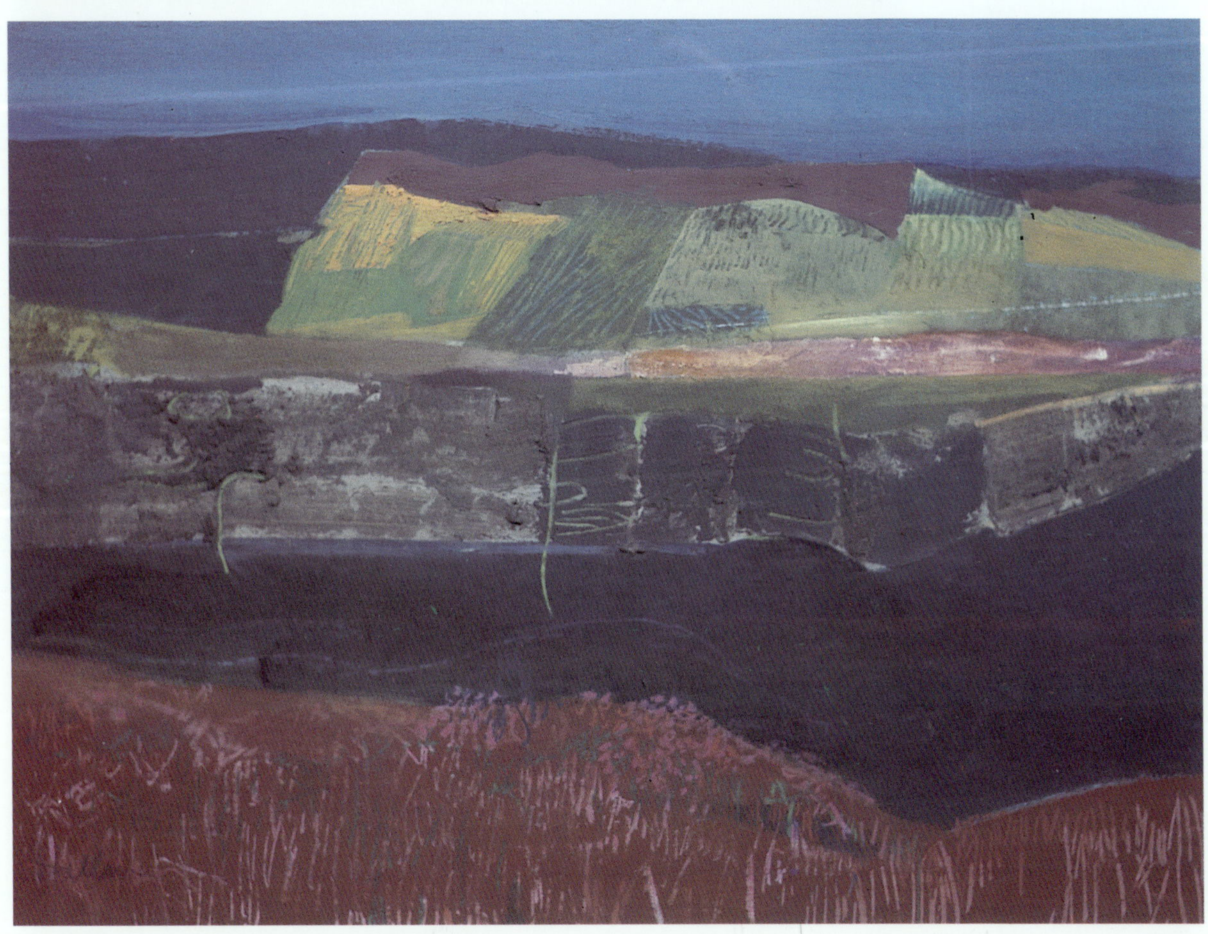

Spanish Corral, 1962
Acrylic and pastel on mounted rice paper, 30 x 40 in.
Collection of Mr. and Mrs. Kerry Lyne

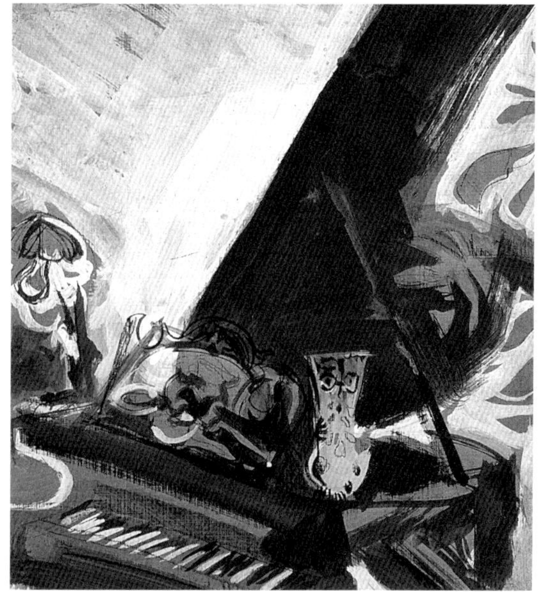

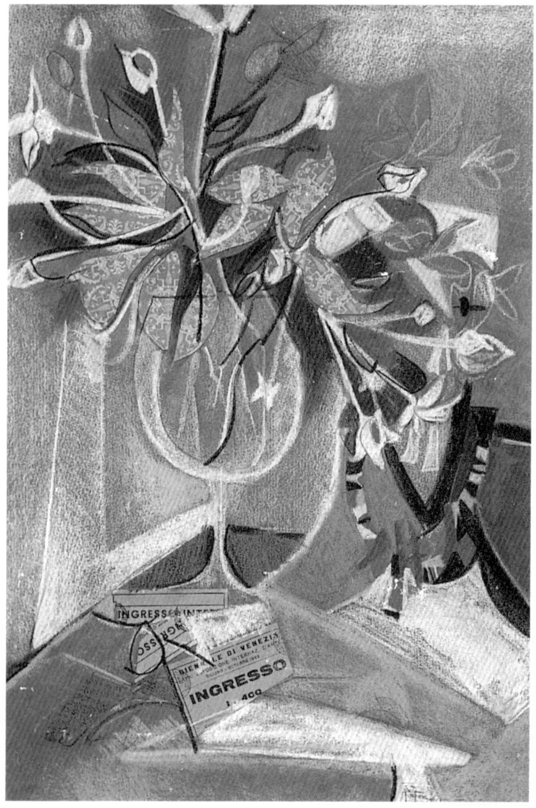

Top: *Vallauris Bird II* (Mougins), 1961
Acrylic & conté on brown Fabriano paper, 15 x 13 in.
Collection of Mr. and Mrs. David L. Linney

Bottom: *Bovardia in Venice,* 1962
Pastel and collage on tan paper
Collection of Mr. and Mrs. John A. Baybut

expressionist—but not, we hasten to add, abstract-expressionist (there is a difference)." He particularly liked a number of flower paintings, "rendered with dash, éclat and in a joyfully exuberant way," and made note of Hallam's "larger, more wonderful canvases, such as 'Pigeons, Piazza San Marco,' or the very handsome 'Glass of Campari.' " A "striking exhibition," concluded the critic, "by one of the most talented women artists in our midst."

The reviewer for the *Christian Science Monitor*, Dorothy Adlow, also had kind words for Hallam's Italian scenes and still lifes. She wrote of the artist's "adventures with the polyvinyl medium, as well as pastels and crayon," and provided a brief explanation of the art of collage. Calling the "general effect of pattern and color" in Hallam's work "gratifying," Adlow praised her "figurations," which are "sometimes quaint or fanciful or saucy," and whose strength "often lies in a sense of delight in performance engendered by this artist." Adlow liked best the small pictures in the show, including *Violets and Camellias*. Of the large work, she mentions *Night Carnations*.

One interior from this period, *Vallauris Bird II* (Mougins), 1961, represents the first appearance in Hallam's work of the Picasso vase she purchased during her stay in France. This lovely object, with the quintessential Picasso bird painted on its side, has been a favorite subject, one which Hallam returns to time and again, most recently in 1994. In the Mougins picture, the bird vase sits on a piano, seemingly ready to take flight at any minute—or at least to burst into song.

After four months in France, Hallam had completed more than 100 works on paper and 7 major canvases. Leaving Mougins, she and Smart drove to Aix-en-Provence, where they visited Cézanne's studio. On a route that took them north over the Alps into Alsace, then north and east of Paris, Hallam took hundreds of photographs for a lecture she was preparing on contemporary churches and stained-glass windows—notably those in Audincourt and Le Corbusier's Chappelle Notre-Dame-du-Haut in Ronchamp; in Franch-Comte, Baccarat, and Alsace; and in Lunéville in the Meuse Valley.

An inveterate gallery and museum visitor, Hallam took in many art exhibitions when she arrived in Paris. An entry in her diary from April 8, 1961, describes a day during which she visits the Louvre, the Sennellier art supply store on the Quai Voltaire, and a show of paintings by American artist Paul Jenkins at the Galérie Karl Flinker.

Hallam met up with Jenkins, who had just been the subject of an article in *Time* magazine. She recalls that they discussed ways of varnishing acrylic paintings and that Jenkins thought it odd that nobody had invented an acrylic varnish with a dull finish. Hallam suggested Krylon transparent spray, which Jenkins had not heard of, but which he planned to order

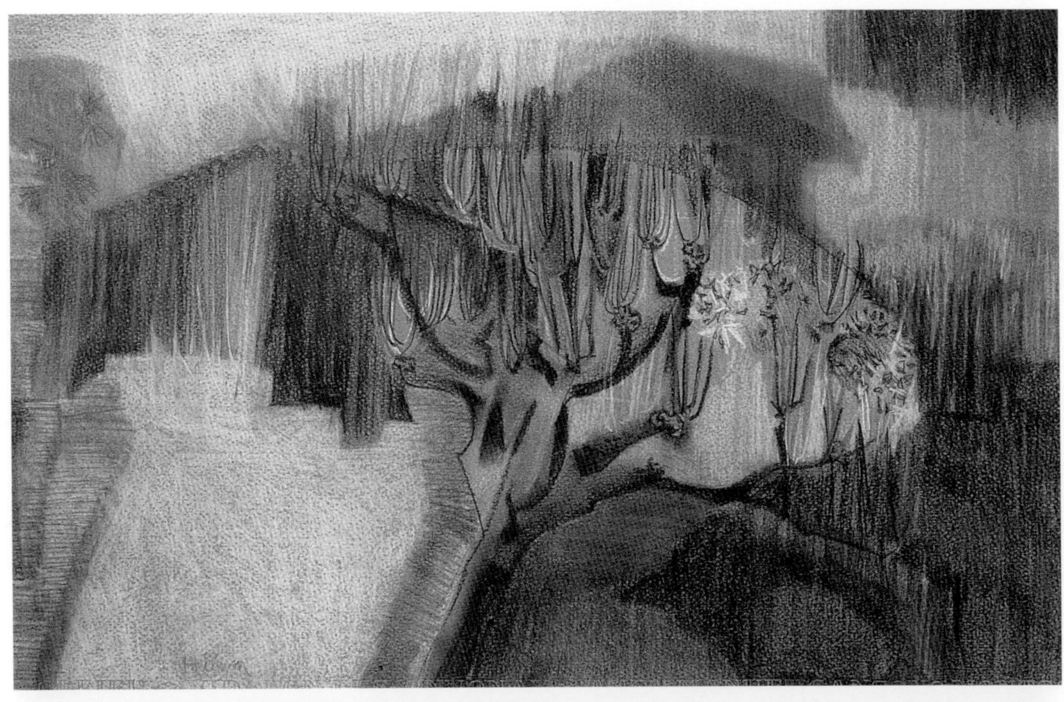

Tilleul Tree in Mougins, 1961
Conté on tan Canson Mi-Teintes paper
19 3/4 x 25 7/8 in.
Collection of Mrs. Thomas D. Masters

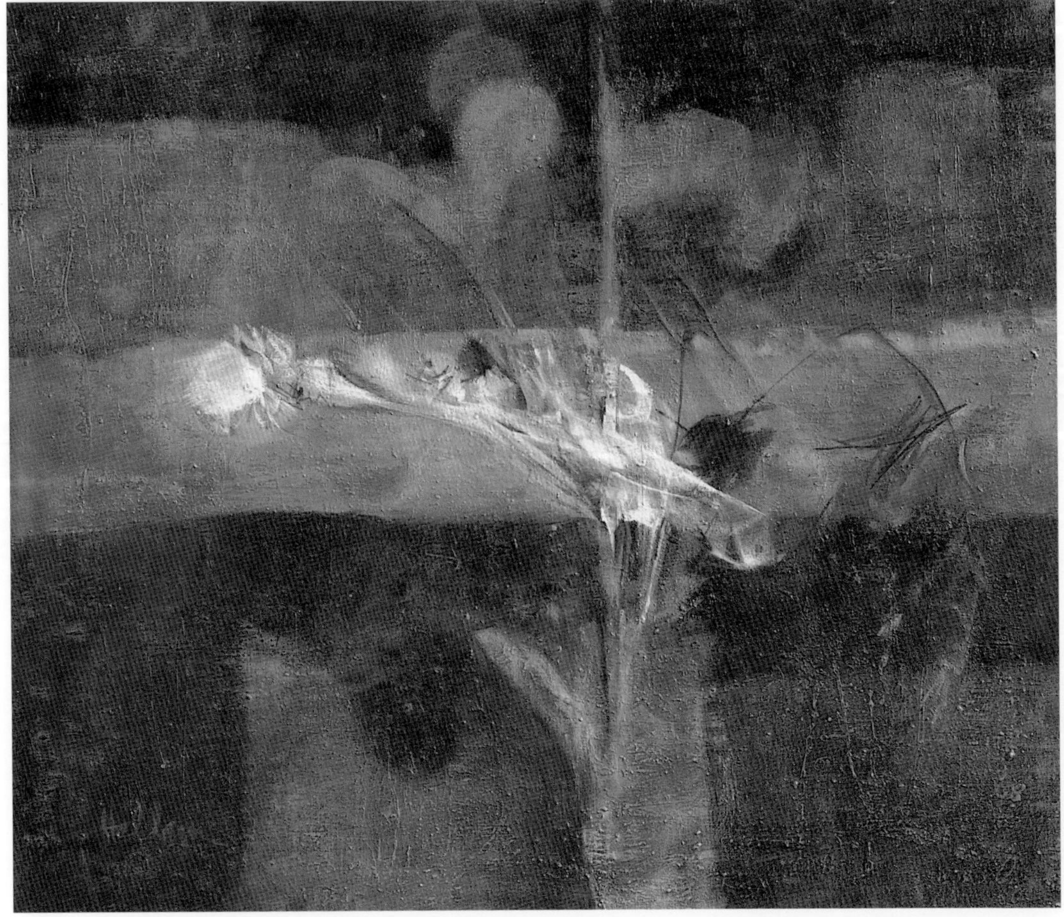

Night Carnations, 1961
Acrylic on Belgian linen, 42 x 50 1/4 in.
Private collection

through his supplier. At the time, he was mostly painting in oils but would soon switch to acrylics.

After Paris, Hallam continued to photograph churches as she headed south through France, then to Spain and Portugal. It was April, and Hallam has distinct memories of passing through the lovely southern European landscape, with verbena, red poppies, tall geraniums, roses, and purple, white, and yellow wildflowers growing on the roadside.

Hallam and Smart also soaked up many memorable meals along the way. Smart, a veteran gourmet cook, introduced her friend to the best city and country restaurants throughout their travels. In fact, one of Hallam's

Mediterranean Sardines, 1961
Acrylic, collage, and conté on paper, 18 x 24 in.
Private collection

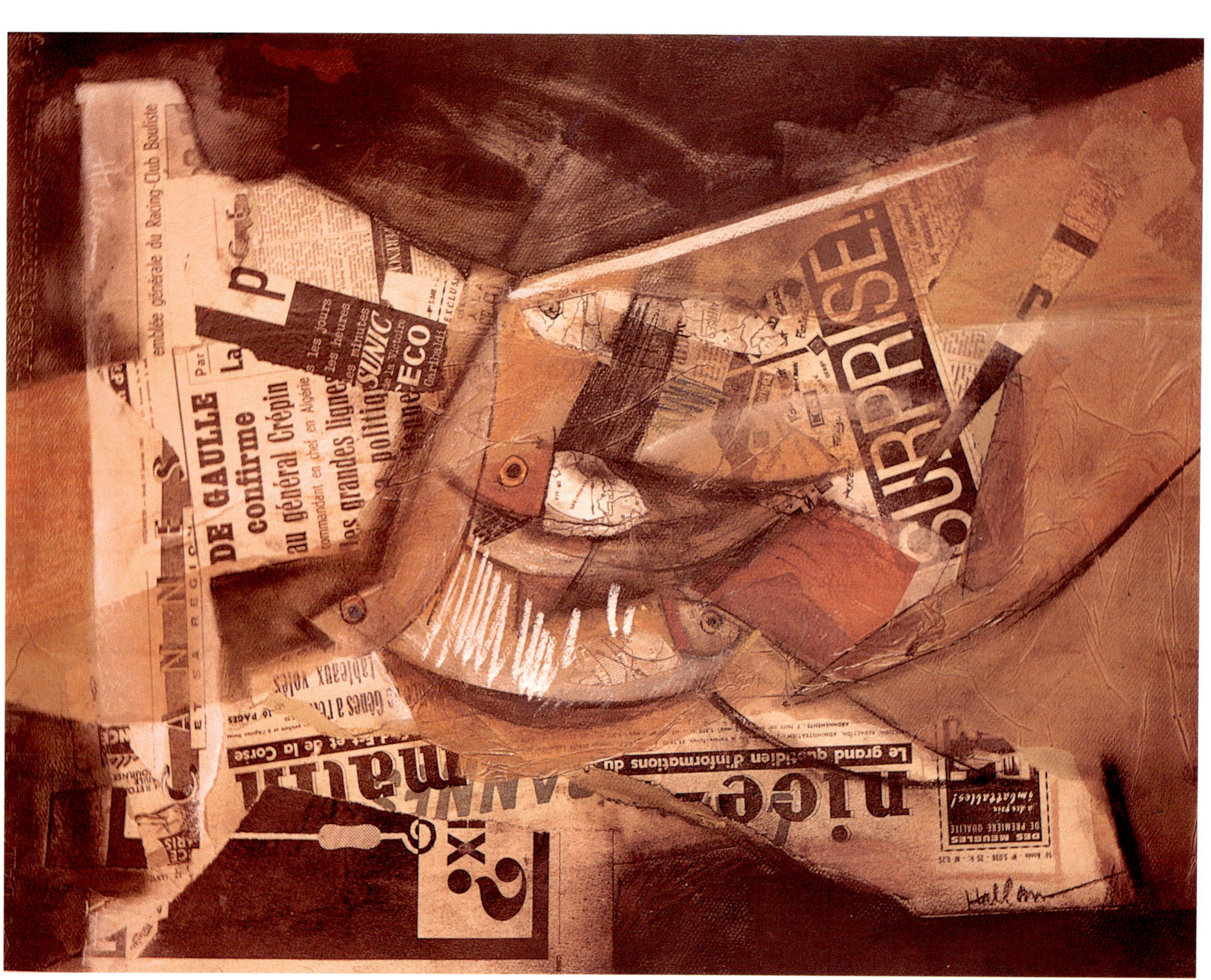

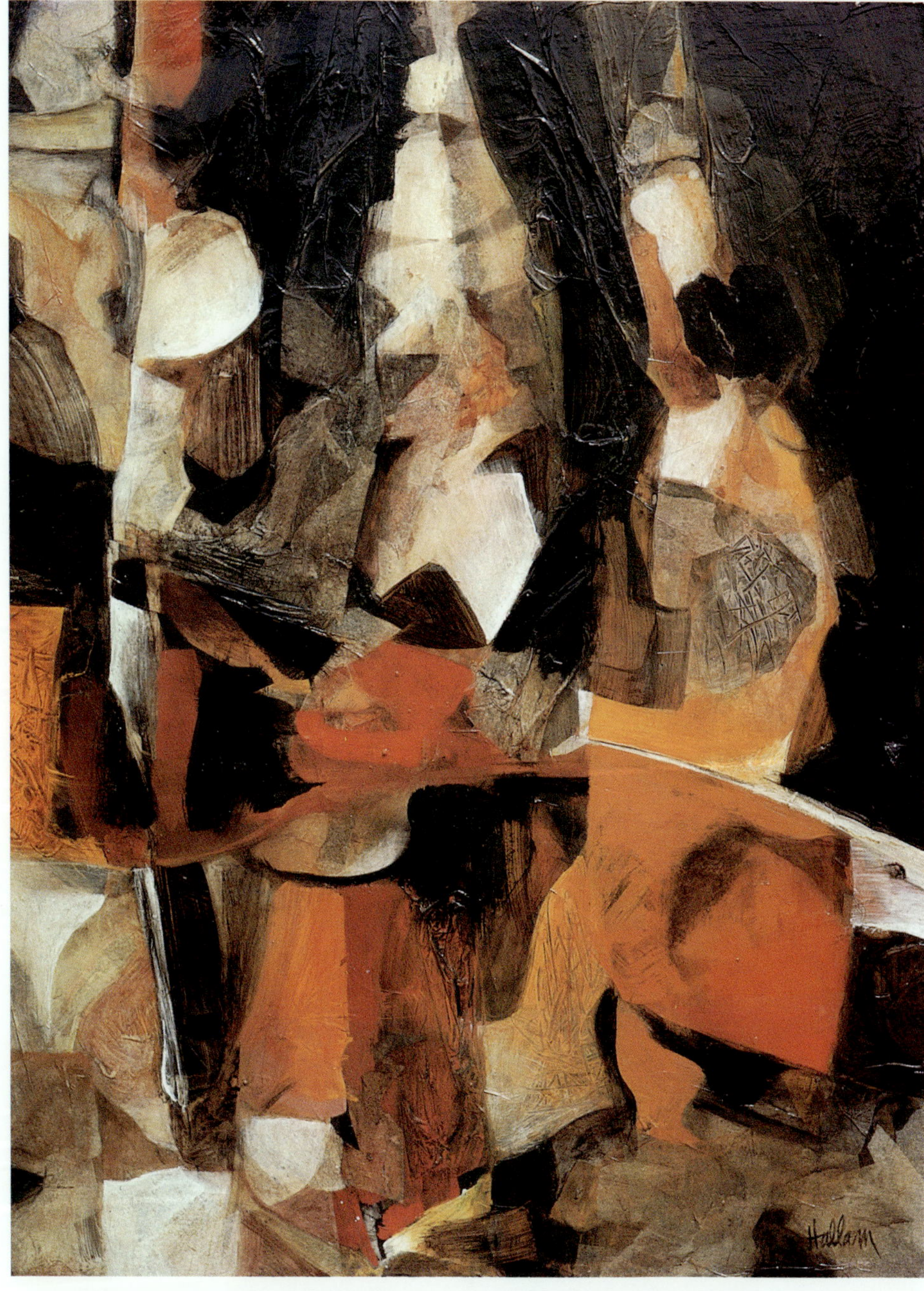

El Torcal, 1962
Acrylic and tissue collage on Belgian linen
48 x 36 in.
Collection of Mary-Leigh Call Smart

most popular illustrated lectures was "Food, France and Italy." Nowadays she chides herself, saying that her food slides remain brilliant while her culinary presentations have tarnished.

One highlight of the trip south was visiting the Lascaux caves in the southwest of France. Hallam and Smart were given a tour by the men who had discovered the caves by accident when they were boys. The Toulouse-Lautrec Museum in Albi, where, she recalls, the horse chestnut trees were in bloom, especially interested her, as did the Mediterranean fishing villages of Collioure, in France, and La Escala, on the Costa Brava in Spain.

In Barcelona, Hallam climbed up a spire of Gaudi's cathedral to photograph it and later took pictures of the cathedral in Madrid. It was in the latter city that she discovered the painter Francisco Farreras. His work was delicate and had a quality and feeling akin to what Hallam had created in the canvases that incorporated tissue paper.

The tiny village of Oropesa, Spain, provided Hallam with subject matter for a later painting now in the collection of the Ogunquit Museum of American Art. She and Smart also visited Tomar—the loveliest city in Portugal, according to Somerset Maugham—and the nearby coastal town of Nazaré, where she photographed the boats and felt that fashion designers had been inspired by the mixed and unmatched patterns of the fishermen's clothing.

In southern Spain, Hallam also went searching for the unusual rocks of El Torcal in Antequera. In retrospect, says Hallam, "it was these rocks that changed my palette." This change is evident in her colorful, vibrant painting *El Torcal,* 1962.

Upon her return stateside, Hallam taught one more year at Mass Art, then returned to France and Italy for two months in 1962. She was immensely interested in what artists in other countries were up to, so again the Venice Biennale was number one on her list of sights, as was Peggy Guggenheim's palace and art collection, which she photographed.

Hallam's continued fascination with rock formations led her to Les Baux, near Avignon. This surreal region, with its deserted medieval citadel and rocky outcroppings, provided material for such canvases as the 4-by-6-foot *Stonecrop,* 1963.

Stonecrop *was a long time in process. It started vertically and was inspired by rock at Les Baux in France and ended on rock in Maine. I named it after my studio in Ogunquit, which was built on the side of a cliff.*

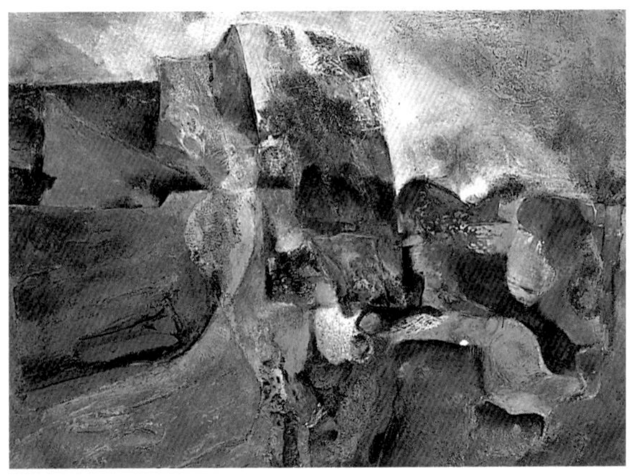

Stonecrop, 1963
Acrylic and mica talc on Belgian linen, 48 x 68 in.
Collection of Mr. and Mrs. Bud Kessler

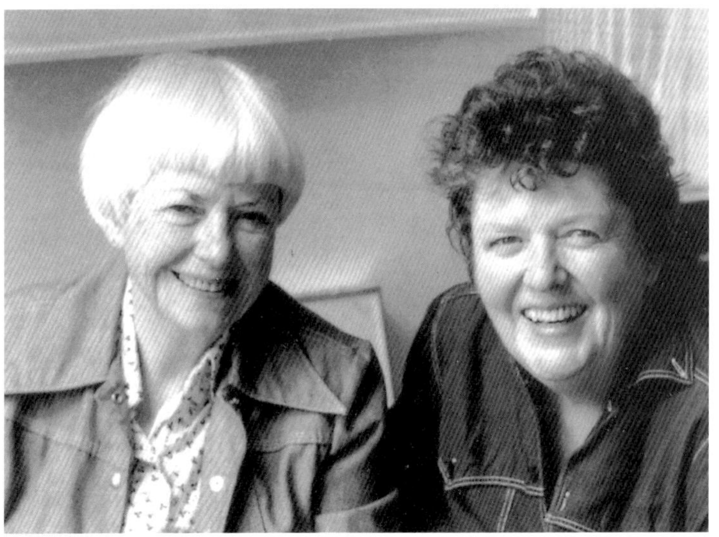

Mary-Leigh Smart and Beverly Hallam

9

Moving to Maine: Coastal Explorations

Returning from Europe in 1962, Hallam moved for good to Ogunquit. She kept her Boston studio for several years, unsure whether she would like living in the country full time. She bought a large studio on the edge of a rock ledge and, with a crew of workmen, winterized it for year-round living. Her new home, called Stonecrop, was a Salem-style house on Shore Road built, as Hallam is fond of saying, "in 1923 to look a hundred years old."

The house, which was featured in *House Beautiful* in July 1929, was the architectural creation of Grace Morrill, its original owner, who used antique materials from a number of different sources in its construction, including a 1770 barn and a 150-year-old house. The design of the house was the work of architects Russell and Little of Salem. Morrill named the place Stonecrop after a tiny, yellow-flowered plant of the genus *Sedum*, the only plant she expected might grow on the rock ledge around her house.

Certain memories of Hallam's sojourn abroad influenced her aesthetic at this time. She had soaked up the latest in European art firsthand. She received permission to photograph the 1960 and 1962 Venice Biennales for lecture purposes and, in so doing, took in a great deal of the avant-garde art of the day—work that, more than 30 years later, still has a new look, pre-empting much of what gets called "cutting edge" these days.

The many-textured landscape of Spain, which she depicted in such pieces as *Spanish Coral* and *El Torcal*, both 1962, found echoes in the Maine coast. The use of crinkled tissue paper in the latter picture led Hallam to pursue even greater texture in her surfaces.

Hallam had been drawn to the work of Francisco Farreras, Jean Dubuffet, Fontana, Alberto Burri, Modest Cuixart, Edmondo Bacci, Luis Feito, and other contemporary European painters who were experimenting with surface textures and out-of-the-ordinary materials such as burlap and burned plastic. "The paint itself has attained full pictorial autonomy," said a critic of Cuixart's work. The same could be said of Hallam's polyvinyl-acetate pieces at this time.

Both Cuixart's work and the robust surfaces of paintings by Antoni Tàpies (see *Gray Relief on Black*, 1959, latex paint with marble dust, from the Museum of Modern Art collection) inspired Hallam to thicken her acrylic medium. Hallam also discovered through experiment a way to bond high relief acrylic medium to large unsized pieces of Belgian linen without having it crack and with reduced weight. While these pieces resemble their igneous models, they are aesthetic objects, resembling to a certain extent some of the work of the Abstract Expressionists, yet with the added dimension of relief.

Now comfortable with the acrylic medium, Hallam achieved remarkable built-up flexible textures on canvas by adding a plasticizer, Resoflex,

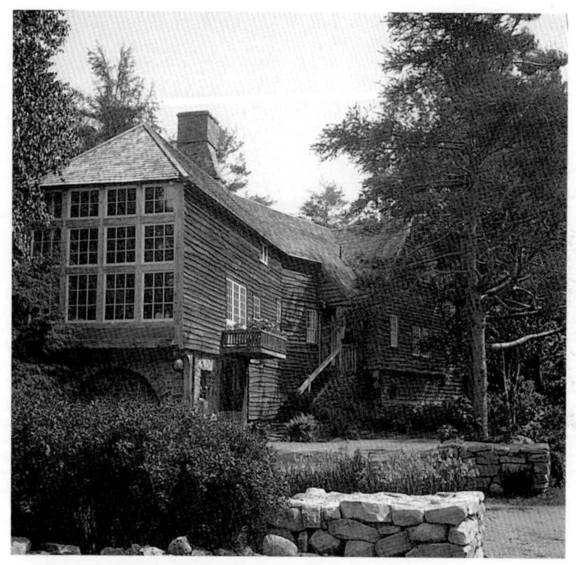

Hallam studio, Stonecrop, on Shore Road, corner of Juniper Lane, Ogunquit

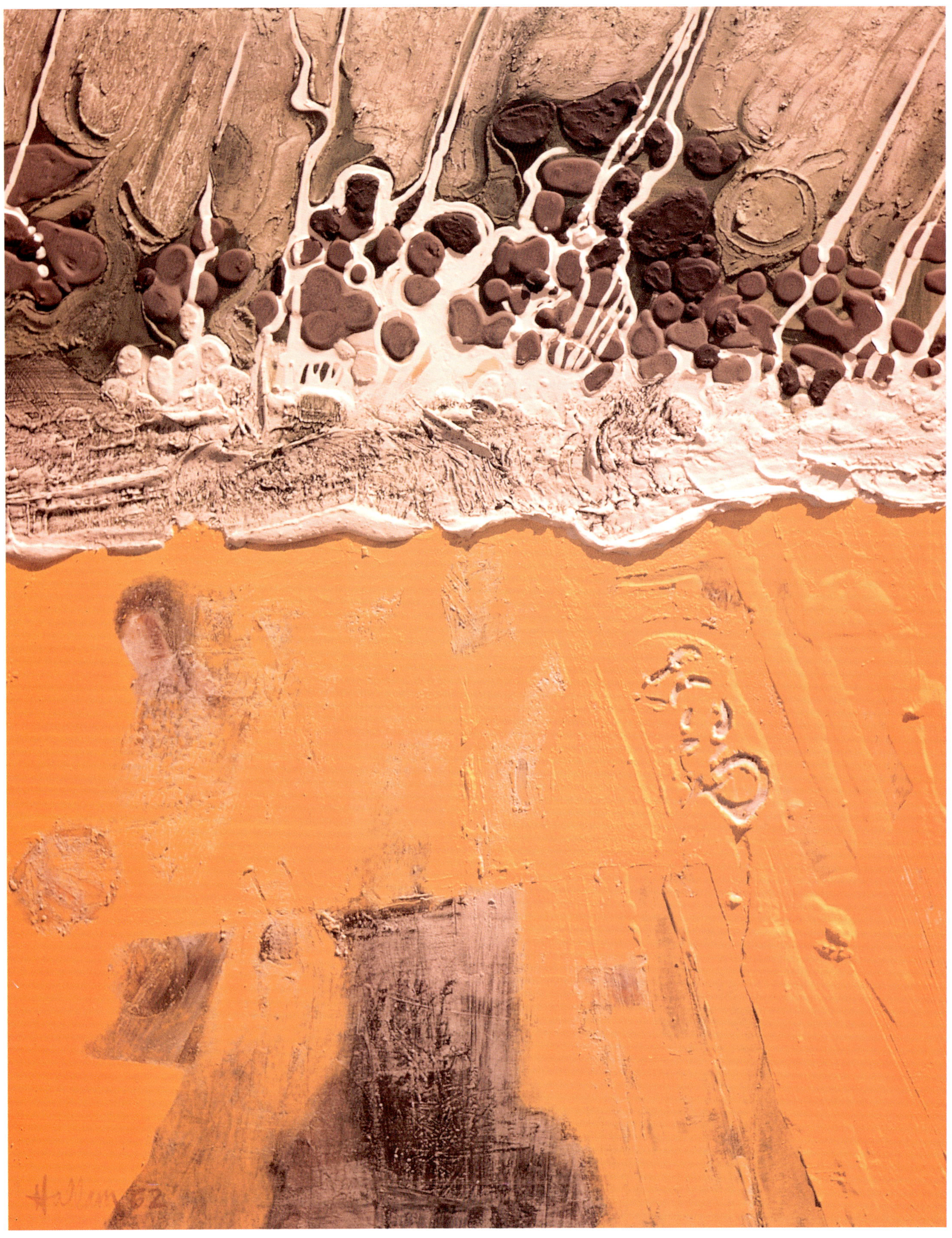

and ammonia to the polyvinyl acetate. She developed the following recipe:

> In a gallon glass jar, pour 8 ounces of water, 8 ounces of Resoflex and 2 tablespoons of 28% ammonia. Stir these together and fill the jar with polyvinyl acetate (P.V.A.). Mix it gently by turning the jar upside down several times and slowly stirring again. The polyvinyl acetate should never come in contact with anything metal as it will cloud the transparent quality. P.V.A. can be obtained from the Borden Company, and Resoflex and other chemicals from a chemical supply house.

To make lightweight "goop," as Hallam calls it, she offered this alternative formula:

> Pour the polyvinyl acetate into a glass bowl. Gradually add powdered mica talc to this medium while mixing with an electric egg beater. A bit of water can be beaten in until the desired consistency is obtained. The mixture should be used the same day.

All of the textured surfaces of Hallam's canvases from this period were prepared in a flat position and, when dry, were painted while upright. The Belgian linen was prepared by nailing the stretcher to the floor (or weighing it down on the corners) and sizing the linen with polyvinyl acetate half diluted with water. Restretching was sometimes necessary to make the canvas tight as a drum, at which point it was ready to receive any kind of aggregate, ranging from tissue paper to corn flakes to thickened mica talc.

I am always mesmerized by the movement of the foam edge of a wilting wave.

In *Tidewater,* 1962, a study of the frothy edge between sea and sand, Hallam used a basting tube and her fingers to build up the acrylic with mica talc, to the extent that the picture begins to resemble a relief.

In the mid-1960s, Hallam focused more and more on phenomena like the tide line, looking for the abstract in nature and, once finding it, translating it into art. "I didn't come here to paint realistic pictures," stated Hallam, in the article "Maine and Her Artists," in the August 1964 issue of *Woman's Day*:

> I came here to get ideas, to fill up the well-springs. I walk on the sand and watch the patterns, I climb over rocks to study the striations. Sometimes a close-up of a section of rock, which looks like an abstraction on canvas, suggests the flavor and essence of Maine better than a realistic interpretation.

(OPPOSITE)

TIDEWATER, 1962
ACRYLIC AND MICA TALC ON BELGIAN LINEN, 50 X 36 IN.
UNIVERSITY OF MAINE MUSEUM OF ART, ORONO
GIFT OF MARY-LEIGH CALL SMART

In the early 1960s, Hallam had returned to photography, using the camera as an aid in carrying out her artistic concepts. She photographed the rock, water patterns, and sea life at Bald Head Cliff, taking many shots from eight inches to a yard away—recording, in her words, "the infinite variations of structure, color, and change of light." A painting like *Bald Head Cliff Magma*, 1962, has the compositional freedom and inventive color one associates with the work of artists like Gino Morandi, Estéban Vicente, or Hans Hofmann, yet the image is derived directly from nature.

In 1963, Hallam did the first of a series of rock reliefs on plywood. She put mica talc aside and bought Jolly King rubber latex by the jar and poured it over rock formations on Bald Head Cliff. Having spread it around, she left the yellowish rubber to set overnight and then returned the next day to pull it off. "No tourists ever touched them. I saw a mother grab her child away from one, saying, 'Don't get near that, somebody was sick!'"

The rubber provided a negative mold into which Hallam poured cast stone. She tried painting the resulting pieces, but it didn't work. The few unpainted ones that remained she threw in the trash. Her friend Mary-Leigh Smart rescued them and they are in her living room today and are among the artist's favorites of her own work.

In *Beach*, 1964, Hallam returned to the tide line for subject matter. She troweled on the mica talc mixture, working up the thickness into visible ridges that divide fields of color. In his book *Creative Seascape Painting* (1981),

(OPPOSITE)

Bald Head Cliff Magma, 1962
Acrylic and mica talc on Belgian linen, 68 x 48 in.
Collection of Mr. Frederick H. Guterman

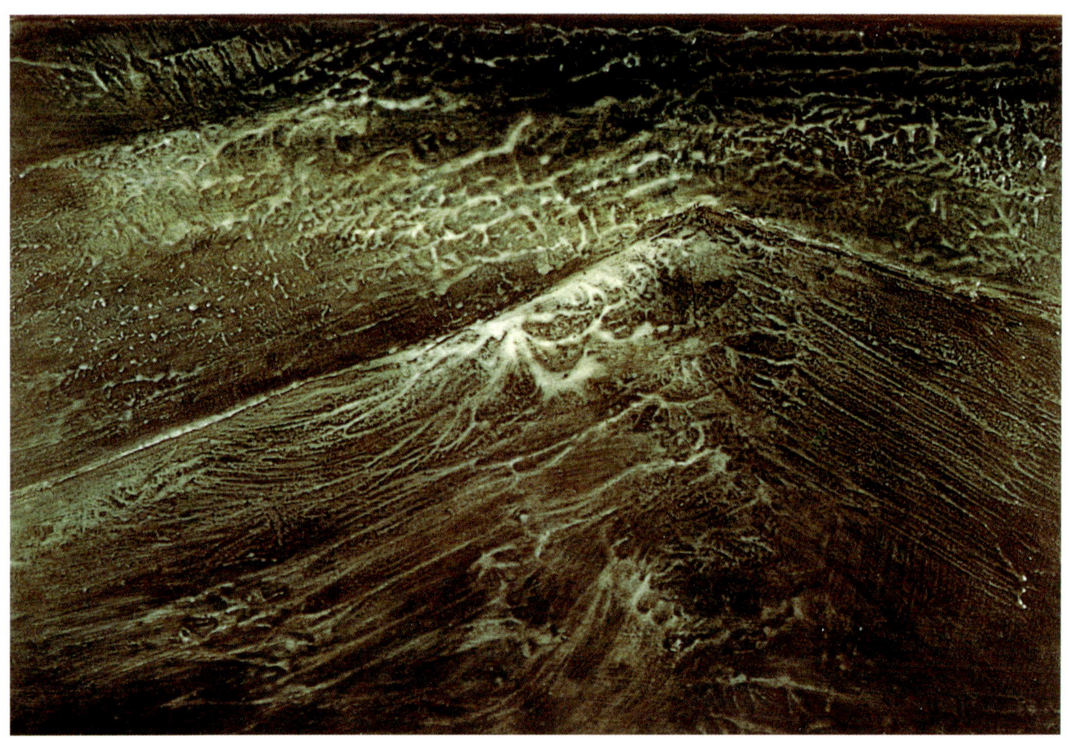

School, 1966
Acrylic and mica talc on Belgian linen, 18 x 28 in.
Private collection

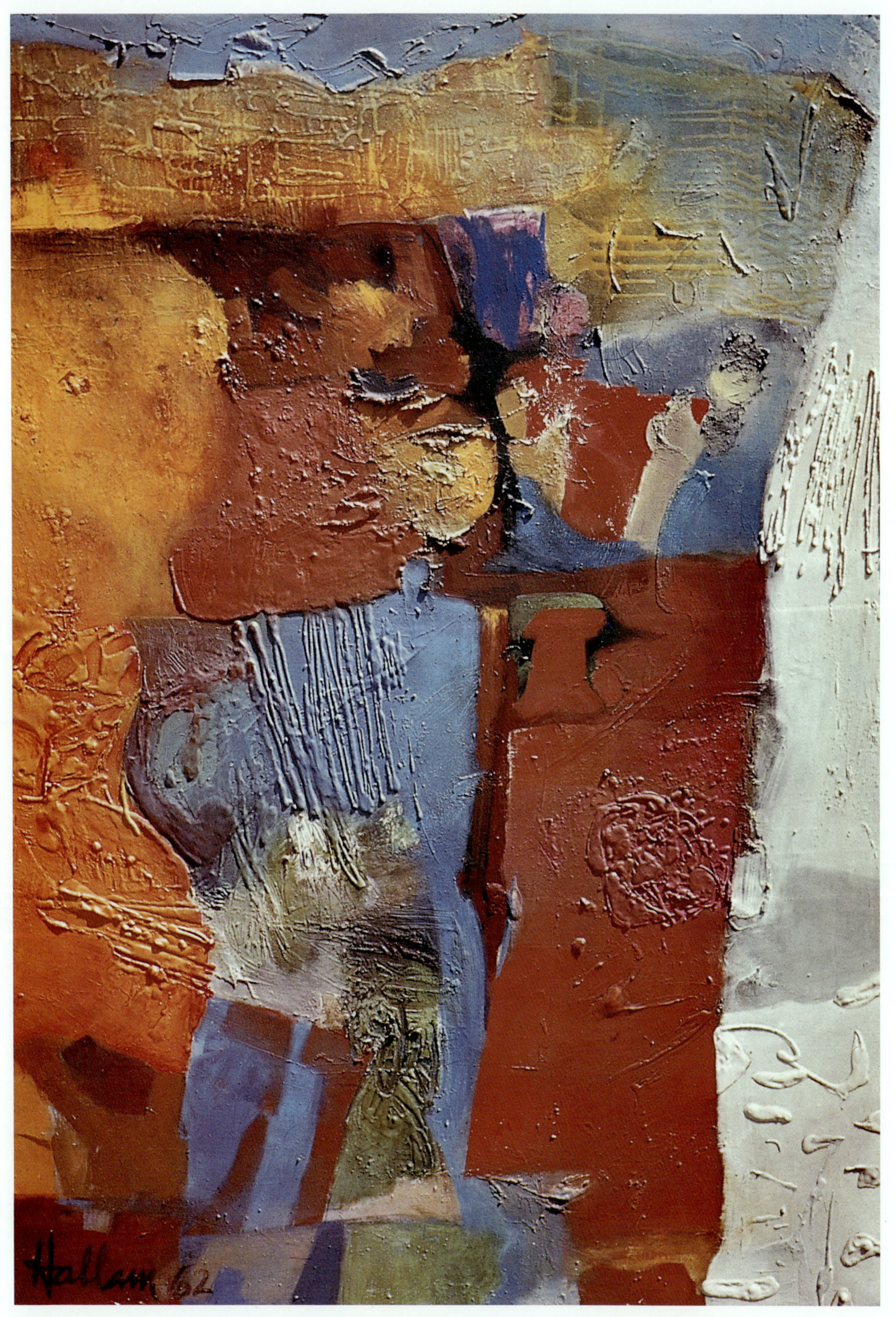
Hallam 62

When I began Ledge *I visualized a different ending. Halfway through I liked it so much I quit.*

Edward Betts describes the complex finish work on this particular picture:

> After drying, the textures were coated three times with white acrylic gesso and then glazed with various colors. When lights were needed, Hallam always sponged back to the original white undercoat; white pigment was never used.

Such a painting reflects Hallam's fascination with how waves end, the overlapping lines of white foam against the dark wet sand. In her own words, "No medium can possibly capture that beautiful performance"; and yet, using acrylic, Hallam could come close to recreating the spirit of the event. As Betts put it,

> The result is a relief painting with a strong sense of weight and tactility that persuasively conveys the sensation of the actual beach itself. The broad, sweeping rhythms and the physical materiality of the surfaces and textures constitute more of a direct identification with the motif than a mere reference to it.

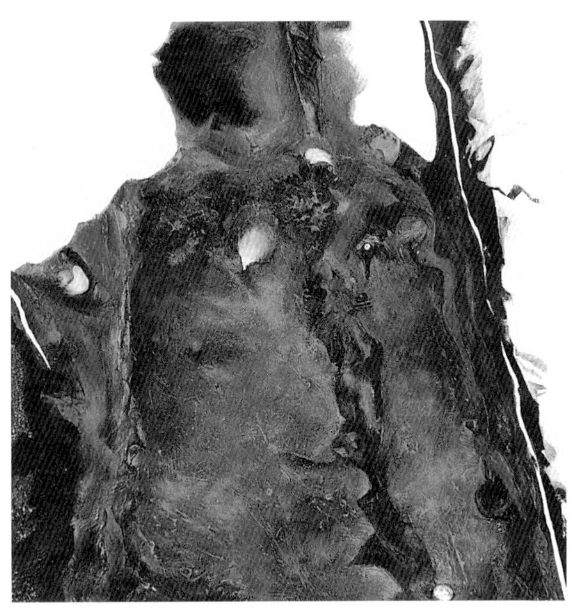

White Sky Pool I, 1965
Acrylic and mica talc on Belgian linen, 48 x 48 in.
Collection of the artist

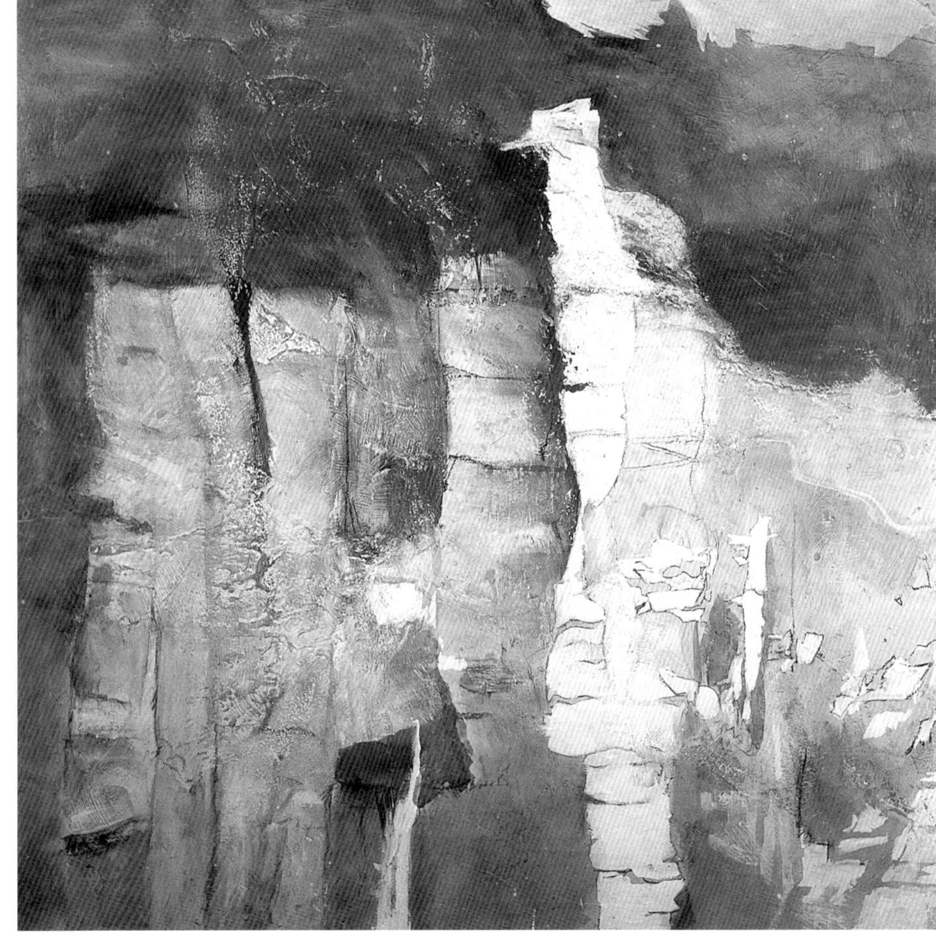

Ledge, 1967
Acrylic, mica talc, and charcoal on masonite, 76 x 76 in.
Collection of Mary-Leigh Call Smart

Throughout the years, Hallam has made photographs of the subjects she has painted for use in her lectures. To demonstrate to her audience what the word "abstract" means, she will show the actual motif and then the painting of it. Not until the airbrush series of the 1980s did Hallam actually follow the photograph closely in her painting, and even then many subtle deviations occur in her complex translations of the photographic image. As the artist has stated, "Photographs are mainly inspirational to me from a color, light, subject, and compositional standpoint, not for the small details they contain."

White Sky Pool I, 1965, captures the multilayered surface of a tidal pool in a variety of surfaces. Hallam worked from photographs taken with a Rolleiflex camera equipped with a closeup lens that allowed for parallax correction. In translating these "gems," as she called them, into acrylic images on canvas, she took a lot of liberties, playing freely with color and composition.

Hallam used the photographs as references, manipulating them by means of projected magnification onto Belgian linen. Thus, an enlarged 10-inch image of sea foam became, in the artist's mind's eye, an astronaut's view of clouds from outer space. Likewise, three inches of rock and moss blown up to 15 times its size was transfigured into "an underwater man." In *White Sky Pool I*, you can make out the shadow of the artist as she peers down into this variegated microcosm of sea life.

While working on these relief paintings, Hallam would listen to such electronic music as Mimaroglu and Stockhausen. The astronauts had just been to the moon and had sent back photographs they had taken of earth. These images were very similar to those Hallam was studying in tide pools, and to the patterns of lichen on rocks that so fascinated her.

Hallam had an exhibition of these paintings at Nasson College in Springvale, Maine, in 1966. She wanted to have slides of the earth as seen from the moon projected all over the ceiling and the floor during the show and have Stockhausen piped in. Such multimedia installations were virtually unheard of in those days.

Perhaps the best-known of Hallam's coast-inspired works is *Big Mussel*, 1965, one of her greatest paintings. In this large vertical work, measuring 83 by 48 inches, the striking blue-black of the mussel shell draws the eye to the center of the picture. Textures abound, particularly in the rendering of the shell's rocky surroundings and the accompanying seaweed.

There is something about this monumental mollusk that brings to mind the floral paintings of Georgia O'Keeffe, yet a sense of the fantastic reigns in Hallam's work. "A two-inch mussel shell was transformed into a space capsule," is the way she once put it, in a statement to accompany an exhi-

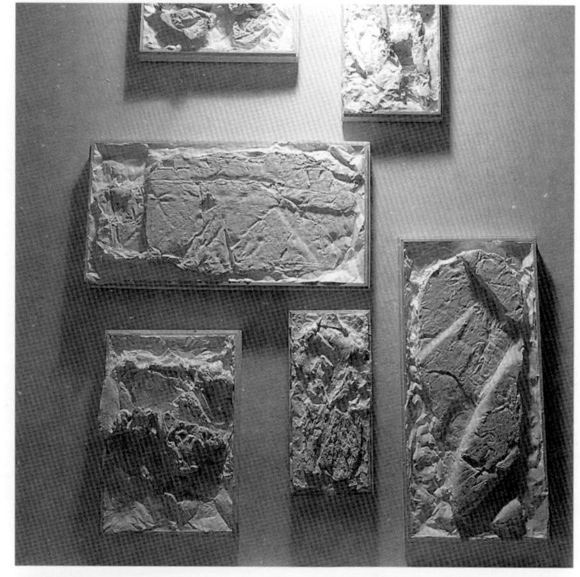

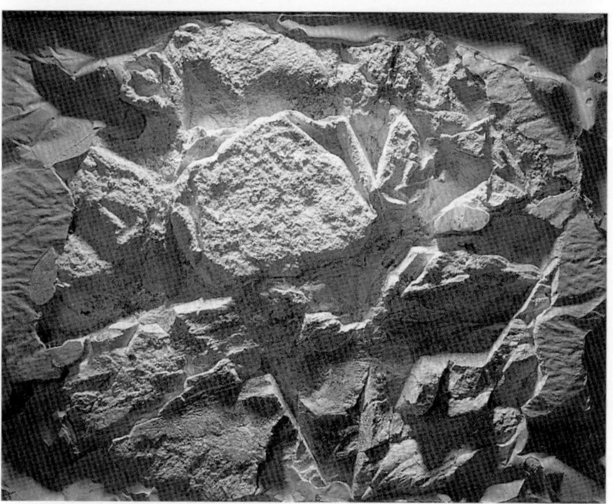

TOP: *FROM BALD HEAD CLIFF*, 1963
CAST STONE

BOTTOM: *CAST STONE IN TWO NATURAL COLORS AND WHITE*, 1965
CAST STONE, 11 1/2 X 14 1/2 IN.
COLLECTION OF THE ARTIST

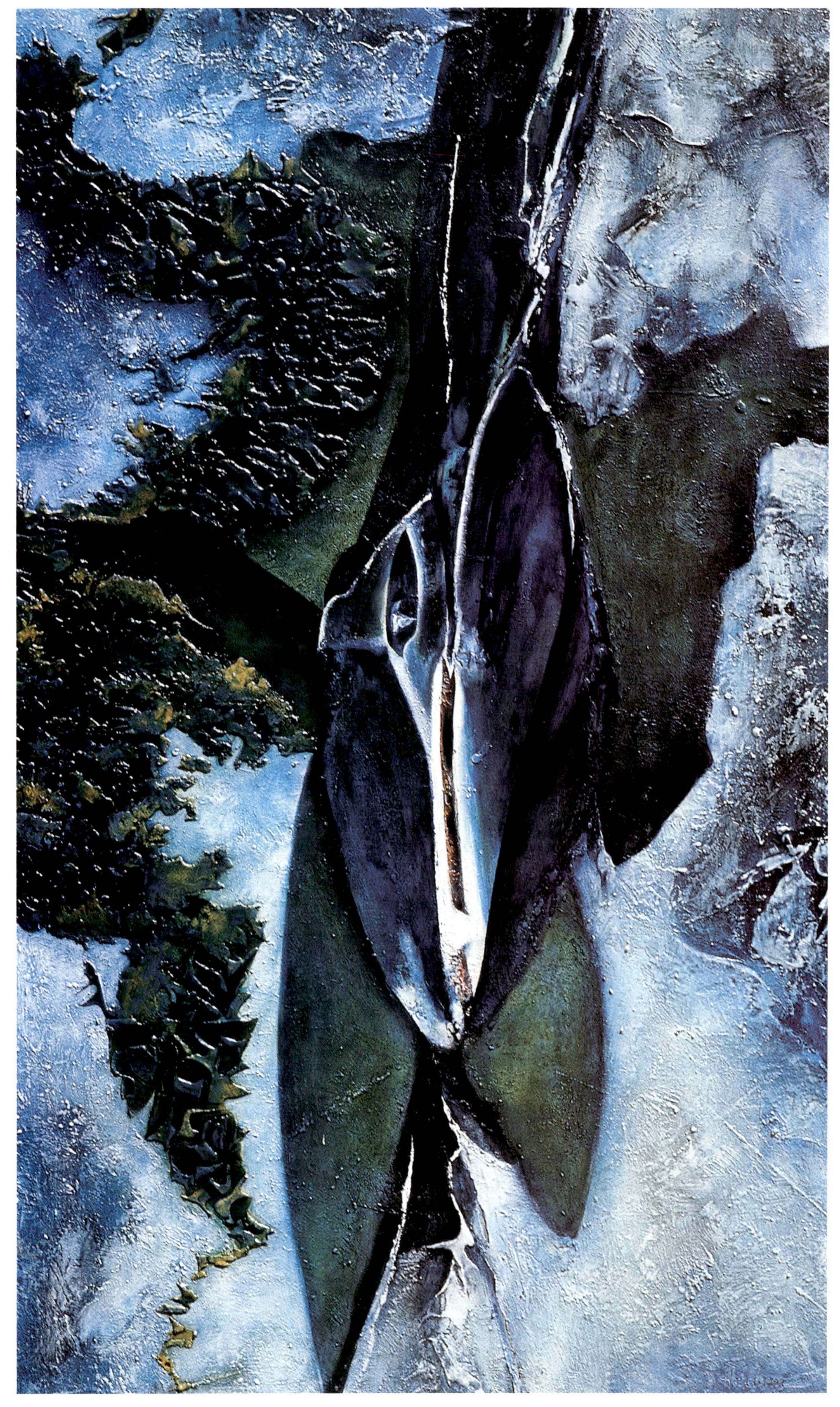

bition of this and other related works at the University of Maine in 1969. "Scale is mysterious," she wrote at the time, "and the shape of nature repeats itself in different forms above earth and under the sea."

Hallam tells an amusing story apropos *Big Mussel*. One night she turned the painting on its side to work on it horizontally. The canvas was brightly lit and could be seen from the road. The next morning two little boys knocked at Hallam's door and asked if they could see the spaceship in her studio.

Calling the picture "heroic in size," Betts described *Big Mussel* this way:

> All the elements have been consistently enlarged to the same degree as the mussel, both in scale and texture, but the forms are so enormous and there is so much emphasis on shape and pattern, that it takes some time and looking before it becomes clear that it is not just a bold abstract composition, that it is a representation of a very small fragment of the marine world.

This canvas and others display a kinship with Max Ernst's pictures of this time. Art historian Diane Waldman has written of Ernst's "profound involvement with nature, in both its rational and irrational aspects"—sentiments equally applicable to Hallam's perceptions of, and aesthetic response to, the Maine coast.

Ledge, 1967, is a closeup depiction of a vein of quartz that runs through Bald Head Cliff. It is also, quite simply, a bold abstraction. The foundation medium for *Ledge* is a thick mixture of polyvinyl acetate and mica talc troweled on masonite. Working with a photograph of the motif, Hallam made a charcoal drawing on the hardened undercoat showing the major cracks and bumps in the rocks. From there she invented, building up texture with a wide whitewash brush and color with a sponge.

Bald Head Cliff, off old Route 1 between York and Ogunquit, is well known to geologists. The shales are said to be the oldest sedimentary rocks in existence, around a billion years old. At Bald Head Cliff, hot moving lava heaved up during volcanic activity and turned on end vertically like a deck of cards, creating remarkable dikes—long masses of igneous rock that cut across the structure of adjacent rock.

The colors and textures of the resulting strata are many. There is one very wide milk-white quartz stripe just south of Perkins Cove that is visible from a long distance at sea. This stripe serves as a landmark for passing boats, and as the inspiration for several of Hallam's canvases.

In *Creative Landscape Painting* (1978), Betts notes that certain of Hallam's rock pictures represent equivalents of what occurs in nature. Speaking of the painting *Cleft*, 1966, he states, "This picture has as much to do with

(OPPOSITE)

BIG MUSSEL, 1965
ACRYLIC AND MICA TALC ON BELGIAN LINEN, 83 X 48 IN.
ADDISON GALLERY OF AMERICAN ART,
PHILLIPS ACADEMY, ANDOVER, MASSACHUSETTS

GIFT OF MARY-LEIGH CALL SMART

STACK, 1968
ACRYLIC ON MILBOURNE PAPER, 40 X 26 IN.
COLLECTION OF THE ARTIST

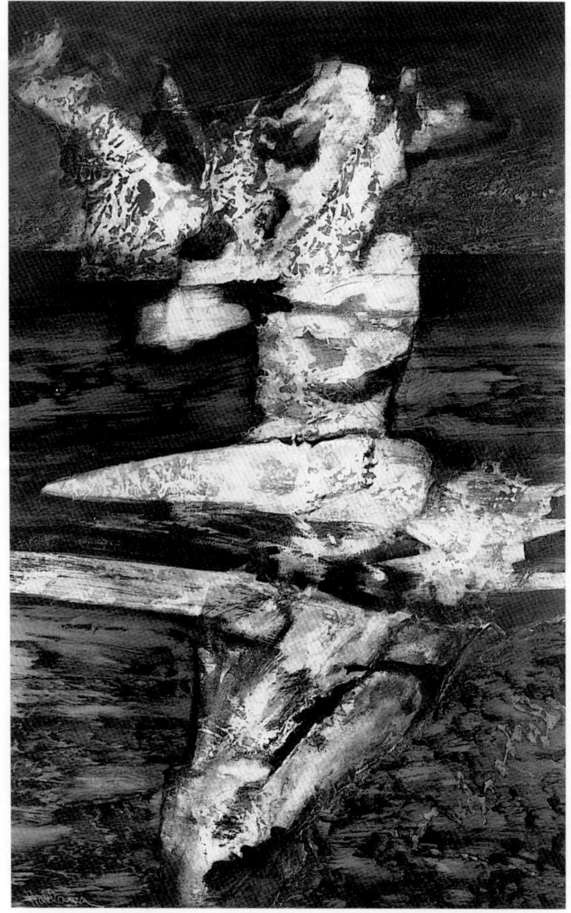

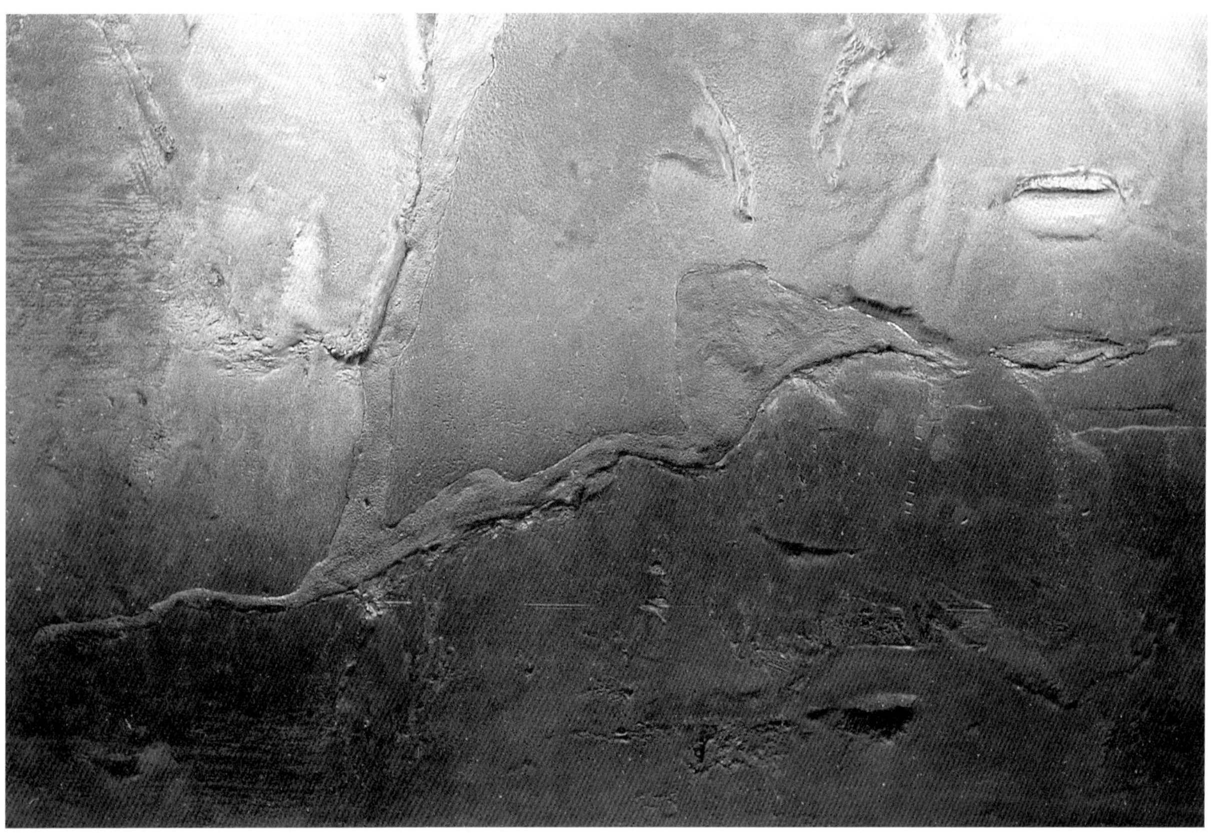

Conceptual Landscape, 1967
Acrylic and mica talc on masonite, 24 x 36 in.
Collection of Mary-Leigh Call Smart

geology as it does with art, a personal response to nature arrived at through the dialogue between the artist's intuitions and her materials."

Pieces like *Stack*, 1968, *School*, 1966, and *Conceptual Landscape*, 1967, demonstrate the artist working at the top of her form to create new textures and striking compositions based on abstract elements of nature and geology. Looking at these and other works from this period, one is reminded of the images of poet Abbie Huston Evans, who was equally taken with the geological elements of the Maine coast. Here are some lines from her poem "The Mineral Collection":

> Rock out of Maine, the ice-like tourmaline
> In shattered spars, pencils of frigid rose
> And chill black-green, of waters most dilute.
> —All these the bright credentials of dark workings,
> Compulsions, interminglings, strangest love,
> Knittings and couplings known but to the atom.

Hallam is still very much taken with coastal motifs. In recent years, she has written that she doesn't dare go and look at the tide pools near her home in York for fear she will be lured away from her flower painting.

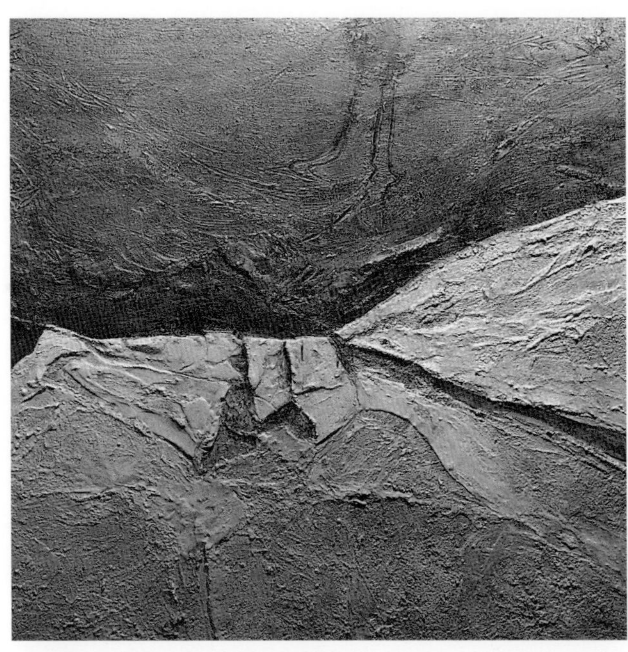

Cleft, 1966
Acrylic and mica talc on Belgian linen, 48 x 48 in.
Collection of the Colby College Museum of Art
Waterville, Maine
Gift of Mary-Leigh Call Smart

Beach, 1964
Acrylic and mica talc on Belgian linen, 20 x 28 in.
Collection of Mrs. Edward F. Dana

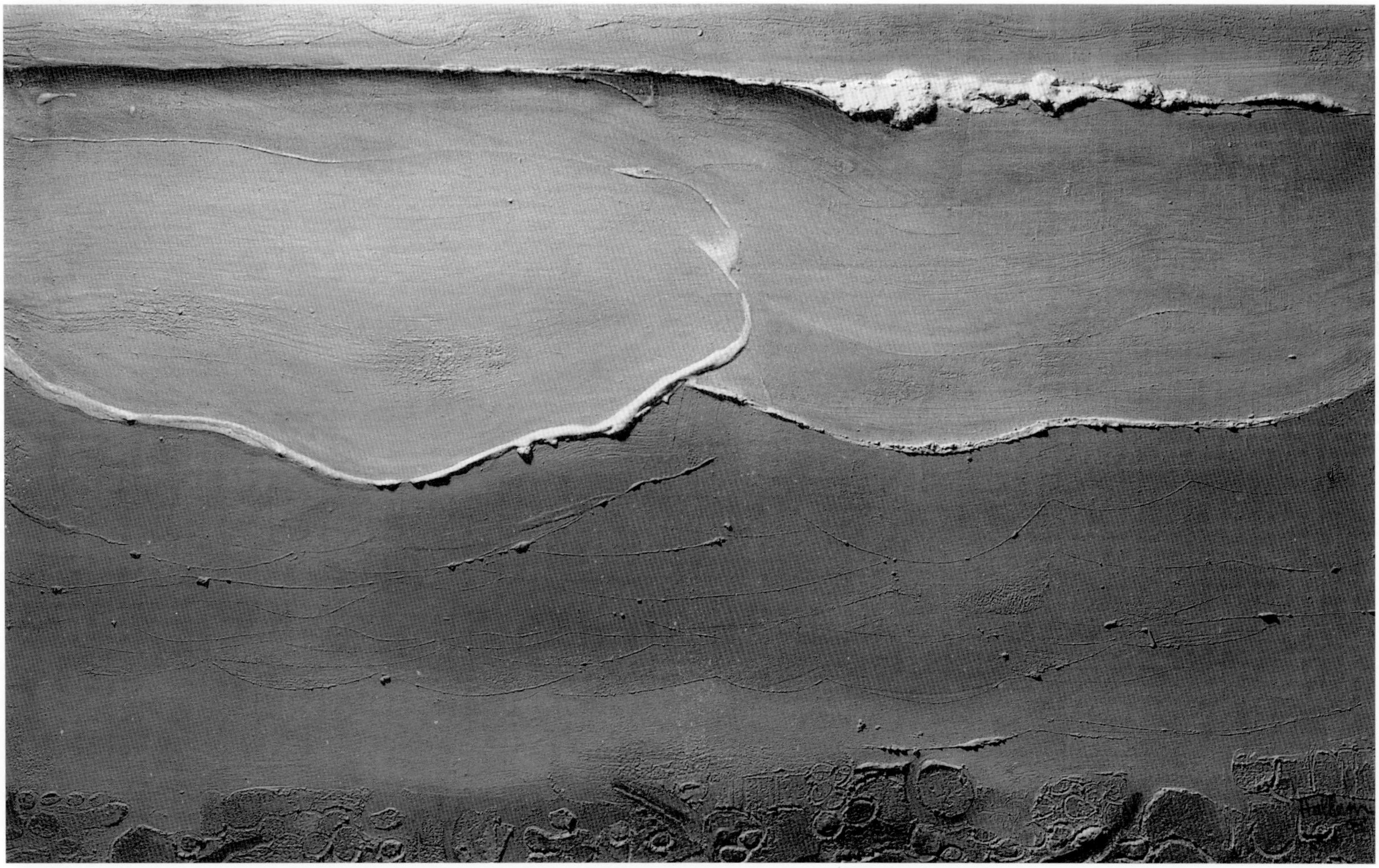

10

Assemblage and Other Avenues of Art

Although absorbed by the many patterns of nature, Hallam also worked with other subjects in these years. *Sydney Littlefield's Looking Toward Wells* is a lovely pastel landscape from 1963. Still lifes remained a passion. Her ability to capture the essence of a form with calligraphic strokes is apparent in *Cleome*, 1967, an energetic homage to this tropical bloom with its conspicuous stamens that give it its other name—spiderflower. These pictures are similar in technique and approach to work done in 1958.

We also witness Hallam's wry and sometimes dark humor rearing its laughing head here and there. *Hallam of Arabia*, 1963, one of the artist's few self-portraits, is a delightful tongue-in-cheek portrayal of the artist as desert wanderer, her head swathed in a white turban. As for mixed mediums, this portrait was painted in acrylic on a dishtowel stretched over cardboard; Marcel Duchamp, for one, would have taken pleasure in this whimsical portrayal.

More oblique, but displaying a similar mischievous manner, are the series of mirror paintings Hallam made in the mid-1960s. The first was a portrait of the actor Bert Lahr, famous for his role as the cowardly lion in *The Wizard of Oz*. Hallam had been introduced to Lahr by her friend Mary-Leigh Smart and her husband, Jack Smart, himself an actor and the famous voice of "The Fat Man" on radio. Lahr and Smart had played together in the original American production of Samuel Beckett's *Waiting for Godot*.

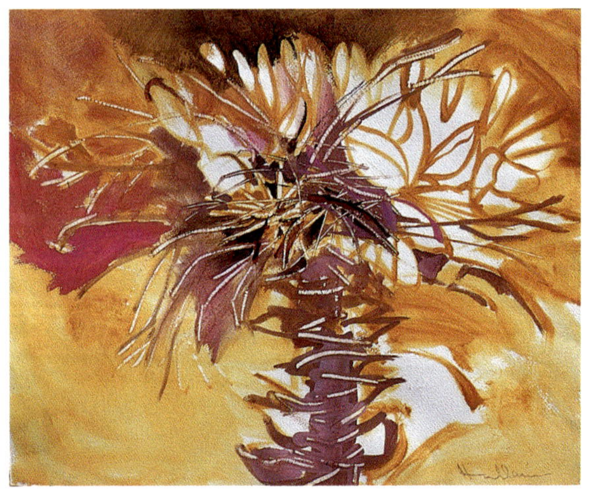

Cleome, 1967
Acrylic on paper, 14 x 17 1/2 in.
Collection of Mrs. Cameron Biewend

Hallam based *Portrait of Bert Lahr*, 1964, on a play the actor-comedian was in at the time, *The Beauty Part*, in which he played five different people. She angled strips of mirror so that the versatile actor could see himself from five different perspectives at once. Hallam recalls that the piece was a big hit when hung in the Boston Public Gardens. People passing it would see themselves and either quickly turn away with an annoyed expression (as they do when they find themselves on television sets in store windows) or go up close and laugh or make faces.

Because the mirror portraits were successful, Hallam actually contemplated spending her life making them. Practical considerations—the weight and fragility of the pieces for shipping, the fact that the mirrors would corrode—led her to abandon the series.

On the other hand, Hallam did not abandon her lobster shells. One night at a lobster dinner, she relates, she noticed that one of the claws looked like someone she knew. The next morning she embedded it in some "goop," put a large glass eye on it, and added a body and two spindly legs. Hallam called the humorous creature "The Yellow-Eyed Money Snatcher."

From this amusement, Hallam created several other striking assemblages, which, according to the artist, were "intended to be satirically

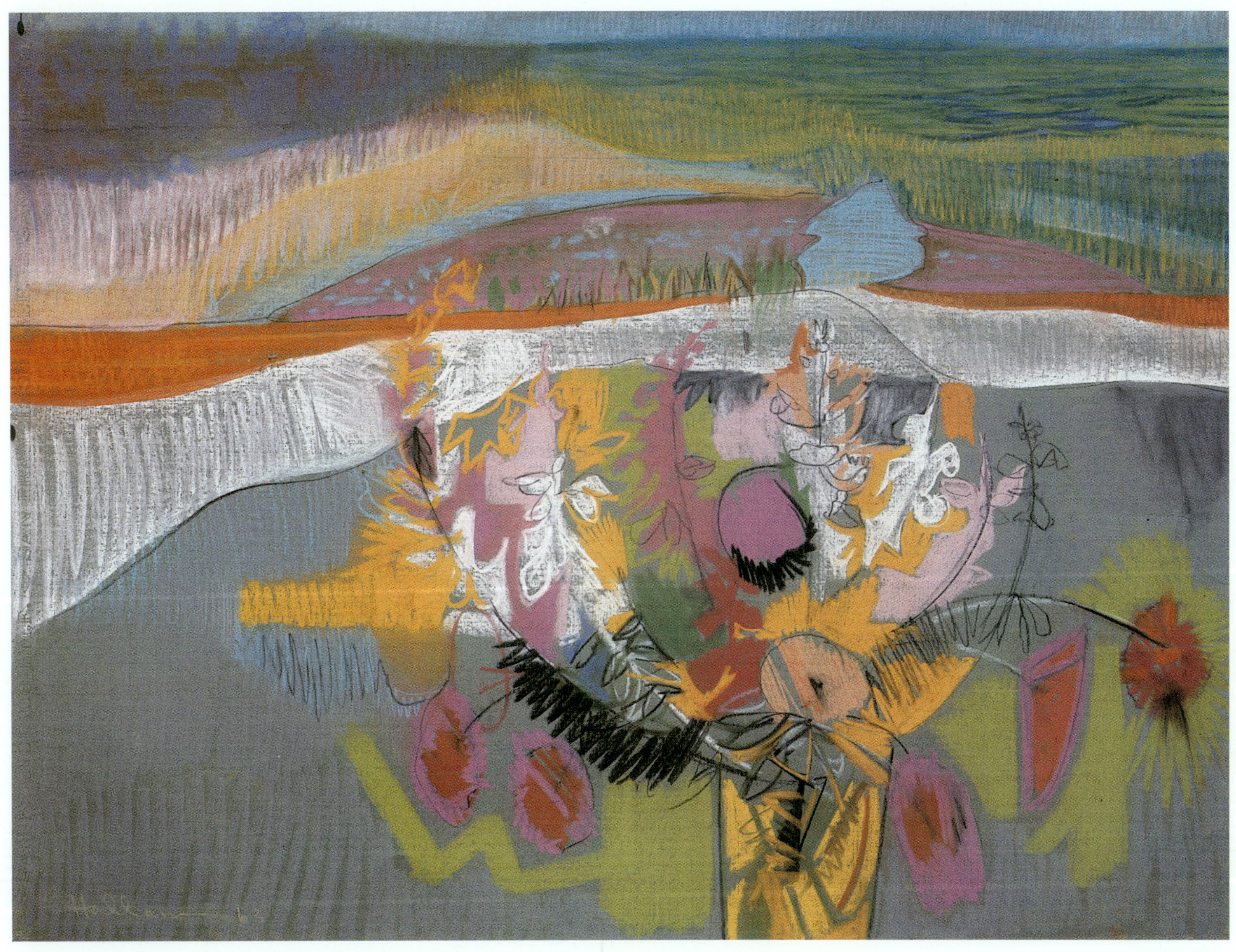

Sidney Littlefield's Looking Toward Wells, 1963
(drawn at Beachmere Place, Three Faces East)
Pastel on San Francisco LMF paper, 22 x 31 in.
Collection of the artist

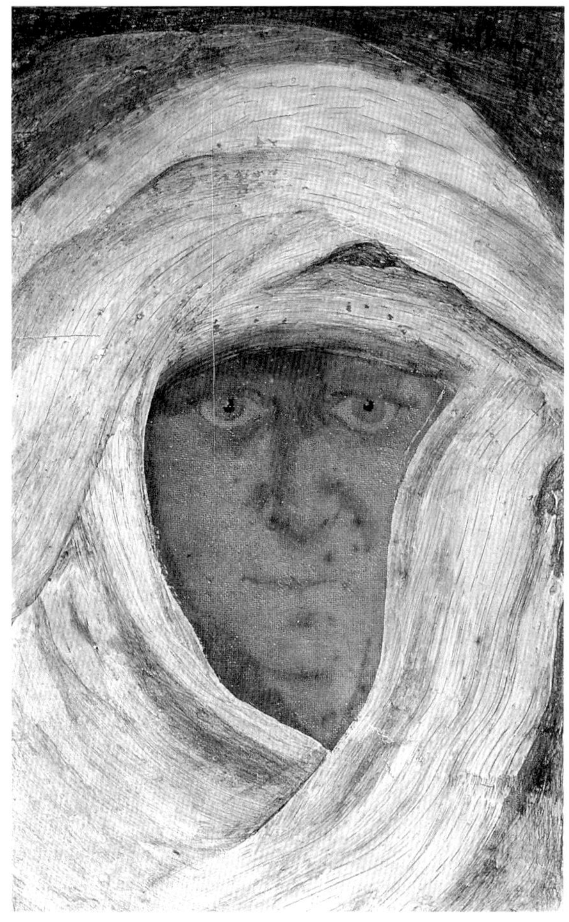

Hallam of Arabia, 1963
Acrylic on saturated acrylic dishtowel stretched on cardboard, with oil monotype frame, 13 x 8 1/2 in.
Collection of Mary-Leigh Call Smart

Jack Smart had a fabulous hat collection. I am wearing one here. Most people enjoy pretending.

frivolous." *Miasma*, 1967, features a tentacled creature made of shell that stares at the viewer with artificial owl eyes.

Miasma's title arose when Hallam painted the protective glass black, then wiped away an area of it in the middle, giving the impression that one is peering through a thick vapor at some otherworldly creature. While a critic for the *Maine Times* called the piece "humorous and imaginative," it also seems to make a point about the fate of the environment and its inhabitants, viewed through noxious man-made veils.

Miasma marked a turning point in Hallam's career. She had met painter Thomas Crotty, a former student of hers at Mass Art, at a cocktail party in Maine. He had started the Frost Gully Gallery in his barn in Freeport and asked Hallam to show there, becoming her first Maine dealer. She showed with him for many years; in those days, she says, "Crotty worked intensively with his artists, traveling with their work all over the countryside."

In 1969 Crotty hung *Miasma* in his barn gallery. The John Whitney Paysons came to the opening and Nancy Payson was struck by the piece. John bought the picture and presented it to his wife as a surprise anniversary gift. They wanted to meet the artist, so Crotty arranged a gathering. This encounter led to a life-long friendship, which later turned into a dealer-artist relationship.

In 1973, the Paysons opened their own gallery in Hobe Sound, Florida. That year Hallam showed her monotypes there, in a two-person show with sculptor William Traber, who worked in plexiglas. She continued with John Payson for 22 years in his Portland and Brunswick, Maine, galleries and then in New York City at the Payson-Weisberg Gallery. Payson later bought Midtown Gallery, which was renamed Midtown-Payson Galleries.

In 1976, the Paysons asked Hallam to create a Christmas show of lobster and shell assemblages for their Hobe Sound Galleries in Florida. Once again, combining mischievousness and found objects, she set about to amuse her audience, using lobster shells and glass eyes and bubbles to create witty cocktail party creatures. Mediums from her past work—cast stone, polyvinyl acetate—were resurrected to simulate sand and water.

With the help of fellow punsters, Hallam came up with rib-tickling titles like *Shell We Dance?* While one couldn't call them social commentaries, some of these lobster-shell pieces have an edge. *The Critic* sports a bulbous nose, which, one presumes, he sticks in places he oughtn't.

We should also note several assemblage portraits Hallam made of friends, using their favorite vice, the cigarette, to stand in for the actual person. *Portrait of May Sarton*, 1966, is a most unusual evocation of the well-known poet, novelist, playwright, and essayist that consists of an assemblage of cast stone, sand, cigarette butts, and an empty pack of the Old

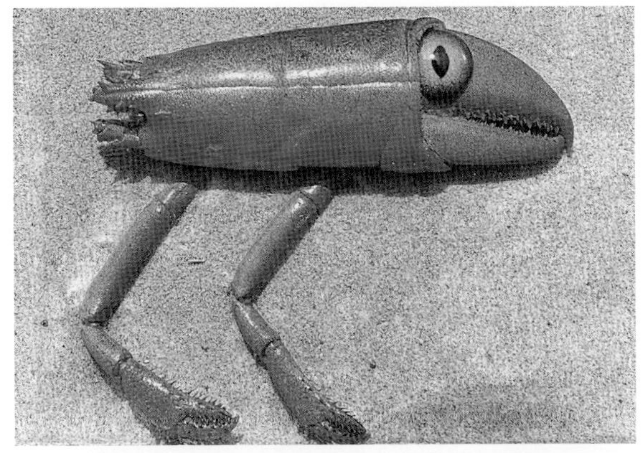

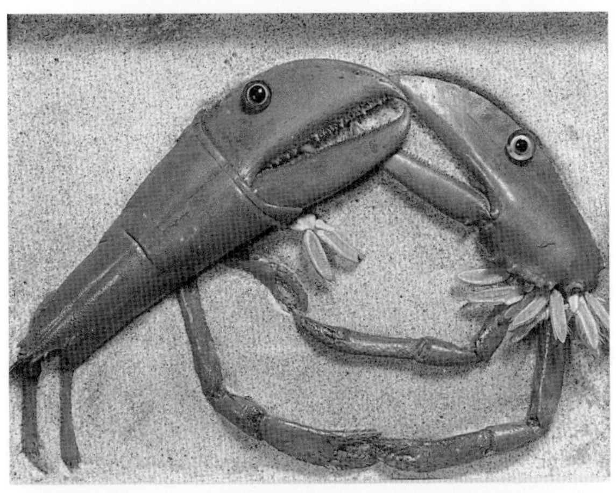

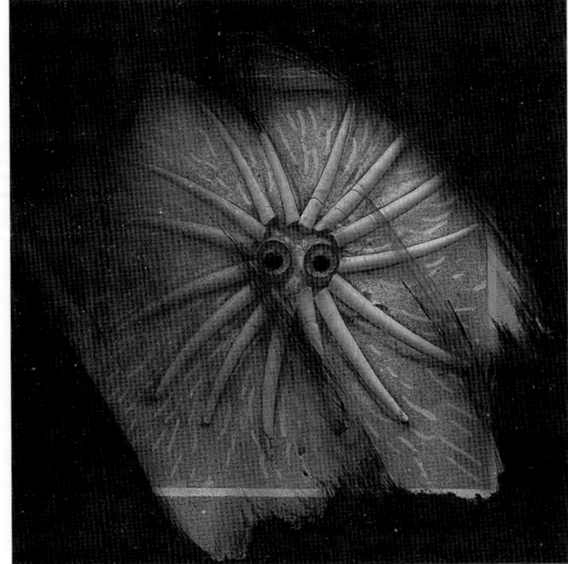

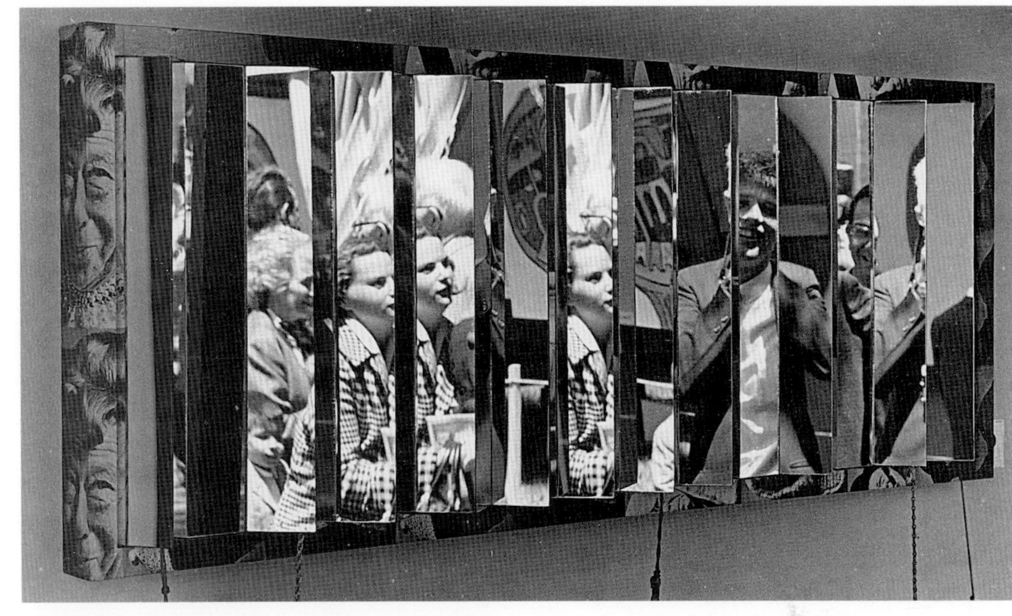

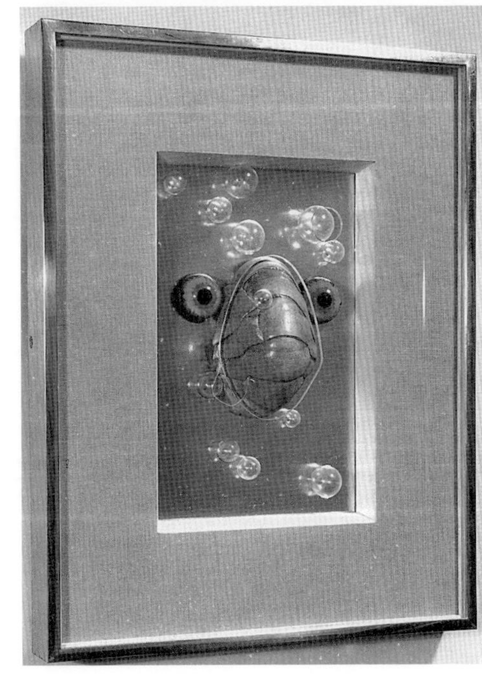

Left top: *Yellow-eyed Money Snatcher,* 1966
Lobster shells, cast stone, and glass eyes
on masonite, 5 x 8 in.
Collection of the artist

Left middle: *Shell We Dance?* 1976
Lobster shells, cast stone, and glass eyes
on masonite, 6 x 8 in.
Collection of Rear Admiral and
Mrs. Ralph M. Metcalf

Left bottom: *Miasma,* 1967
Assemblage of cast stone, shell, glass eyes,
and acrylic on masonite, 18 x 18 in.
Collection of Nancy L. Payson

Top: *Portrait of Bert Lahr,* 1964
Mirror assemblage with collage on wood
19 1/2 x 49 1/2 x 2 1/2 in.
Collection of Mary-Leigh Call Smart

Left: *The Critic,* 1976
Assemblage of lobster tail, glass bubbles, glass
eyes, and gold metallic board
on masonite, 9 x 6 in.
Private collection

Golds that sustained the smoking author.

Likewise, *Portrait of John Whitney Payson*, 1969, incorporates a butt-strewn ashtray, a pack of Pall Malls, and a book of matches with the Mets logo on it to represent the well-known art dealer who was an owner of the New York baseball team. A related piece, *Flight of the Bumblebutts*, 1969, is subtitled *Assemblage of Snuffed Souvenirs from John Whitney Payson's Cigarettes*.

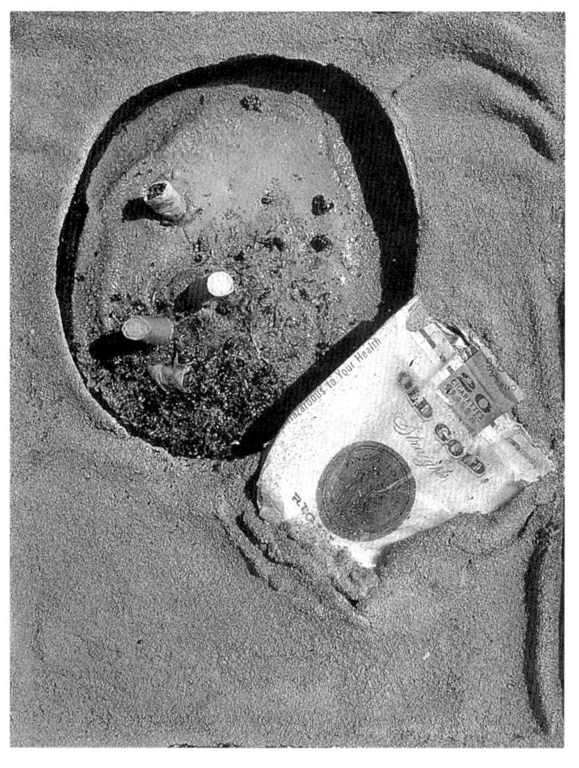

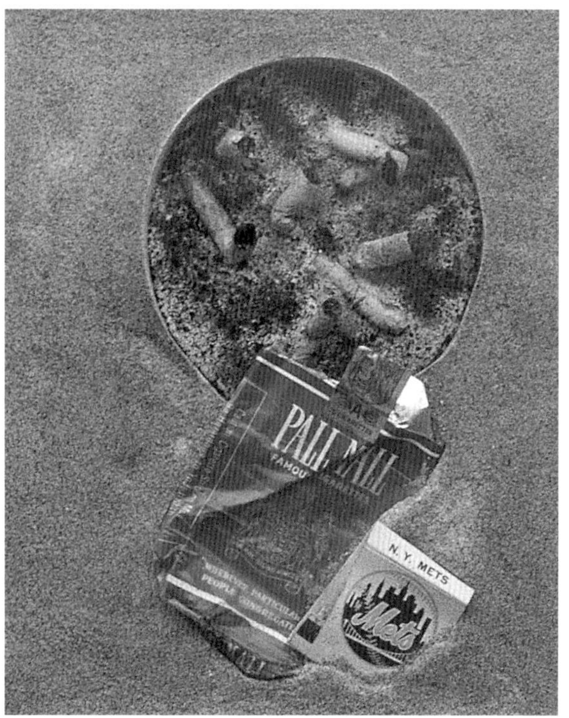

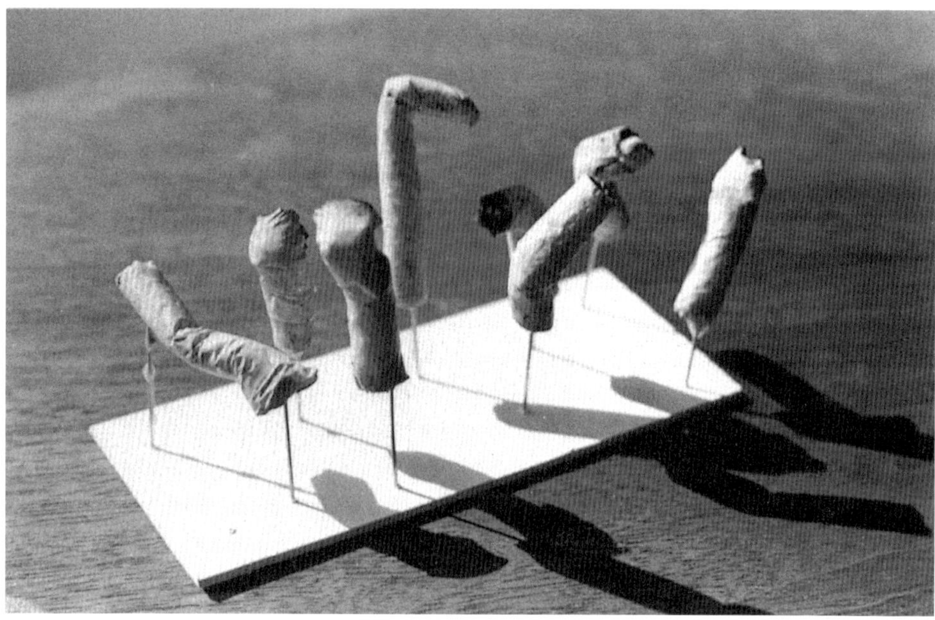

TOP LEFT: *PORTRAIT OF MAY SARTON*, 1966
ASSEMBLAGE IN CAST STONE, 9 5/8 X 7 1/2 IN.
COLLECTION OF THE ARTIST

LEFT: *PORTRAIT OF JOHN WHITNEY PAYSON*, 1969
ASSEMBLAGE IN CAST STONE, 9 5/8 X 7 1/2 IN.
COLLECTION OF JOHN WHITNEY PAYSON

ABOVE: *FLIGHT OF THE BUMBLEBUTTS (ASSEMBLAGE OF SNUFFED SOUVENIRS FROM JOHN WHITNEY PAYSON'S CIGARETTES*, C.1969), 1969
PHOTOGRAPH, 3 5/8 X 5 3/4 IN.

11

The Monotype

In the early 1960s, even as she reveled in the versatility of acrylic, Hallam became interested in monotype. In her inimitable way, through experiment, through chance and change, she mastered this out-of-the-ordinary medium. She brought the same daring to monotype that she had to acrylic.

Hallam notes that in the early 1960s she had reached something of a standstill with polyvinyl acetate. Her work with latex molds and cast stone was verging on sculpture, and she was not particularly interested in this format. It was time, she wrote, "to get back to two dimensions."

It was actually in 1958 that Hallam first became aware of monotype. At five o'clock after a day of oil painting, she was suddenly taken aback by the beauty of her palette. As recounted in *The Boston Sunday Globe* at the time of a show of her monotypes at the Shore Galleries in May 1968, Hallam "placed a piece of paper on the wet colors, rubbed her hand over it and pulled the paper off. 'Like magic the paint transferred to the paper. I had made my first monotype without realizing it.'"

Monotype has a history that reaches at least as far back as the 17th century, to Benedetto Castiglione, who is said to be the originator of the technique. Among the most famous practitioners have been Degas, Whistler, Cassatt, Gauguin, Lautrec, Matisse, and Prendergast.

Today, numerous artists are making monotypes, drawn to its singular qualities and expressive potential. Yet at the time Hallam began her explorations of the technique, it was generally little known. A few printmakers, among them Karl Schrag and Gabor Peterdi, worked in the medium, but many artists didn't know what monotype was, let alone its expressive potential.

As early as 1962, Hallam had familiarized herself enough with monotype to demonstrate the technique to others at the Barn Gallery in Ogunquit. The *York County Coast Star* of July 12 of that year announced that the artist would "show print making in painting and decorative design, demonstrating the use of wooden type, lucite, casein and gesso, oil on glass and vegetables." Hallam ended up demonstrating the monotype process throughout New England and as far afield as Texas. The "medicine man," bearing a new medium, had returned.

In preparation for her first demonstration, Hallam sought out unusual tools and materials. Consulting Peterdi's book *Printmaking*, she came across the address of a company that manufactured gelatin rollers. These hand brayers made of soft yet firm gelatin formed over rods of steel would prove to be ideal for her purposes; indeed, they held her captive for 18 years.

In 1963, the monotype-making began in earnest. Hallam started out using a 50-by-50-inch piece of plate glass, which she would work over with oil paint in tubes mixed with linseed oil and turpentine. She later switched

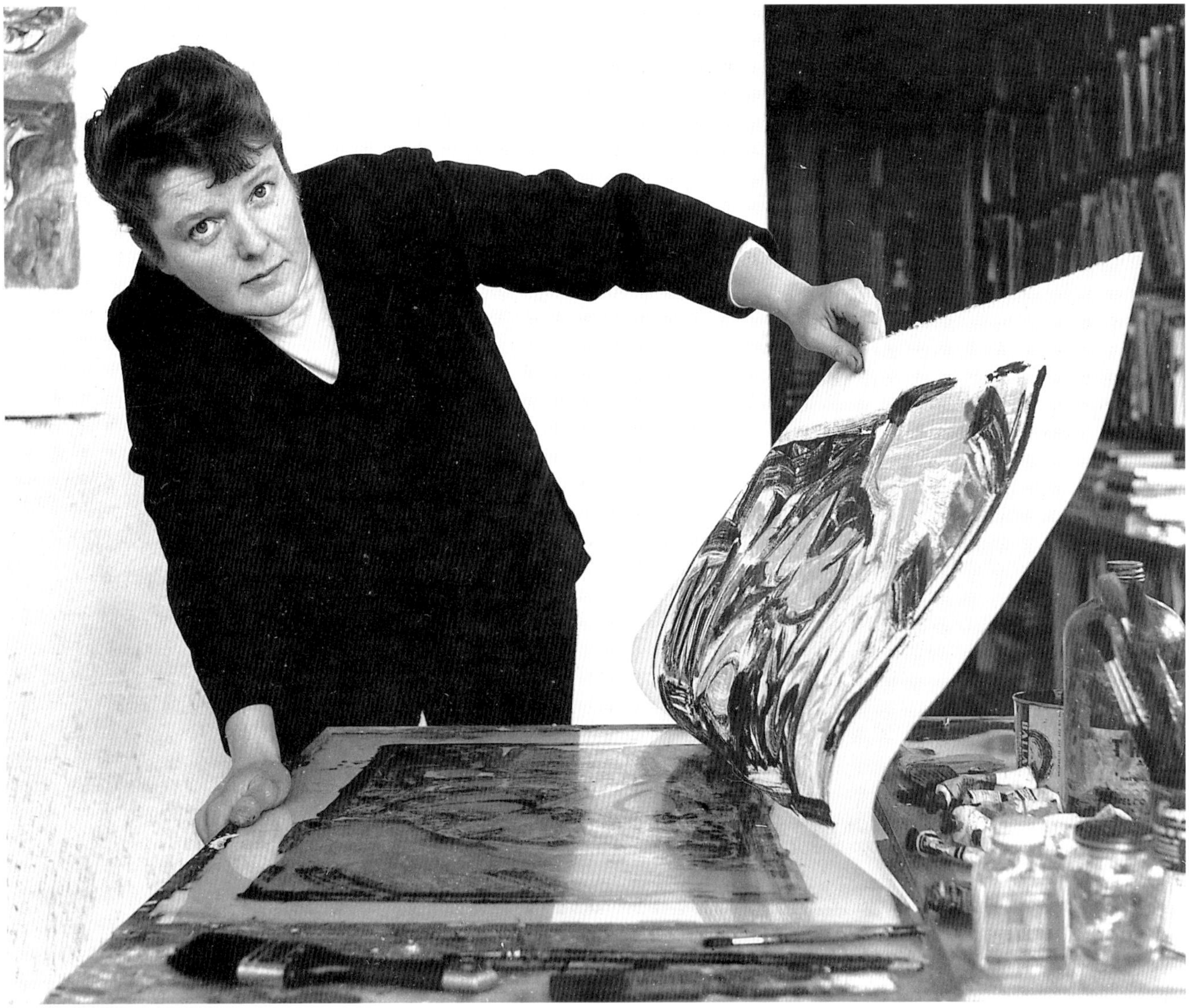

Photographs by Ernestine Mosman Lyman

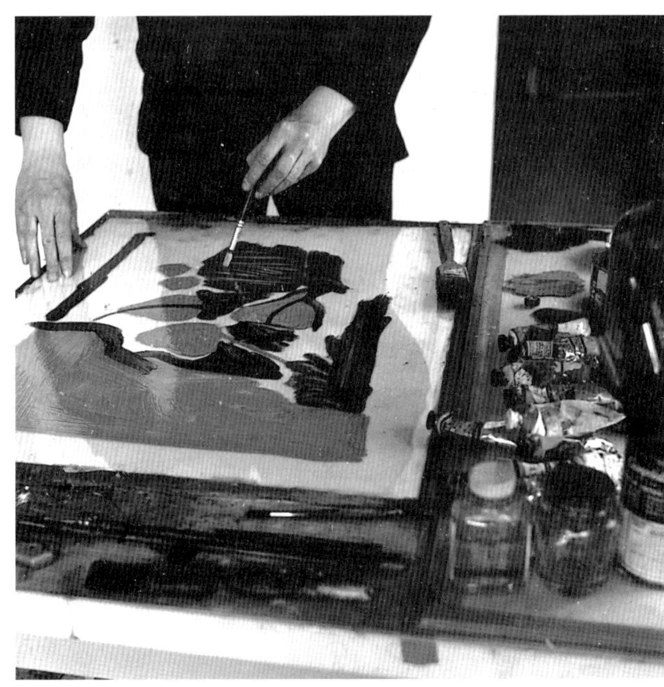

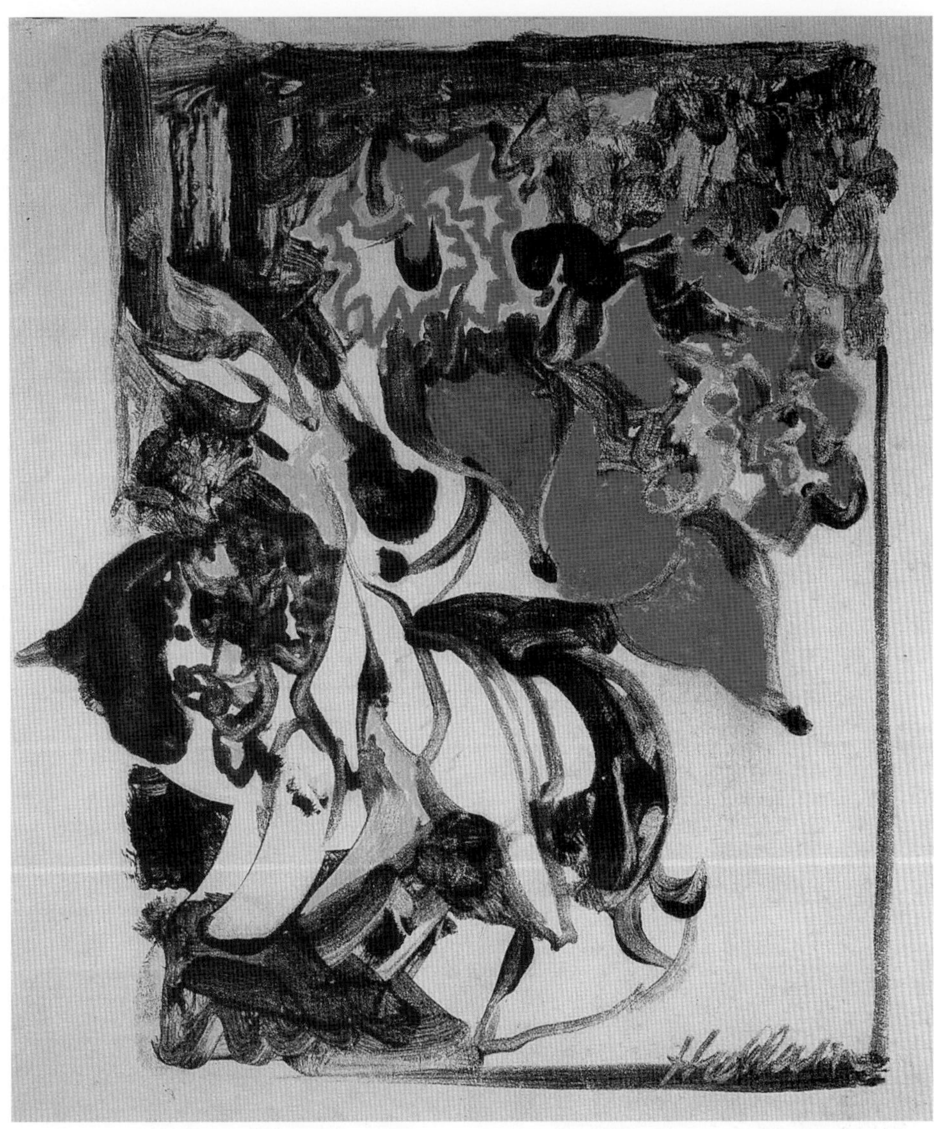

The sculptor Robert Laurent once said to me, "Why don't you frame the glass that you made this monotype from? It's so beautiful." Pity I never did. I thought it might break.

Lilac and Bayberry, 1965
Oil monotype on rice paper
mounted on laid paper, 17 1/2 x 16 1/4 in.
Portland Museum of Art, Maine
Gift of the artist

to oil-based lithograph ink. As for her old friend acrylic, she found that it dried too fast for her purposes.

Using both soft and bristle brushes, Hallam painted on the glass, working very quickly, establishing the entire composition by massing in the negative areas first, then the detail. While the paint was still wet, she placed rice paper or smooth Strathmore over the glass and applied pressure with her hand or a brayer. When the paper was pulled off, there was the print in reverse. Often there was enough paint left on the glass to get a second print. This pale monotype would serve only as a point of departure, with the finished work mostly a drawing. Sometimes she worked on a piece further with pastel or wax crayon. The monotypes were done with dispatch, except for the larger, more involved pieces. Four or five could be completed in a day.

Hallam has confessed to feeling like a "sneak" about working on a

(OPPOSITE)

Bouquet by the Sea, 1965
Oil monotype and wax crayon on Strathmore, 20 x 24 in.
Private collection

I have painted my Picasso owl vase many times. As I feverishly scraped up old paint from my glass work surface the bird movements and feathers came to mind. I added the eyes and made up the title "Fabricillia" for fabrication.

Fabricillia (Slight Fever), 1968
Oil monotype on Strathmore, 23 x 28 in.
Collection of the artist

monotype after it has been printed—until, that is, she acquired a rare volume on Degas's monotypes by Denis Rouart. There she learned that the master had often retouched his monotypes with pastel.

In reviewing the entire body of Hallam's monotype work, one can see that she moved back and forth between the rollers and the brushes, sometimes combining the two. After a day of working with rollers, she would use the leftover ink that was rolled out on the glass. She sprinkled turpentine over the ink and swished a brush or painting knife around in it to create an image. Then she placed a fresh piece of paper over it, rubbed it, and pulled off a monotype. When it was dry, she would occasionally develop the image further with rollers.

Among the monotypes Hallam executed in the mid-'60s (before the advent of the rollers) were *Lilac and Bayberry* and *Bouquet by the Sea*. These pictures are marked by a freewheeling approach, the oil paint brushed on

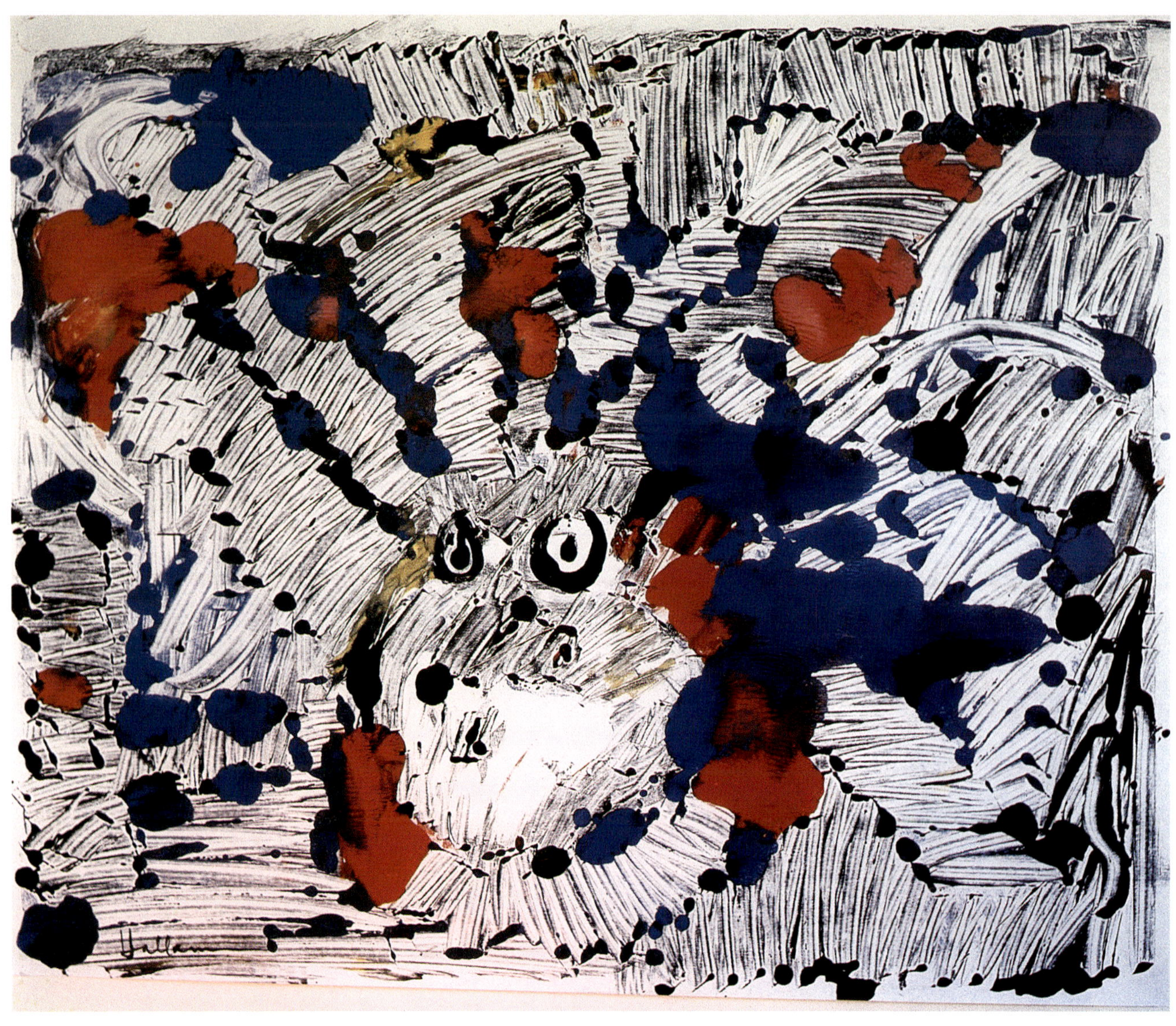

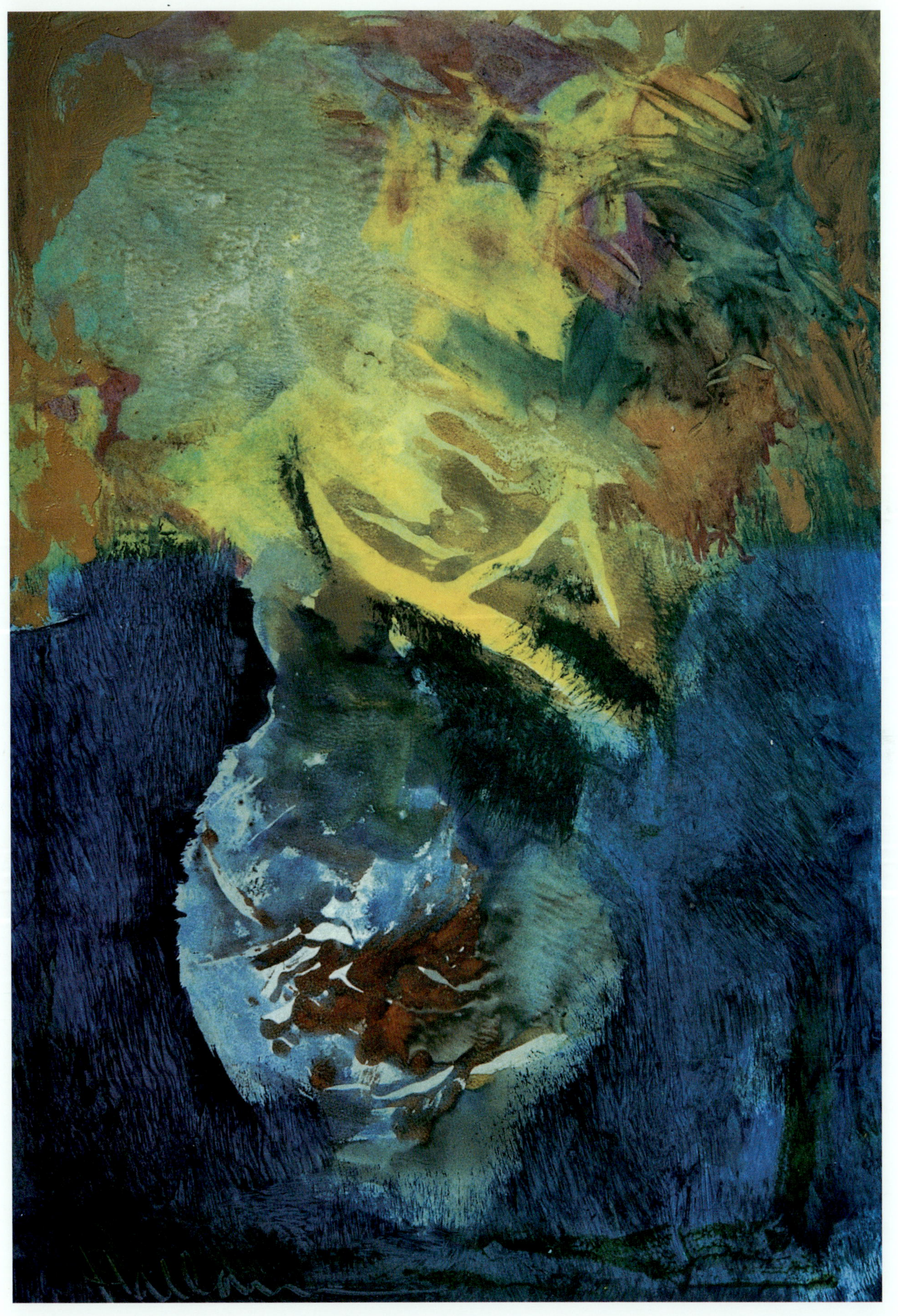

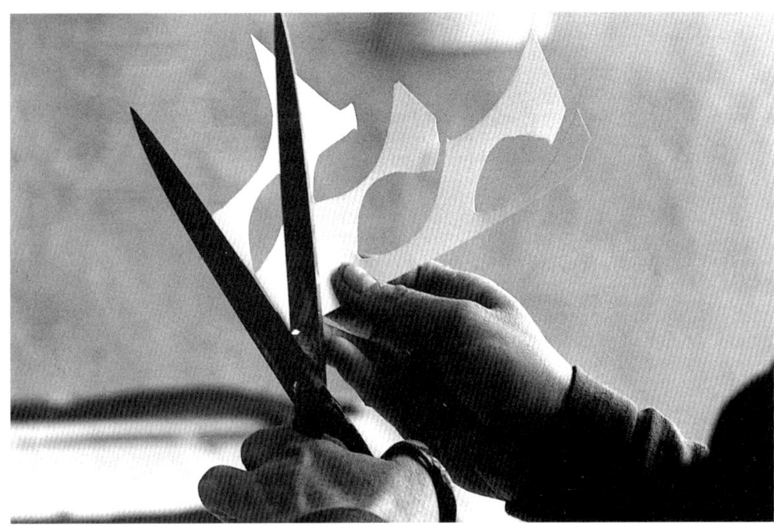

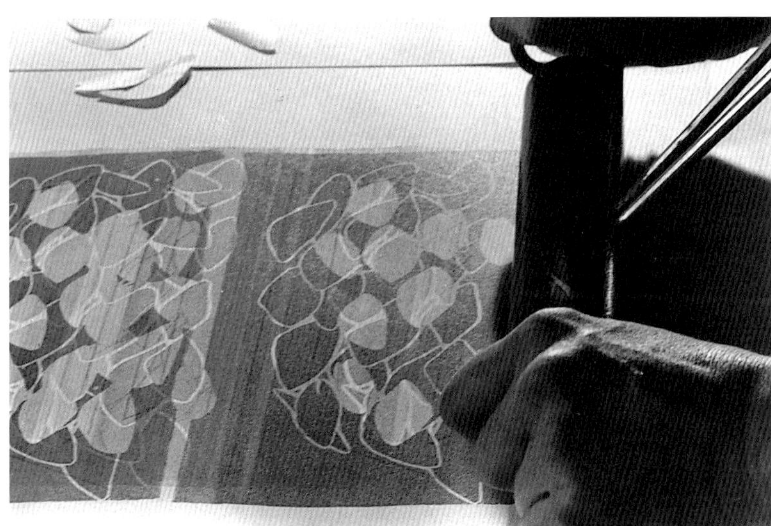

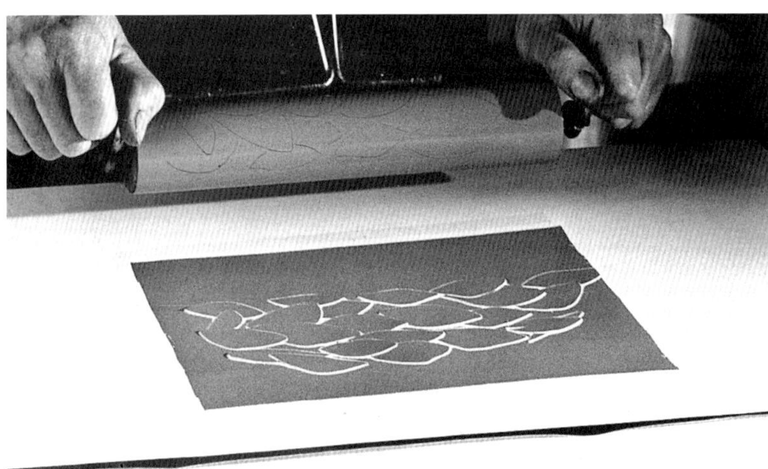

Photographs by Betsey Baybut

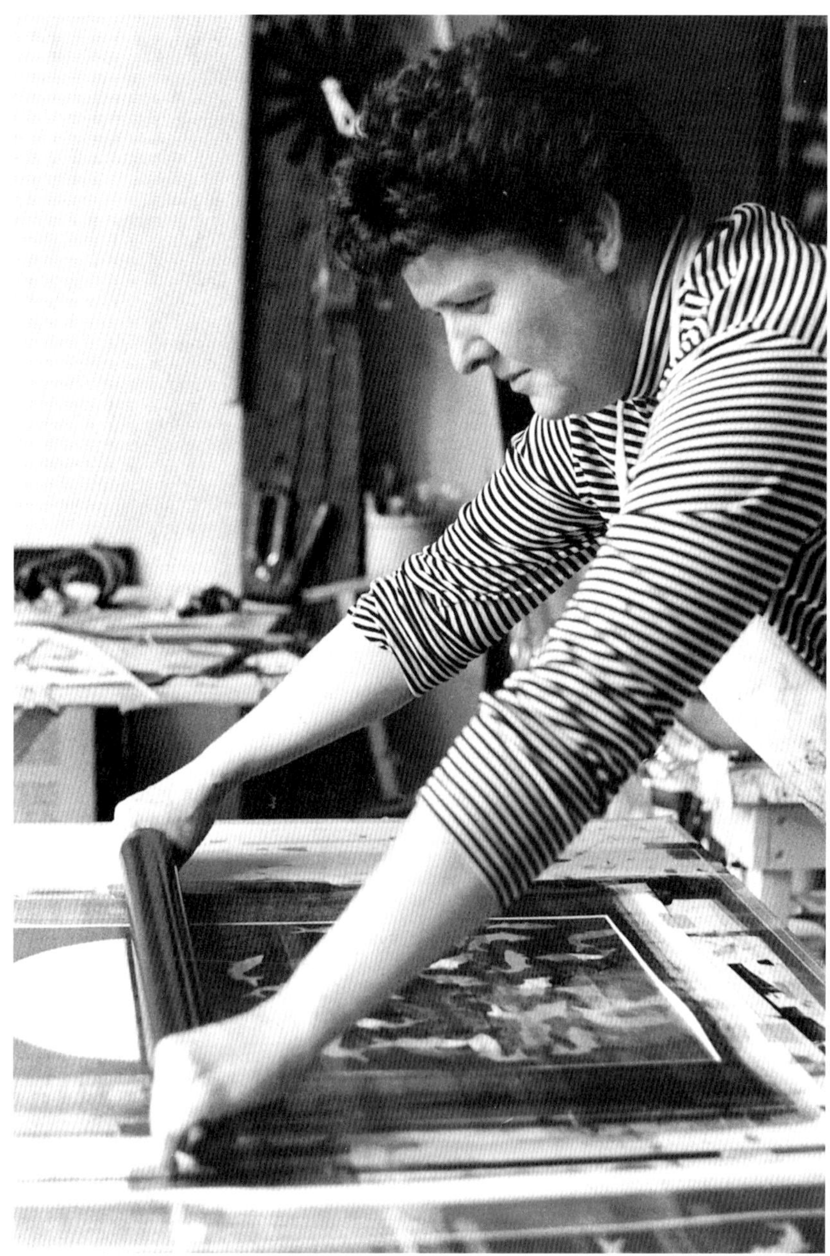

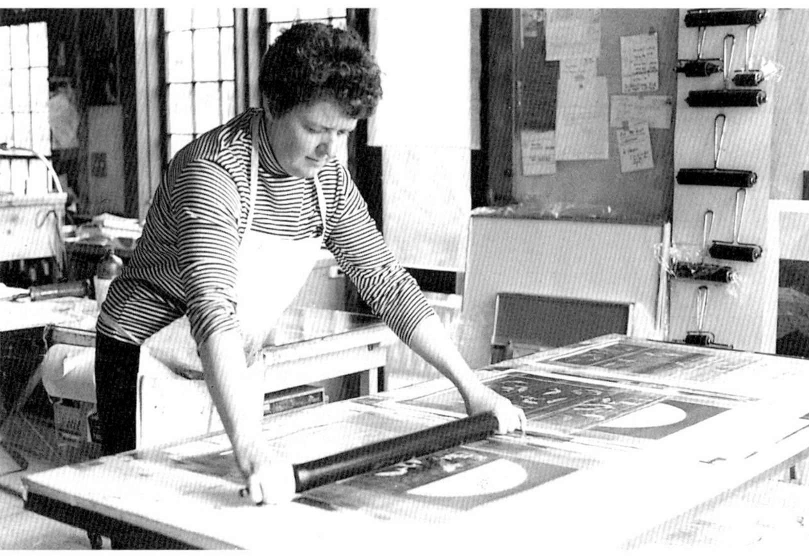

glass with expressive verve. Hallam added pastel to *Lilac and Bayberry* and wax crayon to *Bouquet by the Sea*.

Following the use of brushes, the gelatin roller allowed Hallam to produce intricate hard-edged patterns in a matter of seconds. The method she developed resembles that of offset printing, except by hand, not by press. She rolled the ink onto glass with the brayer until the medium was the correct consistency. Precut paper shapes or stencils were then taped onto the paper with double-stick tape. The inked roller was then run over the whole thing.

After the ink dried, the paper stencils were shifted on the paper or new ones were added, and a second, third, or fourth transparent color was rolled over. Hallam worked from light to dark, constantly remembering to cover over all elements that she wanted to keep in the final composition. A transparent silk screen base was added to the ink for brilliant color or transparent variations.

One characteristic of the gelatin roller caught Hallam's eye and held her fascinated throughout the many years working with this tool: when inked, the brayer had a good memory. After the roller passed over a stencil, it retained the image. Fainter duplicate shapes appeared as the roller moved up the paper.

Hallam called these duplications "ghosts" and found them very exciting. All manner of relatively smooth textures, such as a metal grill or folded tissue, could be "lifted" for patterns. The artist sometimes made her own devices to roll over. She cut shapes out of heavy Strathmore paper, glued them to a glass, and rolled them with ink. This inked device would be rolled over with a fresh, dry roller, making one revolution, then applied to the paper. If she kept the roller going, the pattern would be repeated over and over until the ink on the roller ran out.

At first, the monotypes were abstract, with technical concerns outweighing those of subject matter. Gradually, leaf and flower shapes appeared, then the sun and moon and rocks. Except for a few bouquets, most of the monotypes came out of Hallam's imagination.

The Picasso bird that Hallam has been obsessed with over the years makes an unusual appearance in a 1968 oil monotype *Fabricillia (Slight Fever)*—a fine example of cleaning off the glass after a day of working with rollers and making use of residues. A multitude of knife strokes and splashed clots of paint have been applied in a feverish manner, creating the milieu for the wild-eyed creature from Vallauris.

One of Hallam's first prints using just gelatin rollers was *Floating Leaves*, 1967, where the shapes of several leaves appear to float in and on the evenly textured surface of the print. In 1969, Hallam received, as a gift, a roll of

Floating Leaves, 1967
Oil monotype and collage on rice paper, 9 1/8 x 8 7/8 in.
Collection of Mr. and Mrs. Burton L. Shatz

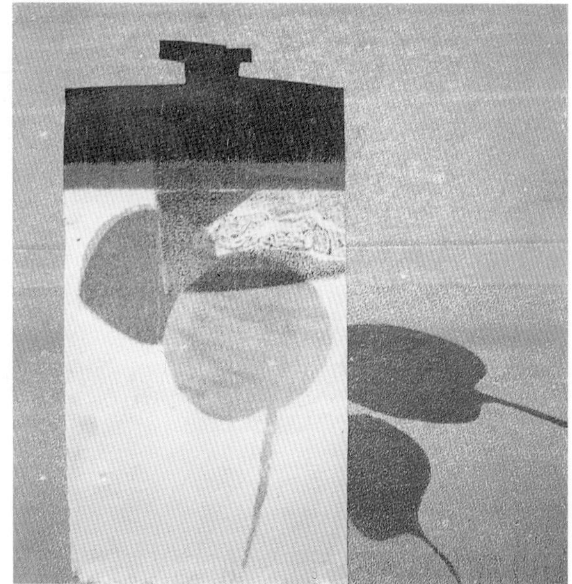

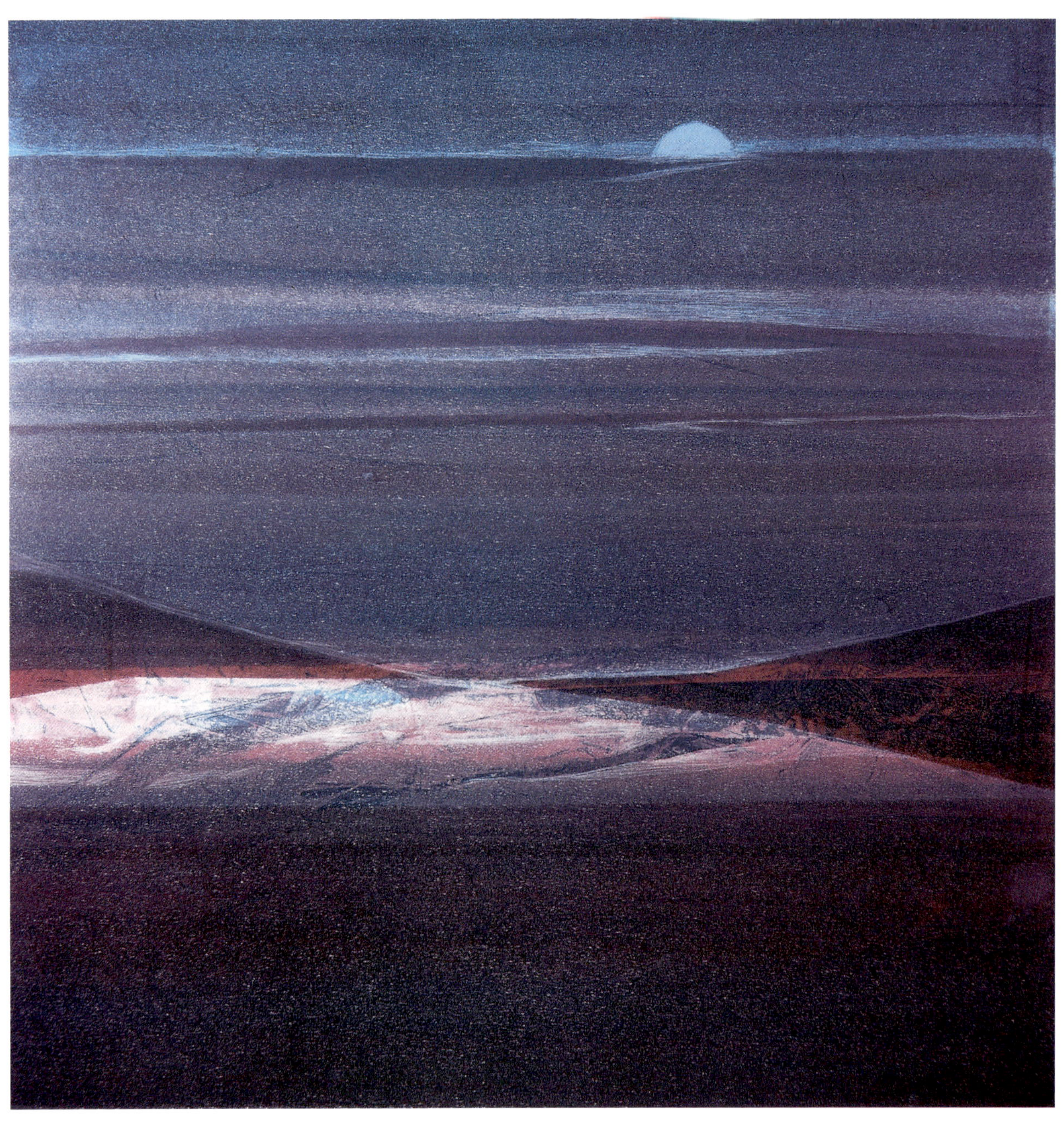

Blue Moon, 1968
Oil monotype on Strathmore, 9 x 9 in.
Collection of Lucy and Carter Jefferson

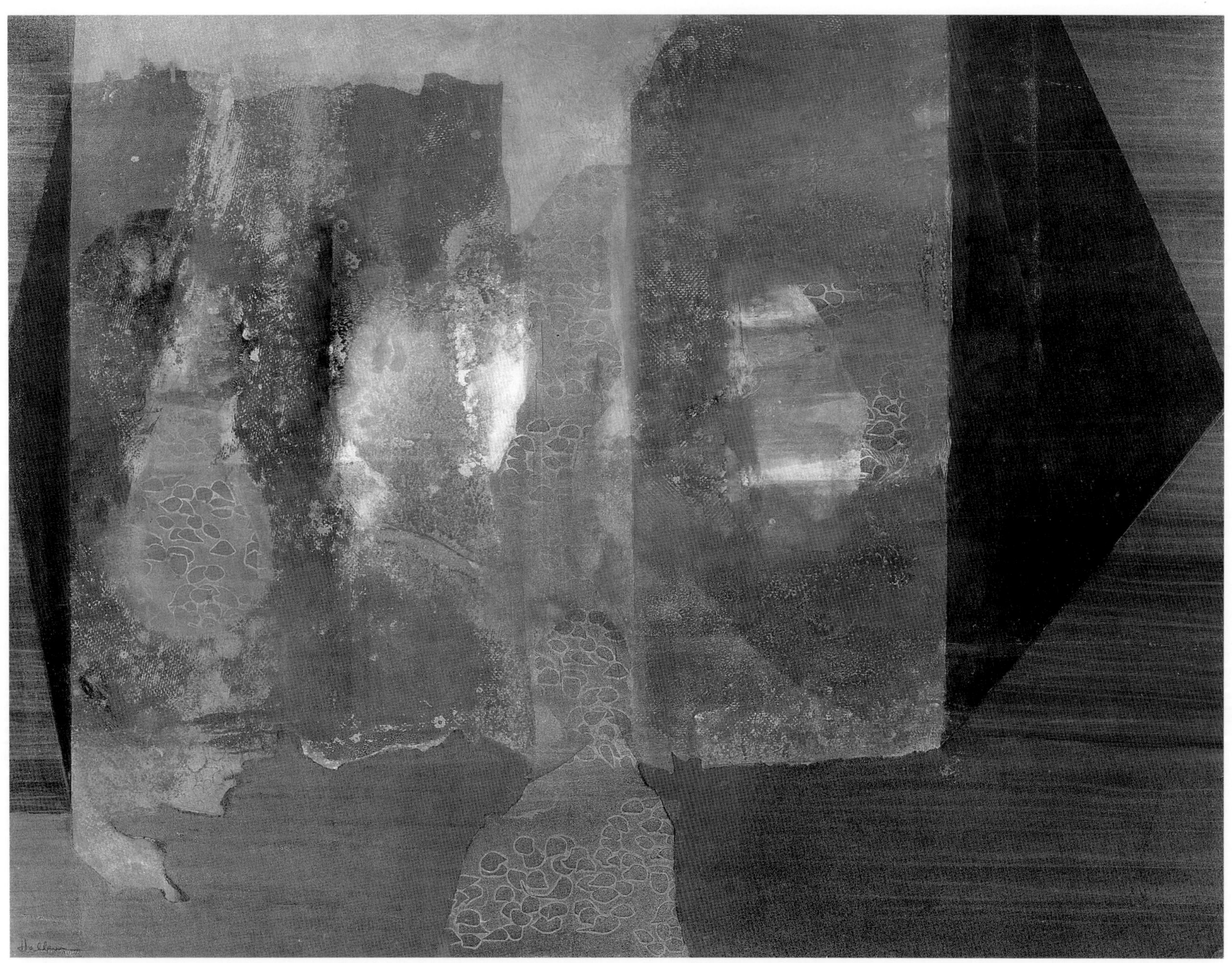

Sand Plan, 1969
Oil monotype on synthetic paper, 30 x 40 in.
Collection of Mary-Leigh Call Smart

Texoprint paper manufactured by Kimberly-Clark. The paper was smooth, tough, and synthetic, a perfect surface for the gelatin roller. One of the largest oil monotypes, *Sand Plan*, 1969, was made on this synthetic paper. Incorporating shell shapes, this "hard-soft edge" monotype was one of a series of 30-by-40-inch sheets that were carefully planned from the start. Its subtle and soft fluent effects are achieved in a deceptive manner through the transfer of the texture of paper towels.

Many of Hallam's monotypes have a stylized quality, in which a formal design reigns. Take *Blue Moon*, 1968: This landscape, somewhat oriental in feeling, conjures up a moonlit coastline through a series of horizontals that lend the piece a subtle sense of depth. Hallam would return to this kind of stratified seascape many times.

As a child I could never jump rope. Probably because I was left-handed. I liked the jingle "...the lowest one is out." Memory can spark the imagination.

At the time of Hallam's solo show of monotypes at the Shore Galleries in Boston in 1968, Eugenia Parry Janis mounted a Degas monotype exhibition at the Fogg Art Museum. On May 5, both exhibitions were reviewed by Edgar Driscoll, Jr., in *The Boston Globe*. "Clear, clean forms and bright-clear colors abounded," wrote Driscoll of Hallam's exhibition; he went on to describe the artist's happenstance introduction to monotype and her subsequent mastery of the medium.

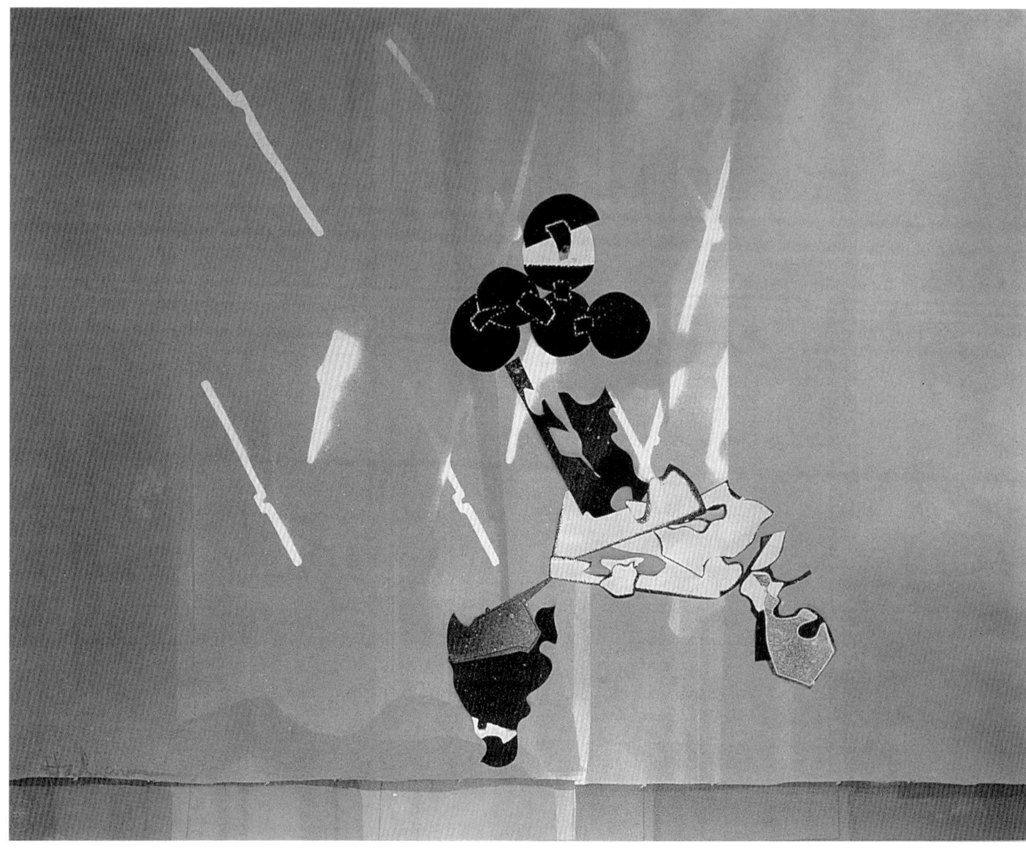

The Lowest One Is Out, 1968
Oil monotype and collage on Strathmore, 23 x 29 in.
Collection of the artist

The artist herself once described monotype as "an instinctive art, stemming from the most primitive maneuvers." As she evolved into a master of the medium, Hallam increasingly drew on her instinct; and her maneuvers, while sometimes primitive, also evidenced the highest levels of aesthetic sophistication.

The artist was making progress toward pure abstraction. *Stack*, from 1968, follows the compositional format of an acrylic picture of the same name painted in 1965, while *The Lowest One Is Out*, also 1968, witnesses the artist moving into wholly inventive territory. In this particular monotype, we sense a playful sensibility at work, Klee-like in its formulation of imaginary scenarios. Here, she glued pieces of old used stencils onto the rolled-ink surface.

This inclination toward the abstract led Hallam down some unusual byways. From 1969 to 1972, she contributed several cover designs and illustrations for *Stamping/Diemaking*, a trade magazine published by William Stanger in New York City. For these, Hallam rolled ink over items that had been produced by means of photochemical machining. In one, the bits and pieces of flat, cut-out metal are caught in a spider web; in another, they form patterns and grids. The last piece using stamped-out metal pieces was quite fittingly titled *Curtain Call*.

Elements from this graphic design work reappear in some of Hallam's finest and purest abstract creations, such as *Electronic Eggs*, *Programmed Choreography for Eggerator*, and *Power Plant Pollination*, all completed in 1973. In making the last-named monotype and collage, wrote Martin Dibner in his foreword to the catalogue *Expressions from Maine 1976*, "Hallam moves into Miró-like dimensions, a departure from earlier, more formalized renditions."

The titles of two of these monotypes bring to mind one of Hallam's favored motifs, the egg. Something about this simple oval shape and its association with Easter has appealed to her over the years. The subject reached perhaps its fullest expression in a series of monotypes from 1969 and, later, in *Twelve Eggs and Golden Trees*, 1973, a lovely monotype that features intricate abstracted overlays. For years, Hallam made monotypes of eggs on Easter Day. As the artist observes tongue-in-cheek, "Some people blew their eggs. I rolled them, but not on the lawn!"

Entering nonrepresentational realms, Hallam never lost sight of nature. Indeed, two of her most impressive monotype series from the late 1960s to the early 1970s were based on elements of the natural world: the milkweed pod and the chrysalis. The latter was brought to her attention by artist and writer Isabel Lewando and her young son, Benjamin, who gave Hallam a cocoon and showed her how to care for it until it hatched. She stayed up all night at the appointed time to watch the butterfly emerge.

Stages (Butterfly), 1969
Oil over negative master stencil on Strathmore, 23 x 12 in.
Collection of Robert S. Johnson

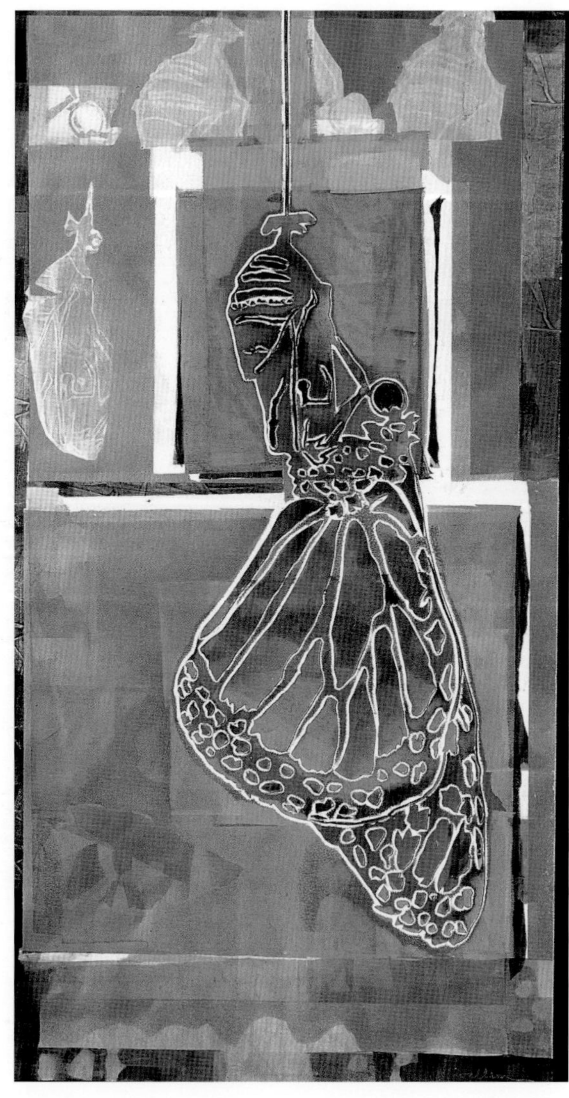

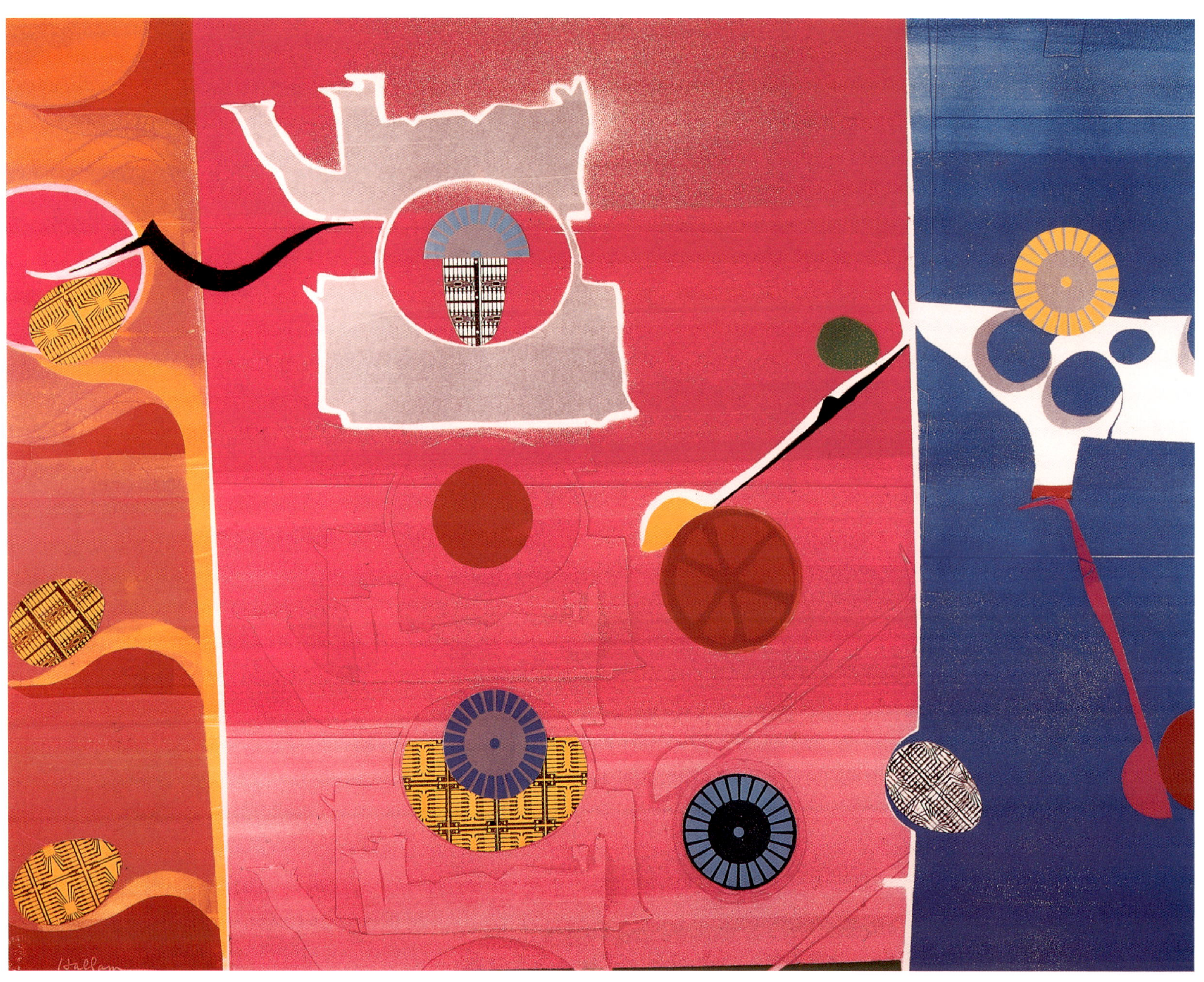

Programmed Choreography for Eggerator, 1973
Oil on synthetic paper, 23 x 29 in.
Collection of the artist

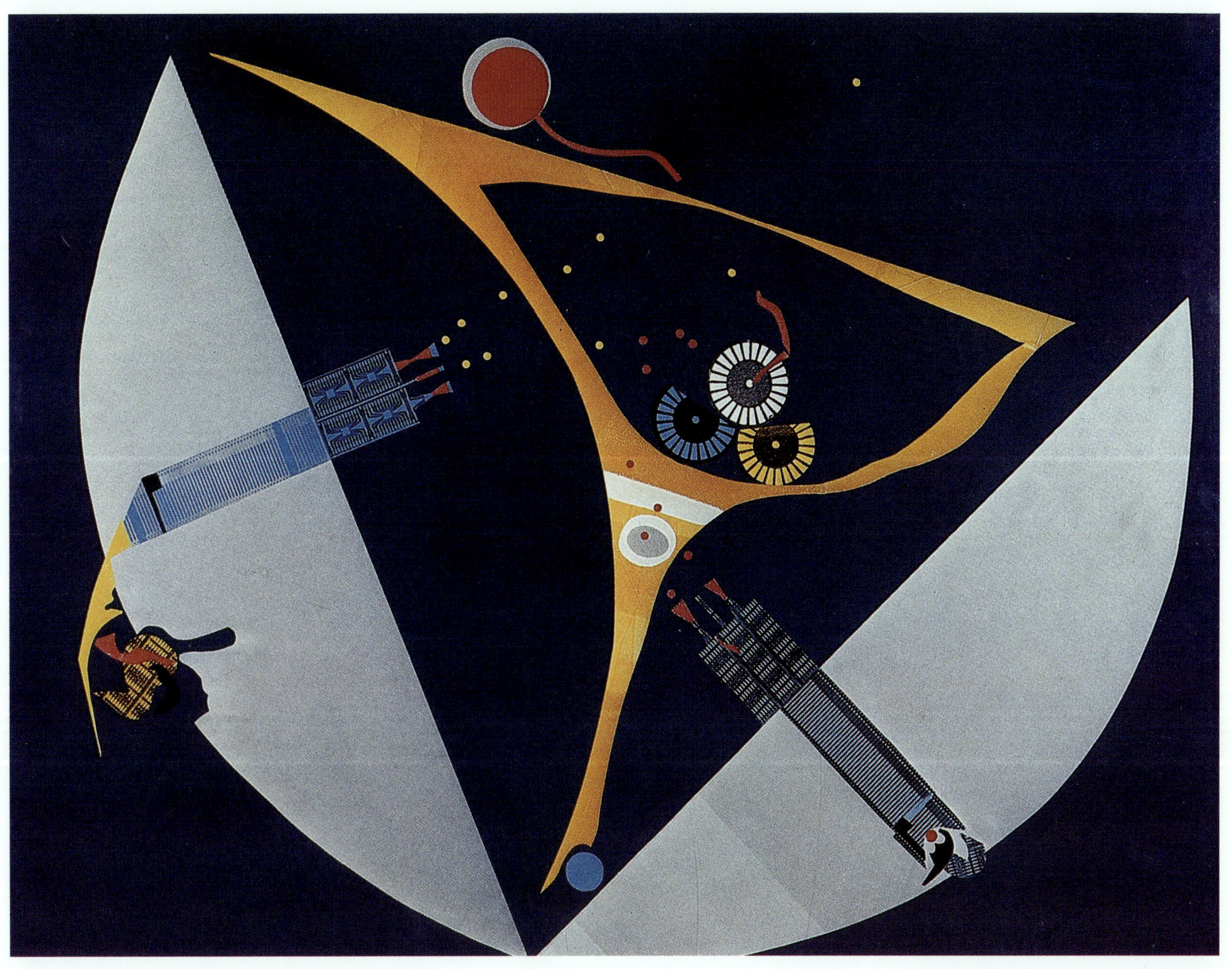

Power Plant Pollination, 1968-1973
Oil monotype and hand-printed collage on foam core board, 30 x 40 in.
Collection of Mr. and Mrs. John Whitney Payson

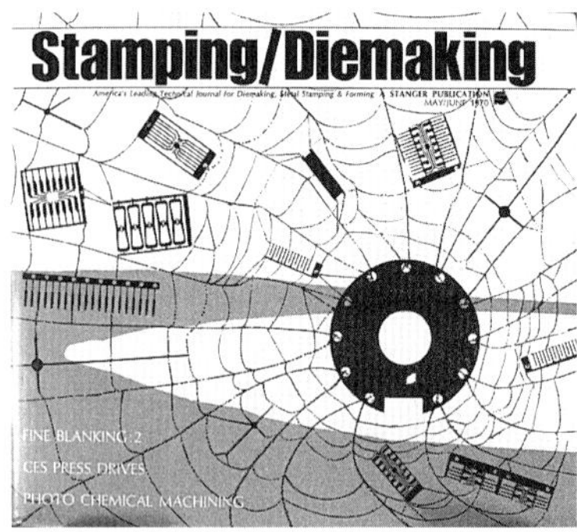

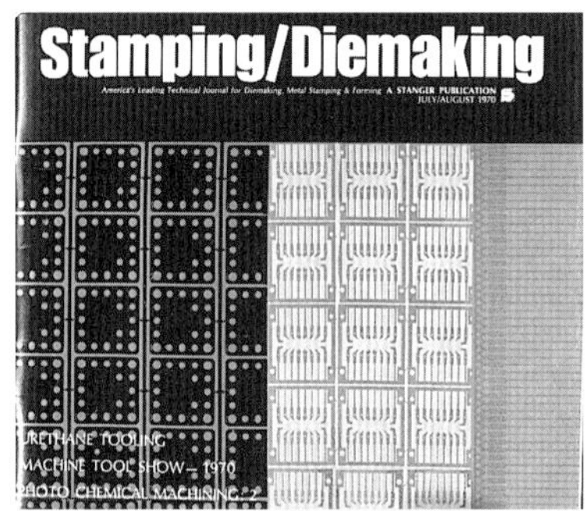

Stamping/Diemaking Magazine covers,
May-June, July-August, 1970
Oil monotype on Strathmore
7 1/4 x 8 1/2 in.
Collection of Stanger Publications Inc., New York

Twelve Eggs and Golden Trees, 1973
Oil monotype on synthetic paper backdrop with Strathmore overlay
29 x 23 in.
Private collection

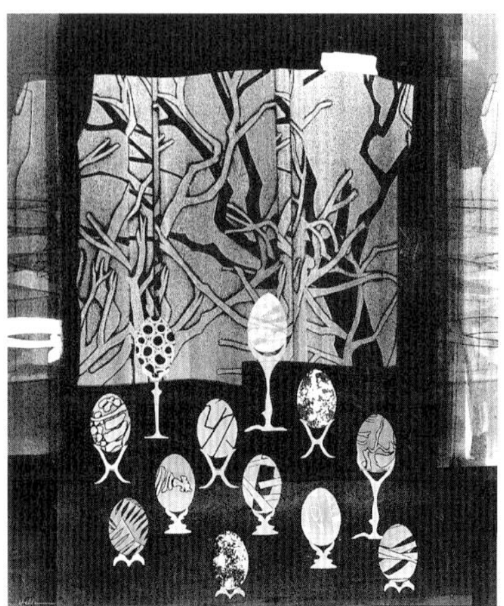

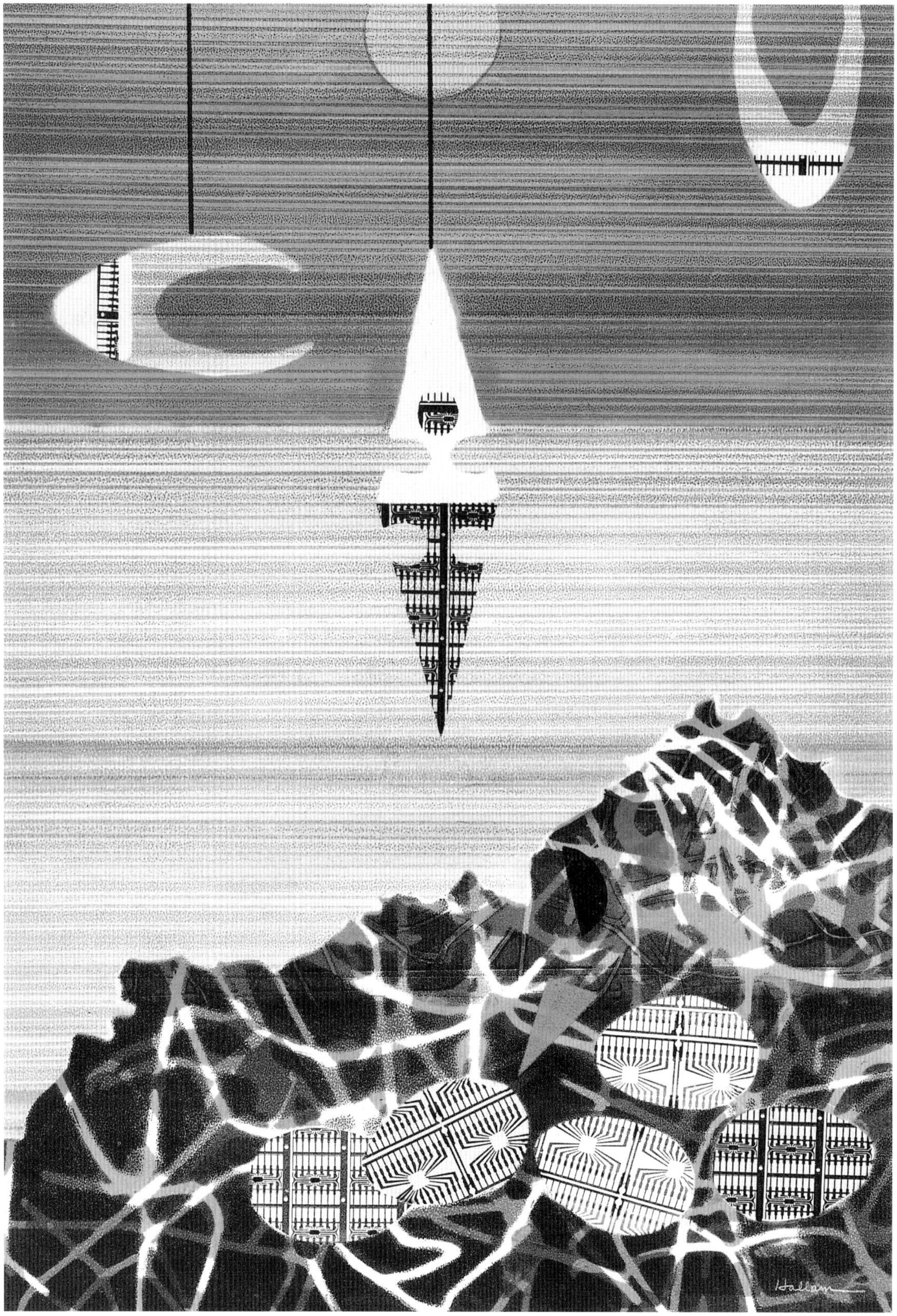

(Opposite)

Electronic Eggs, 1973
Oil monotype on Strathmore, 20 x 14 in.
Private collection

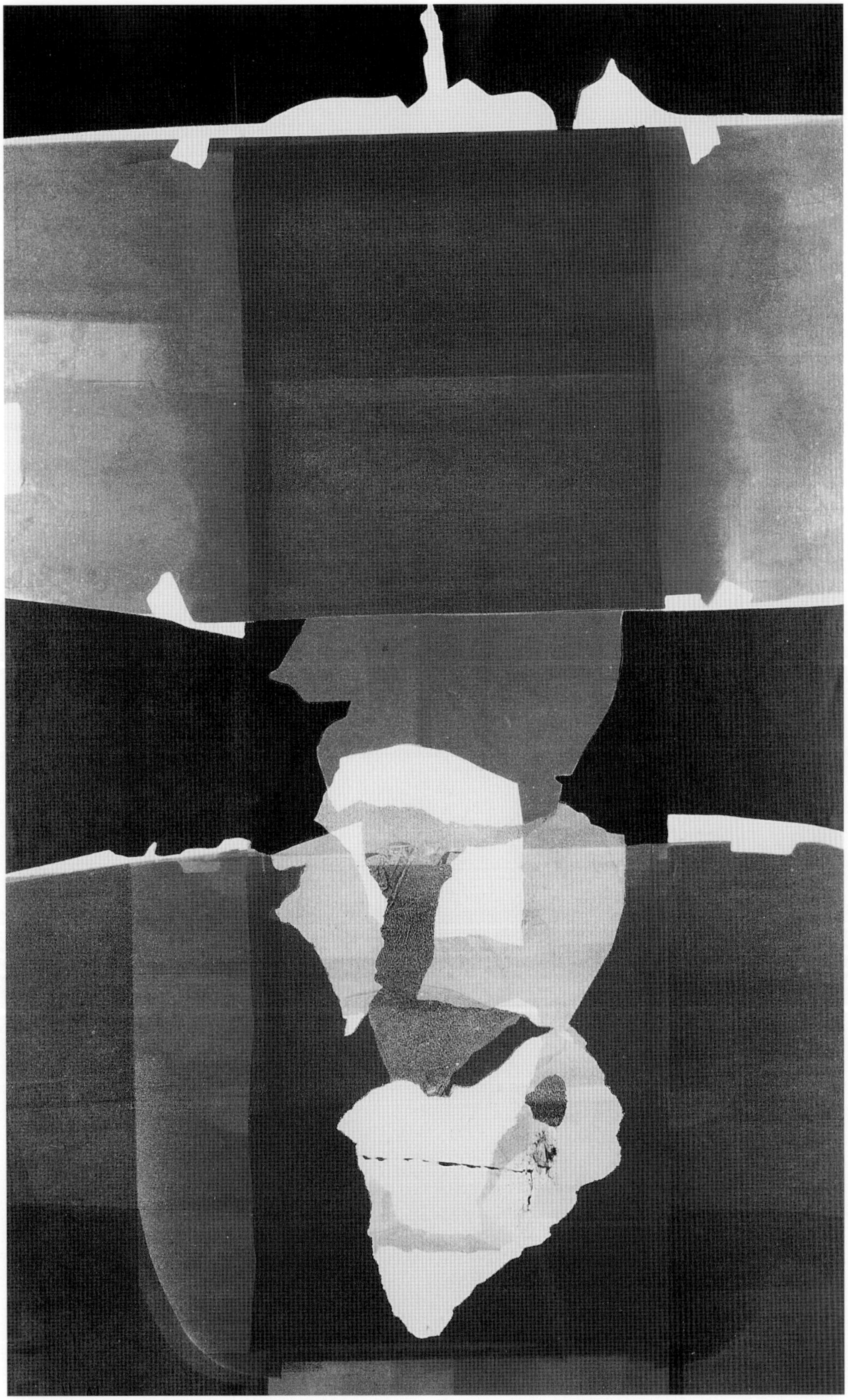

Stack, 1968
Oil monotype on Strathmore, 30 x 20 1/2 in.
Addison Gallery of American Art
Phillips Academy, Andover, Massachusetts

Sea Vigil, 1970-1971
Oil monotype on Strathmore, 20 x 14 in.
Collection of Mrs. Storer G. Decatur

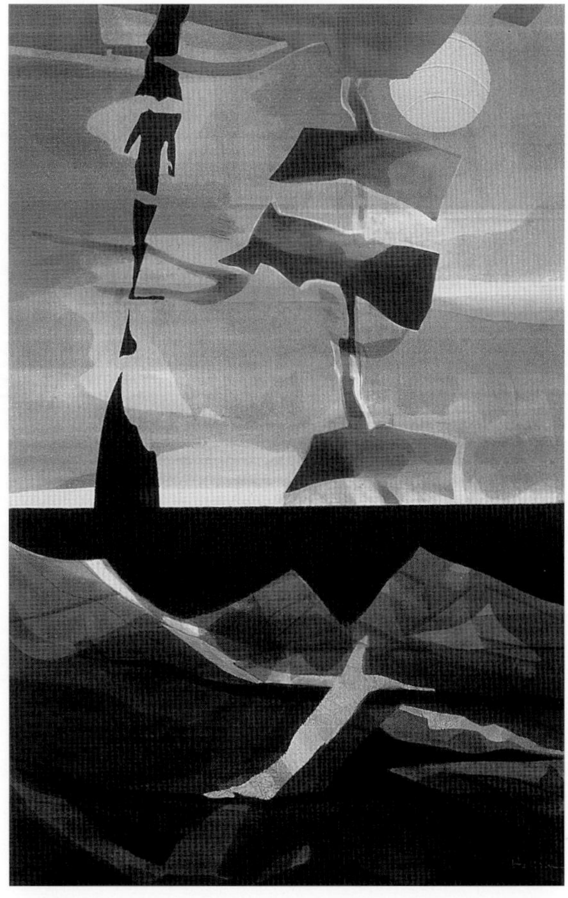

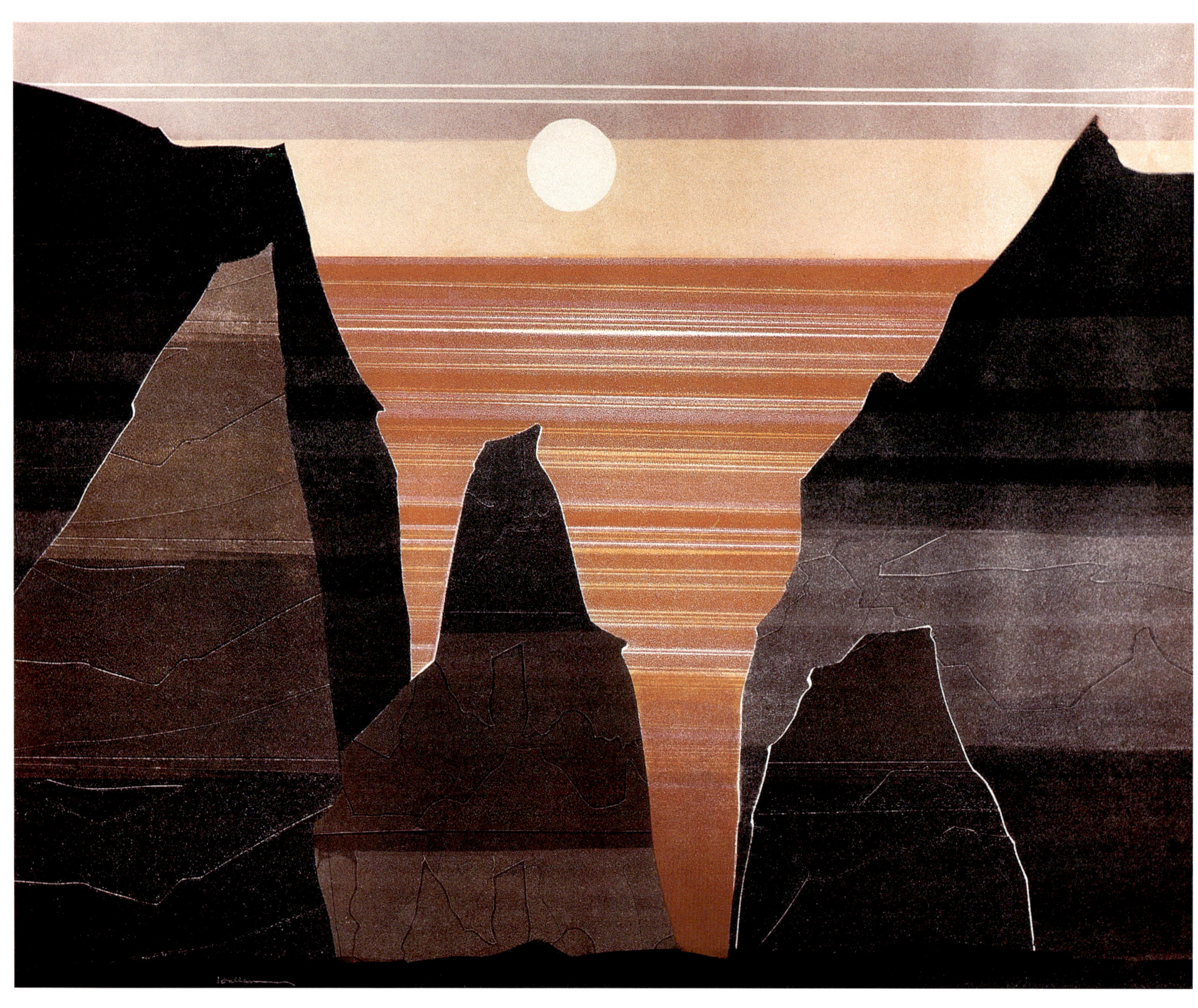

Settling In, 1972
Oil on synthetic paper, 24 x 30 in.
Collection of Mr. and Mrs. Barron F. Stallman

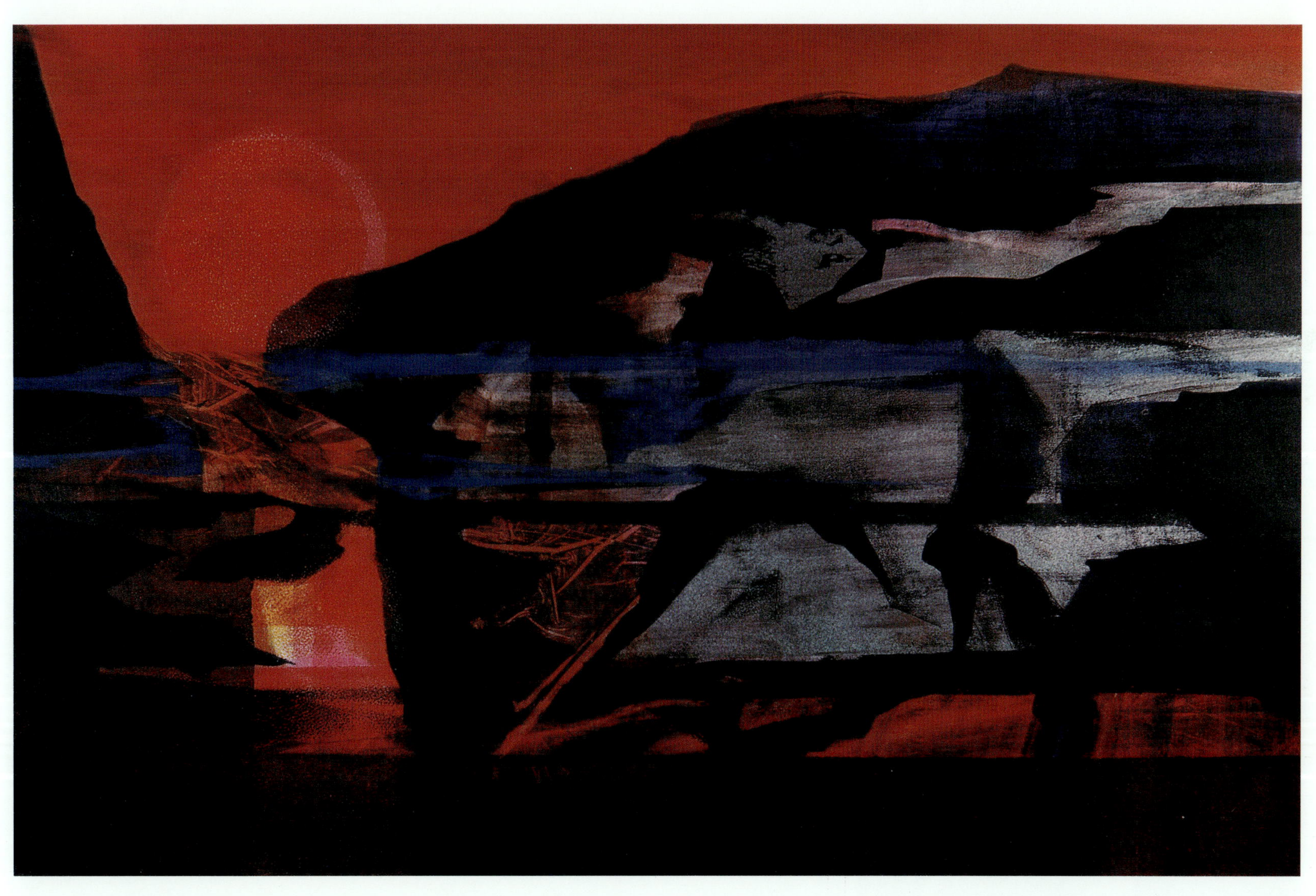

Extinct Brink, 1970
Oil monotype on Strathmore, 12 1/2 x 20 in.
Collection of Ernst & Ernst, Chicago

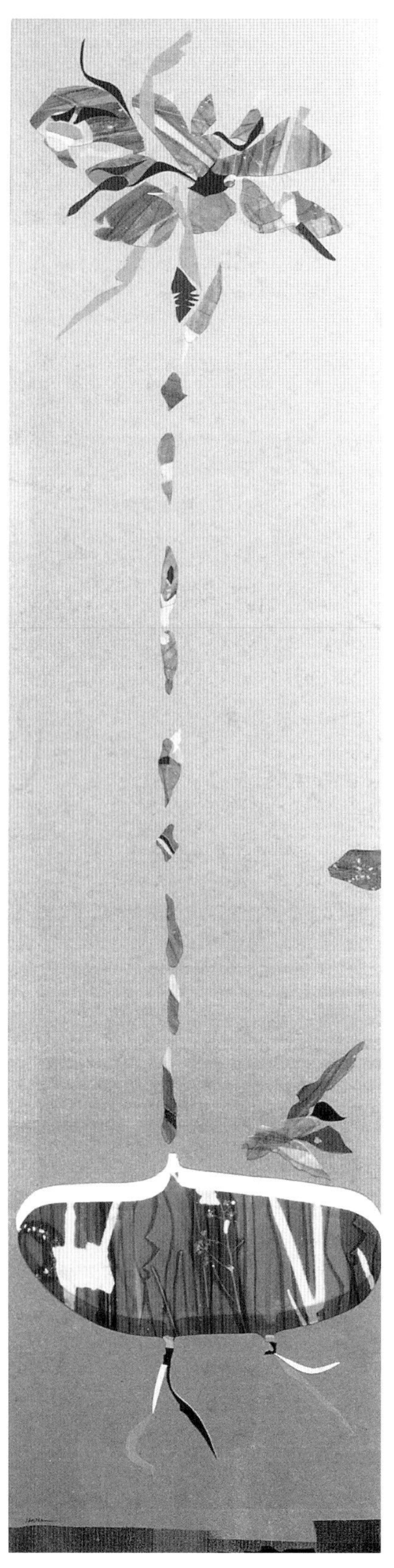

This witnessing of the birth of a butterfly led to *Stages (Butterfly)*, 1969, an oil monotype that incorporates the abstract-organic shape that so fascinated Hallam. Using stencils, she went on to render the stages of the chrysalis. Several pieces in this series were not completed until 1979.

The seacoast milieu Hallam lived in continued to exert its influence on her art. A number of oil monotypes from the early 1970s—*Sea Vigil*, *Settling In*, *Extinct Brink*—respond to coastal scenes and atmospheres. They also reflect the influence of such Max Ernst pictures as *Reflections* and *The Marriage of Heaven and Earth*, both 1962, and *Yellow Sea and Blue Sun*, 1964, an oil on canvas.

Hallam's first full-scale retrospective exhibition, mounted at the Addison Gallery of American Art in 1971, featured 131 works, including paintings, assemblages, monotypes, and drawings dating from as early as 1956. By this time, Hallam was taking part in exhibitions all along the eastern seaboard, from Maine to Washington and on to Florida. The list of private and public collections that owned her work was growing each year.

Hallam continued to produce monotypes throughout the 1970s. In an interview with Robert Taylor in the September 10, 1972, issue of *The Boston Sunday Globe*, the artist explained to the critic that her enthusiasm for the medium derived in part from the fact that she had "never made more than one of anything" in her life.

"The artists she admires, such as Max Ernst, Gyorgy Kepes, Tàpies, Yves Klein," wrote the perceptive Taylor, "are characterized by an ability to get outside the confines of formula, to grow and change rather than reiterate." Hallam emulated these artists' innovative ways, following her own creative avenues.

An oil monotype, *Featherbed Creek*, 1974, recalls the complex renderings of tide pools Hallam painted in the early 1960s. It also bears out something Taylor wrote in a review of the show *Sixteen Maine Artists* at the Shore Galleries in January 1974: "Beverly Hallam has made of the monotype an expressive medium of infinite capacities, contrasting hard-edge forms and a soft textural counterpoint of subtle tonal transitions."

Many of the monotypes from the late 1970s include collage, as Hallam continued to practice the kind of interdisciplinary art she thrives on. The last monotypes incorporated what she calls her "dregs," bits of old stencils that she had held on to. Such recycling was a signal that the artist was getting ready to move beyond the medium that had kept her occupied for so many years.

Among the outstanding monotypes from the end of the decade are *After Tsai*, 1978, and *Basket of Strawberries*, 1979. The former is a narrow vertical piece—an unusual format for Hallam—featuring collage elements arranged on a metallic silver to render a kind of long-stemmed flower swaying in a floating vessel. The effect is oriental, delicate, and evocative—and reminiscent of the sculptor Tsai's work. The latter, *Basket of Strawberries*, makes clever use of collage, featuring cut-out photographs of strawberries neatly arranged in a basket—a seamless and becoming illusion.

Blue Window Bouquet, 1978, makes similar use of cut-out material, in this case stencils Hallam had used for a group of monotypes in 1972. Large pieces were given a renewed identity with scissors. Ever the painter of flowers, she used essentially abstract means to recreate the essence of blooms in a dynamic scheme. It is fitting that flowers would serve as the subject for many of her great paintings of the next decade, and that the stencil device used to create the monotypes was to be the bridge for her next body of work in airbrush.

(OPPOSITE)

AFTER TSAI, 1978
OIL MONOTYPE AND COLLAGE ON SYNTHETIC PAPER
39 1/4 X 9 7/8 IN.
COLLECTION OF MR. AND MRS. DEAN R. FRIEZE

Before me, the road leading to Perkins Cove in Ogunquit was called Featherbed Lane because of the smooth beach stones one drove over to get there. I liked the name and imagined the look of it.

FEATHERBED CREEK, 1974
OIL ON SYNTHETIC PAPER, 30 X 40 IN.
COLLECTION OF MR. AND MRS. KENNEDY BUELL

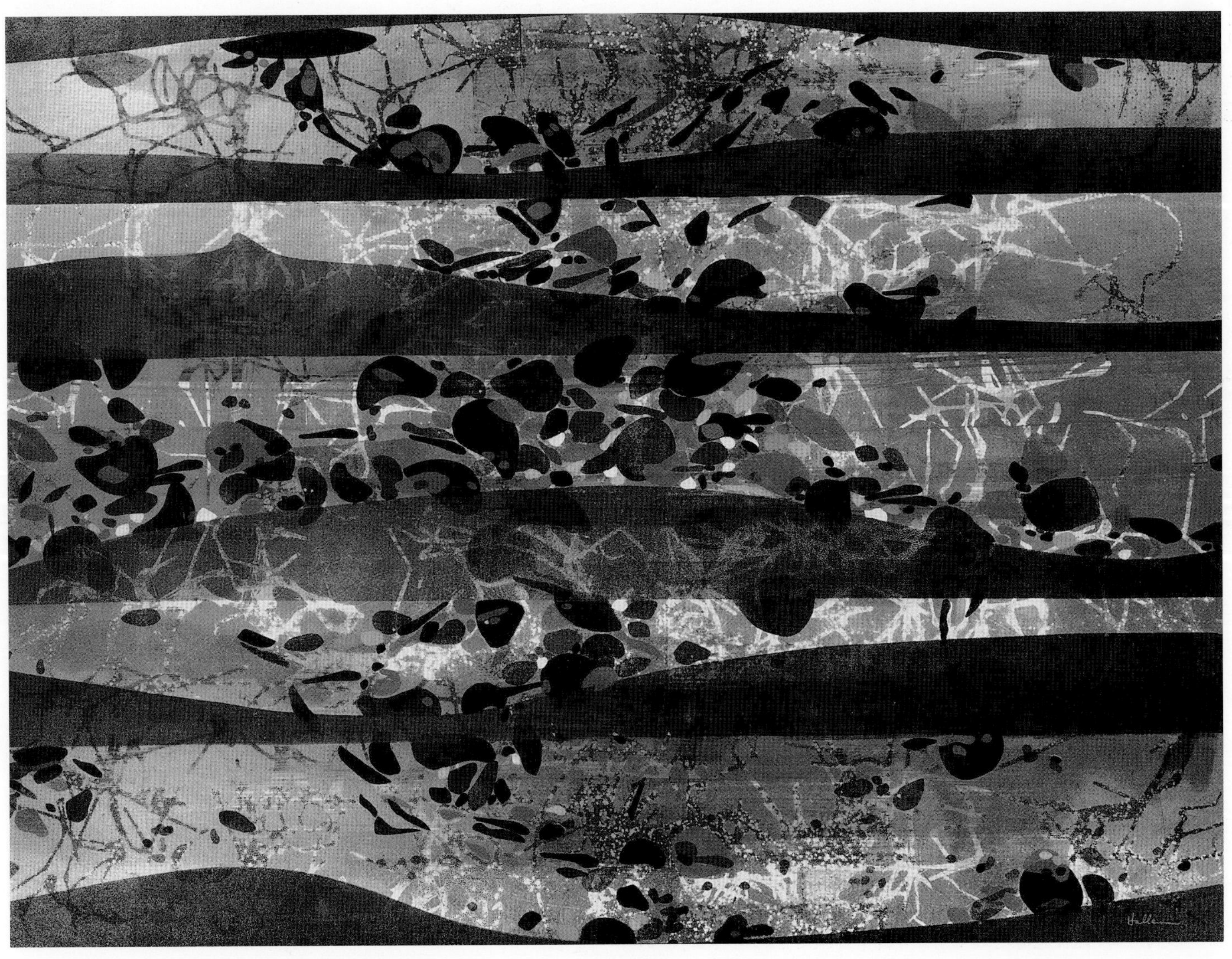

There is never-ending delight in pushing little haphazard cut-out shapes around to make an impression. It can't go wrong. Nothing is final until it's pasted down.

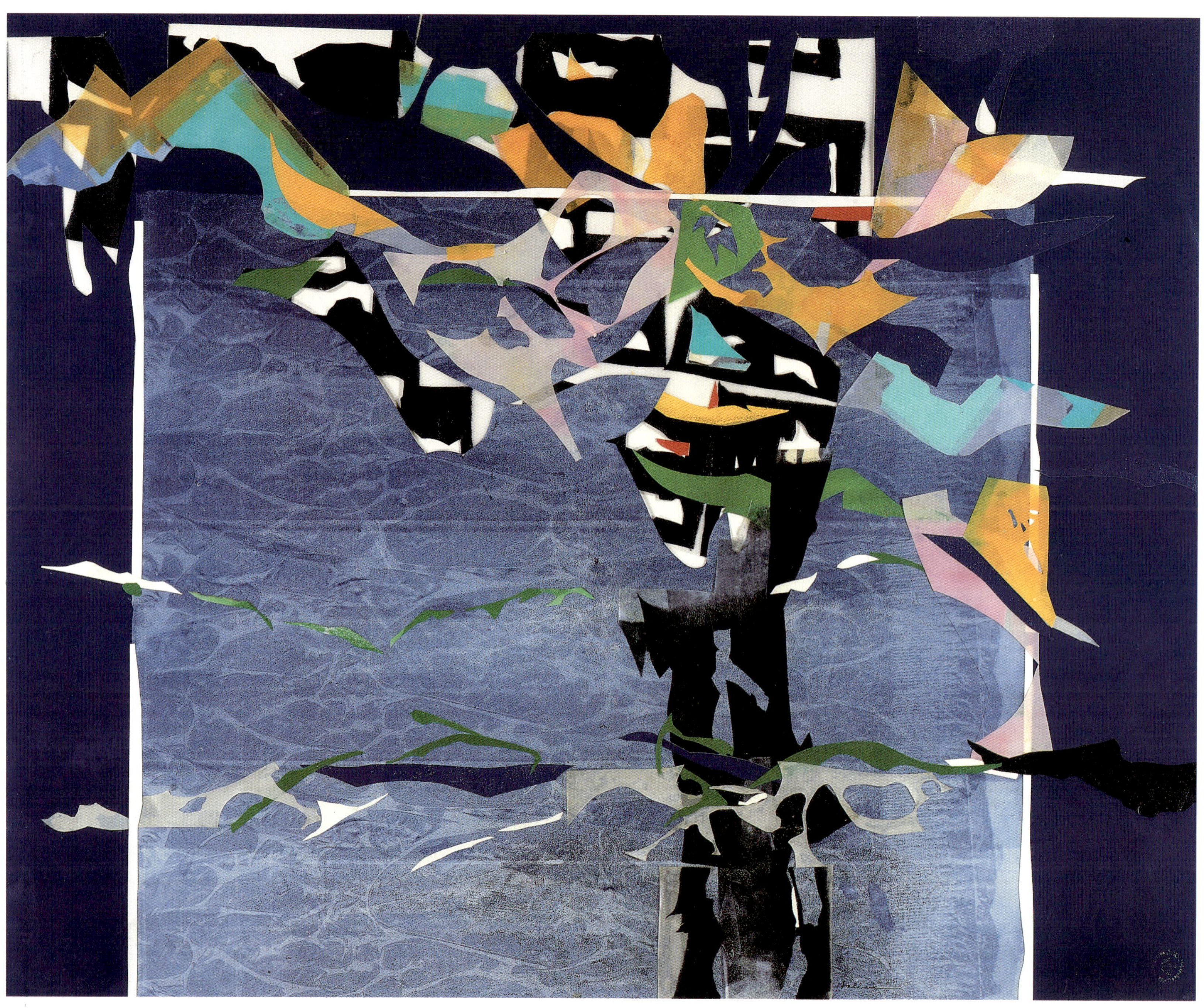

Blue Window Bouquet, 1978
Oil monotype and collage on Strathmore, 29 x 23 in.
Collection of Michael Palmer

(opposite)

Basket of Strawberries, 1979
Oil monotype and collage on Strathmore, 11 x 17 in.
Collection of the artist

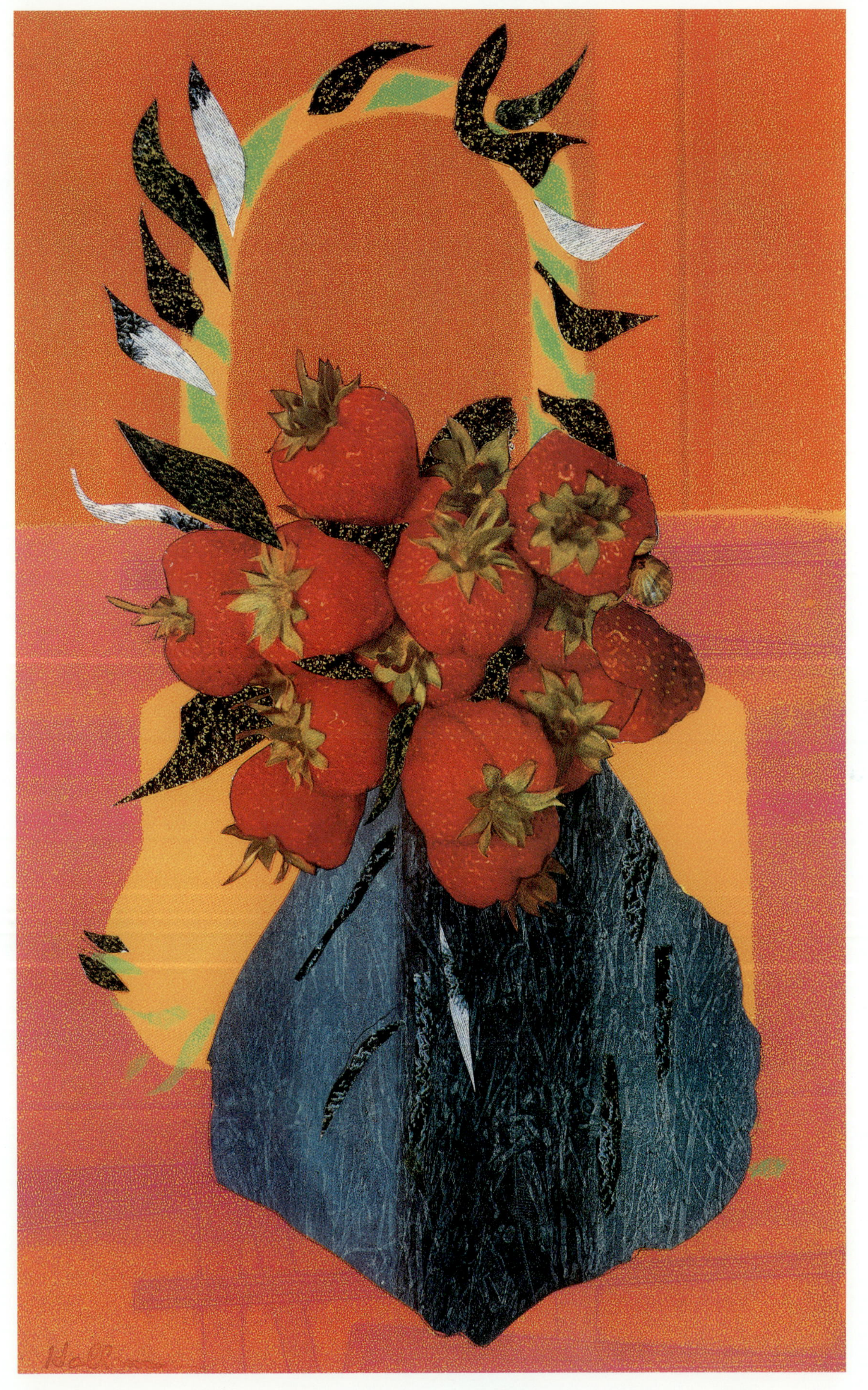

12

Airbrush: Beginnings

> Beverly Hallam...took the winding road through modernism before arriving at her current style. Her lengthy and fascinating evolution was capped by a dramatic, fairly recent transformation from painter of muted, subtly suggestive organic abstractions to creator of brilliantly hued, spectacularly patterned flower paintings that are as sharply focused, precisely rendered and startlingly "accurate" as any Photo-Realist images, but that make their point with considerably more imagination and flair.
>
> —Theodore Wolff, *On the Edge: Forty Years of Maine Painting*, 1991

At the end of Robert Taylor's article about Hallam in *The Boston Globe* in 1972, the artist made a revealing statement about her approach to art. "I'd get bored with painting if it lacked spontaneity," she states. "Yet everything is based on what I see and everything is in the mind, waiting, too. A painting makes itself as it goes along. I wait quite a while for the right solution."

In 1980, the right solutions to Hallam's next move in art would appear in a serendipitous sequence of events that took place in her dining room, her flower garden, and her studio. By that year, Hallam had been making monotypes for nearly two decades. "I was beginning to be bored," she has admitted, and felt ready for a change.

Interviewed by *Maine Life* in February of that year, Hallam discussed her plans. "I want to paint bigger things," she said, noting that the width of the rollers she used to make her monotypes limited her to 30-by-40-inch surfaces. She also expressed a desire to simplify and to pursue what she called a "mysterious quality" in her work, by means of shadows.

As the eminent art critic and historian Theodore Wolff points out, Hallam's transformation from monotype maker to airbrush artist was dramatic, yet it did not occur overnight. It arose out of a cyclical experience Hallam has undergone throughout her career: reaching something of a stalemate in a medium, she gradually but systematically moves into new aesthetic territory, reinventing her art and rediscovering herself as an artist.

The way Hallam tells it, the transition to airbrushed work began one day in the spring of 1980 when the late afternoon sun hit a bouquet of red poppies and iris. The incredible shadow that the flowers cast across her dining room table fascinated Hallam, and she quickly photographed the arrangement. She went on to arrange and photograph floral setups through the summer, adding such "props" as a black velvet tablecloth and mirrors. Out of this poetic and extravisual concatenation of events arose a body of work simply amazing in its power and presence.

The monotype period came to an end with the creation of six oil floral pieces in 1980-1981, inspired by Hallam's photographs. The first five of

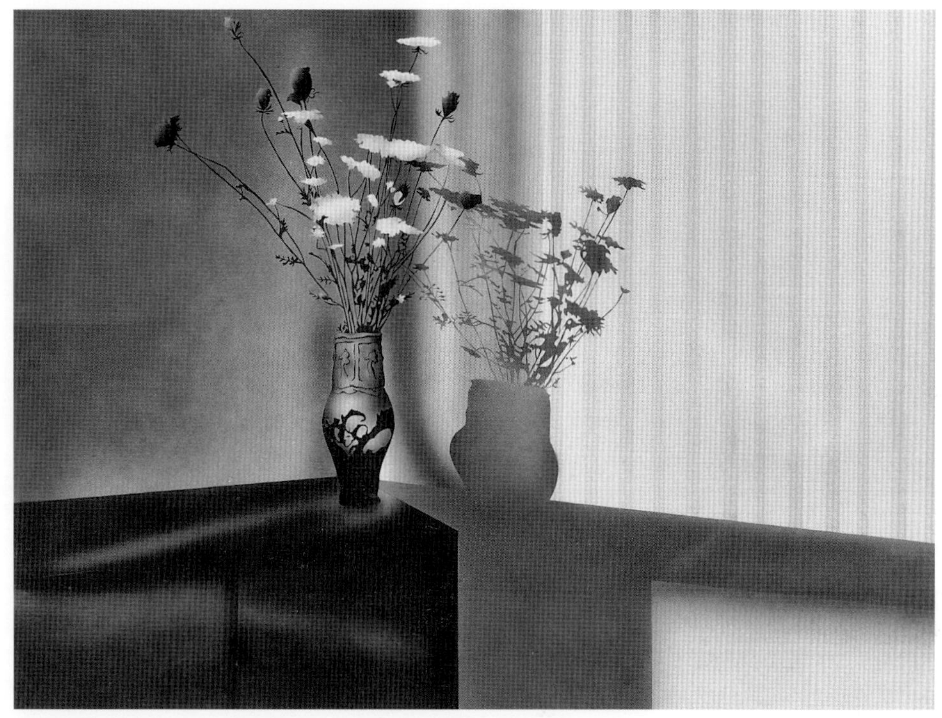

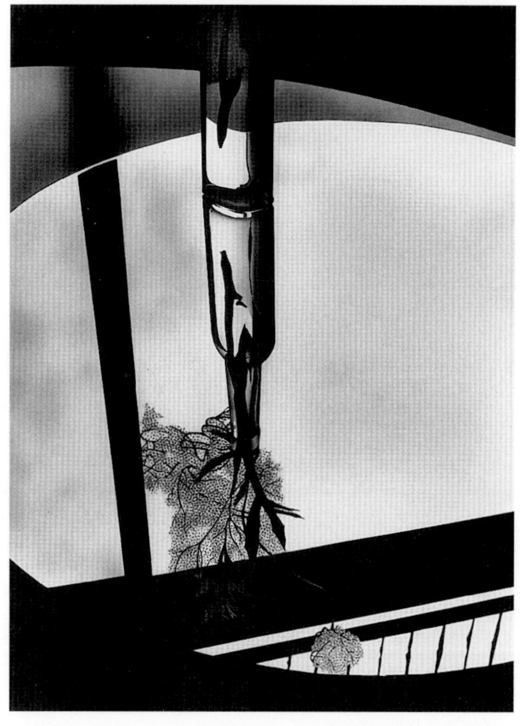

Left: *Queen Anne's Lace in John Natale's Raku*, 1981
Oil on Strathmore mounted on ragboard
30 x 40 in.
Collection of Hind's Industrial, Tulsa, Oklahoma

Right: *Martha Washington's Plume*, 1981
Oil on Strathmore and silver mylar mounted on ragboard, 40 x 30 in.
Collection of the artist

these transition pieces were created with gelatin roller and airbrush; the sixth, *Queen Anne's Lace in John Natale's Raku*, 1981, is completely airbrushed. The realism in this last piece is extraordinary: the earthenware vase seems tangible, as if you could reach out and pluck it from the painting.

For the third floral piece in the series, *Martha Washington's Plume*, Hallam wanted to create some cloud shapes, but the gelatin roller wouldn't serve her purposes. She remembered a Thayer & Chandler airbrush that someone had given her but that she had never had the occasion to use. She read the instructions, purchased a can of compressed air and an adapter, and went to work.

The results were so successful that Hallam decided to add airbrushed flowers to both *Japanese Iris and Freesia* and *Japanese Iris and Freesia II*, the first two of the aforementioned six floral pieces. *Poppies in Picasso Vase*, number four of the six, was entirely airbrushed except for the green grass, which was rolled on, then softened by airbrush. Below the table, one can see the pattern of octagonals that will recur in future pictures, coming to the fore in the extraordinary *Tulips on Carpet*, 1986.

Pink Poppy in Blue Picasso Vase, 1981, was also largely airbrushed, with just a faint pattern on the table, courtesy of the roller. According to Hallam, this picture represents the last time she used the gelatin roller. Quite fittingly, one can just make out, on a wall in a background, three of

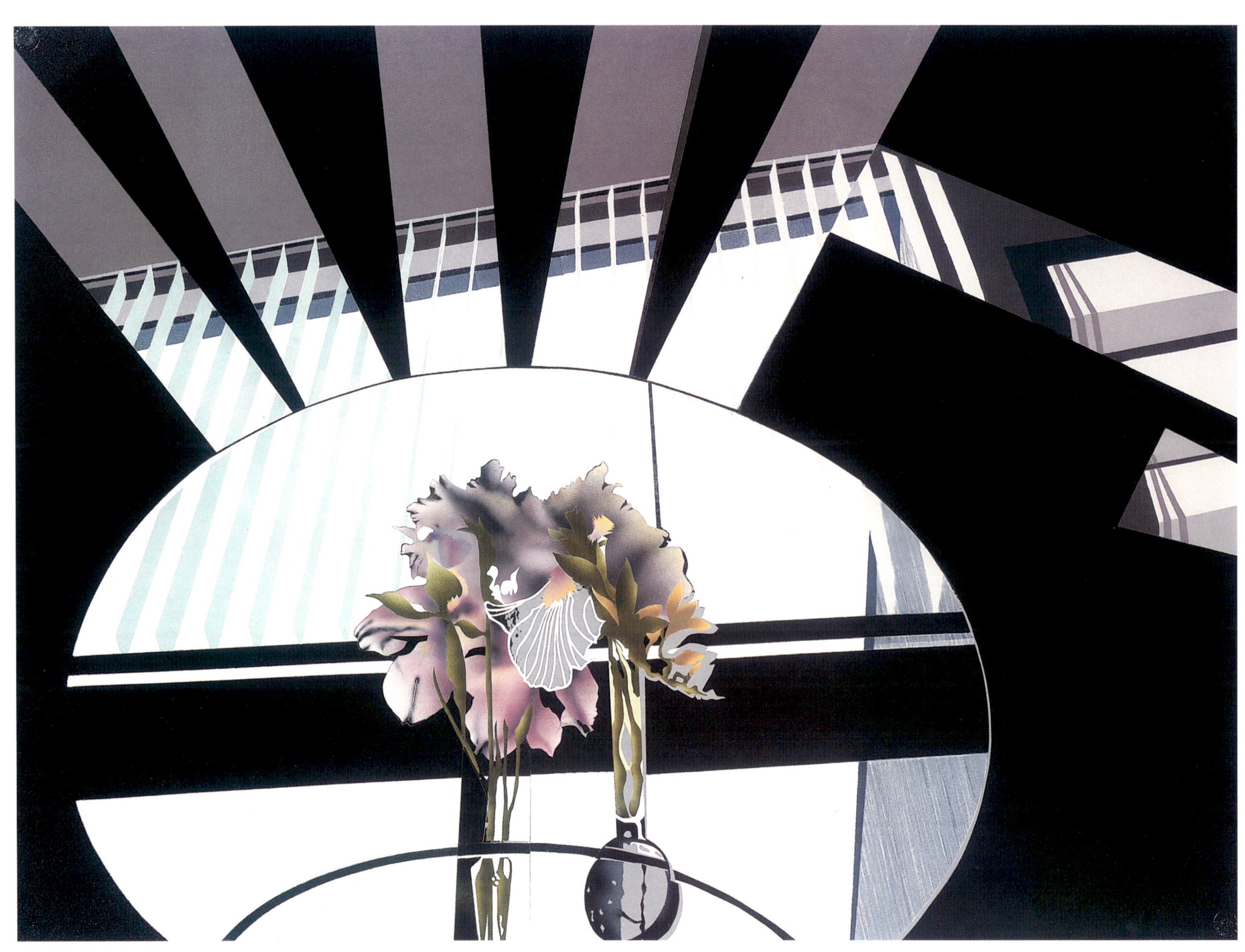

Japanese Iris and Freesia, 1981
Oil on Strathmore and silver mylar mounted on ragboard, 30 x 40 in.
Bowdoin College Museum of Art, Brunswick, Maine

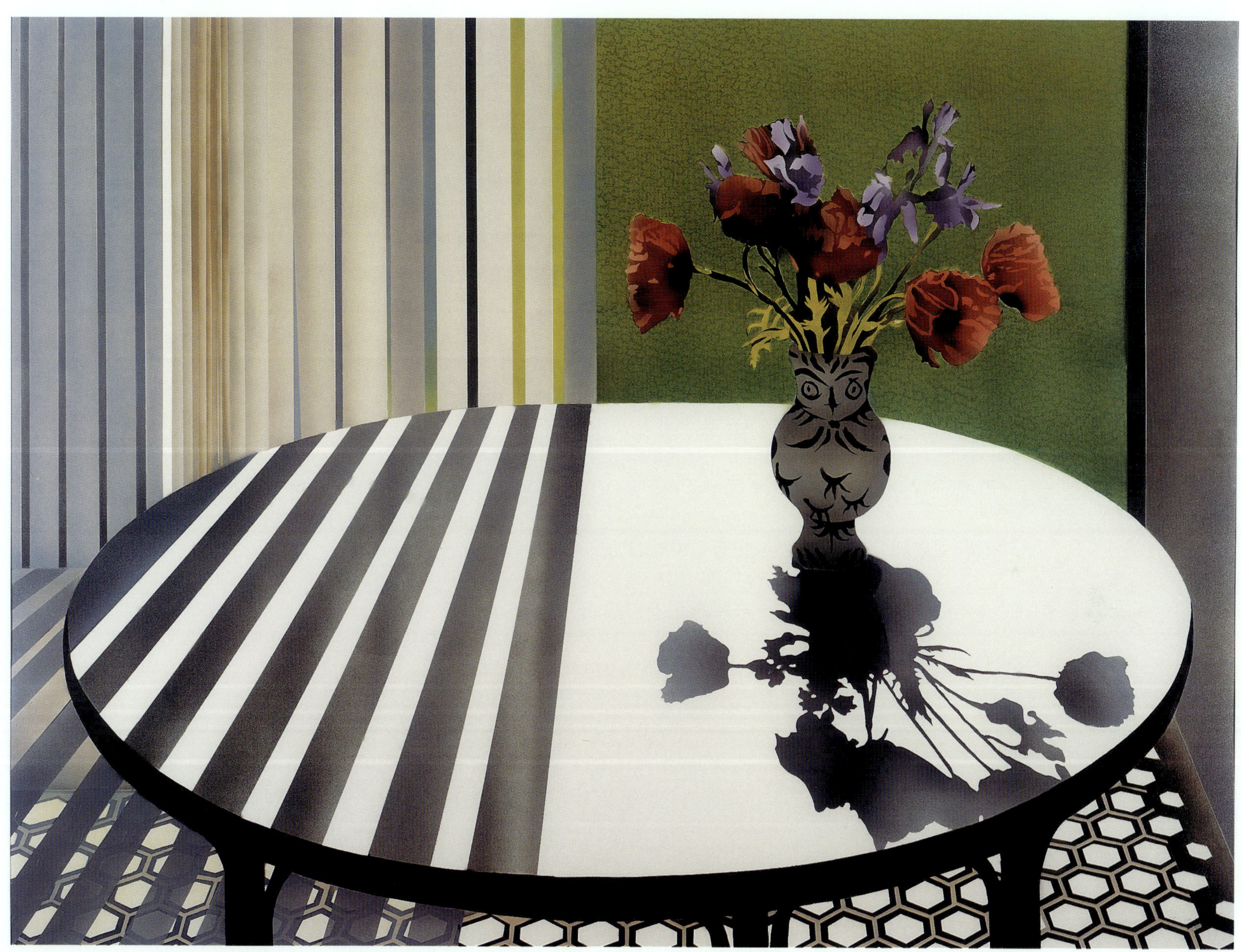

Poppies in Picasso Vase, 1981
Oil on Strathmore, 30 x 40 in.
The Art Gallery, University of New Hampshire
Gift of Mary-Leigh Call Smart, 1981

Hallam's framed monotypes. They hang off stage in the dark, while the main, and new, attraction, an exquisite flower arrangement, catches the late afternoon sun.

One of the beauties of these six pictures is the way in which the straight lines of certain elements in the setting play off against the natural configurations of the centerpiece blossoms and the remarkable shadows they often cast. In *Japanese Iris and Freesia*, for example, rectangular and circular mirrors, vertical blinds, and hard-edge areas of negative space provide a geometric milieu for the cluster of showy blooms. The space is broken up in such a way that one isn't quite sure what's up or down, although the flowers in their narrow vases serve to orient the eye.

As with her acrylic and monotype work, Hallam was meticulous in her preparations. For the six floral pieces, for example, she had her framer mount 30-by-40-inch sheets of three-ply Strathmore paper onto heavy ragboard. After rolling white lithograph ink onto the surface, she airbrushed the picture, holding the airbrush parallel to the paper, which resulted in beautiful suede-like surfaces. Unfortunately, the fumes from the sprayed oil paint led Hallam to switch to acrylic, which doesn't allow for the napped finish she so loves, but which nonetheless spurred her to manufacture a whole range of new textures.

About this same time, Hallam produced a lovely group of pastels, using some of the same bouquet-in-vase setups, with variations of the same flora, such as *Oriental Poppies, Iris and Rhododendron in Picasso Vase*, 1980. All of these were drawn on a lovely green Mi-Teintes paper and display an open, spontaneous hand. Hallam often sought relief from the intensity of the exacting airbrush work by making fast pastels from the same subject.

Although confident with her new art tool, Hallam proceeded cautiously; she felt more experimentation and increased facility were required before she could go on. In February 1981, for the sake of practice, she purchased a can of black automotive spray paint and set out to make some rapid pictures using this simplified version of an airbrush. She placed some old Narcissus bulbs directly onto large pieces of rice paper, using common pins to keep their wilted leaves from blowing away. She then "blasted away" with the spray paint. Afterwards, a few strokes of pastel were added to several of these pieces. *Paperwhite's Farewell I* and *II* are ethereal, mysterious pictures created with the simplest of means. The glowing bulb shapes with their reed-like leaves assume different poses in their shadowy setting.

In April 1981, Hallam was ready to tackle the airbrush in earnest. Still, she proceeded with care, beginning with acrylic Liquitex paint in jars (fluid colors made by Golden were used in the 1990s), which she applied to 6-by-8-inch sheets of heavy rag paper. For subject matter, she chose a few

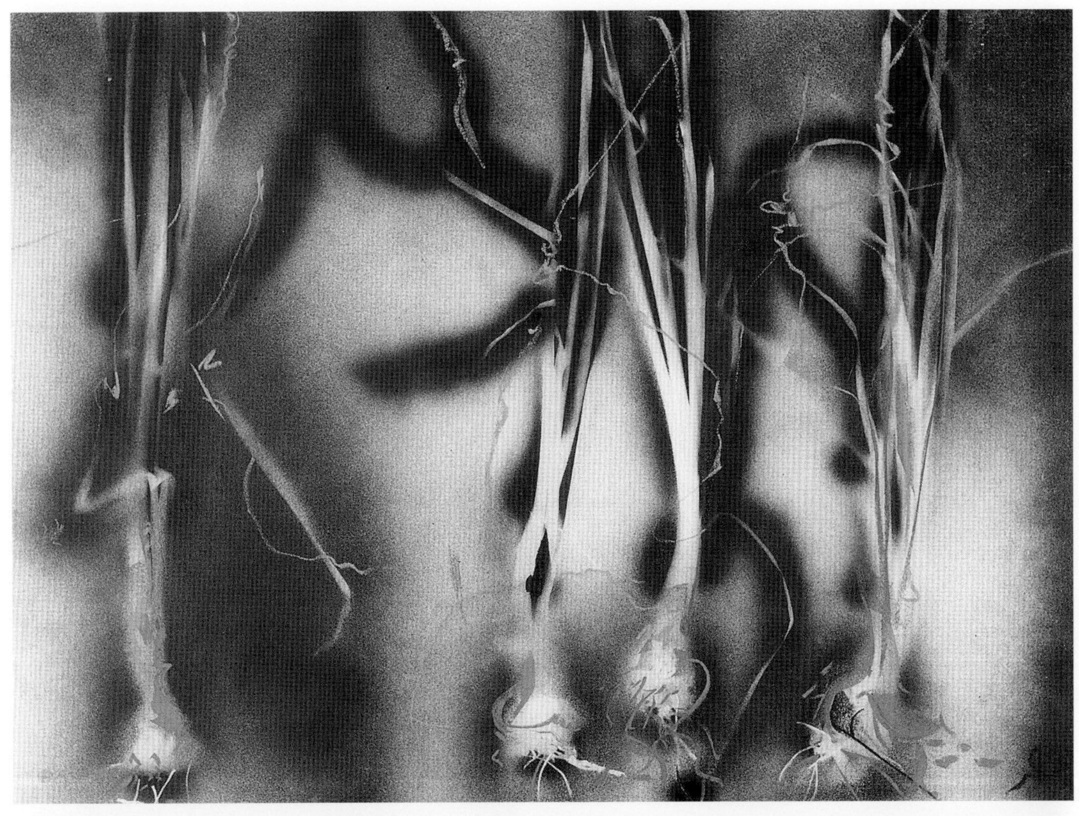

Paperwhite's Farewell I, 1981
Oil and pastel on rice paper, 21 x 29 in.
Collection of the artist

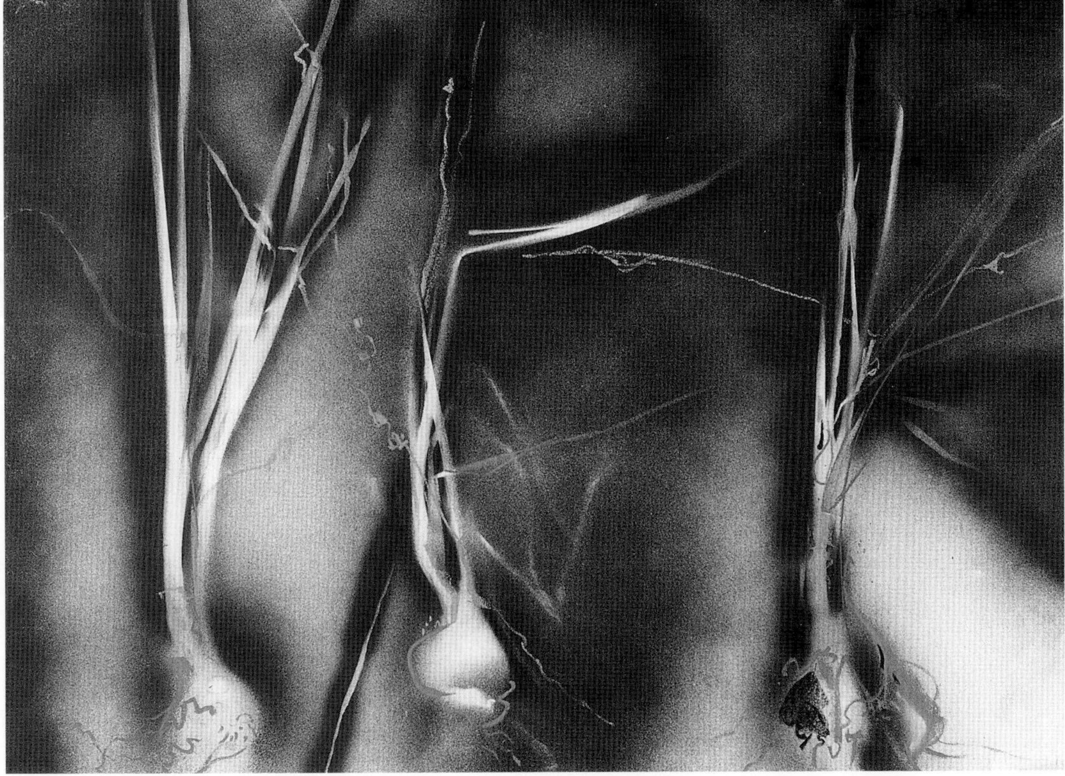

Paperwhite's Farewell II, 1981
Oil and pastel on rice paper, 21 x 29 in.
Collection of the artist

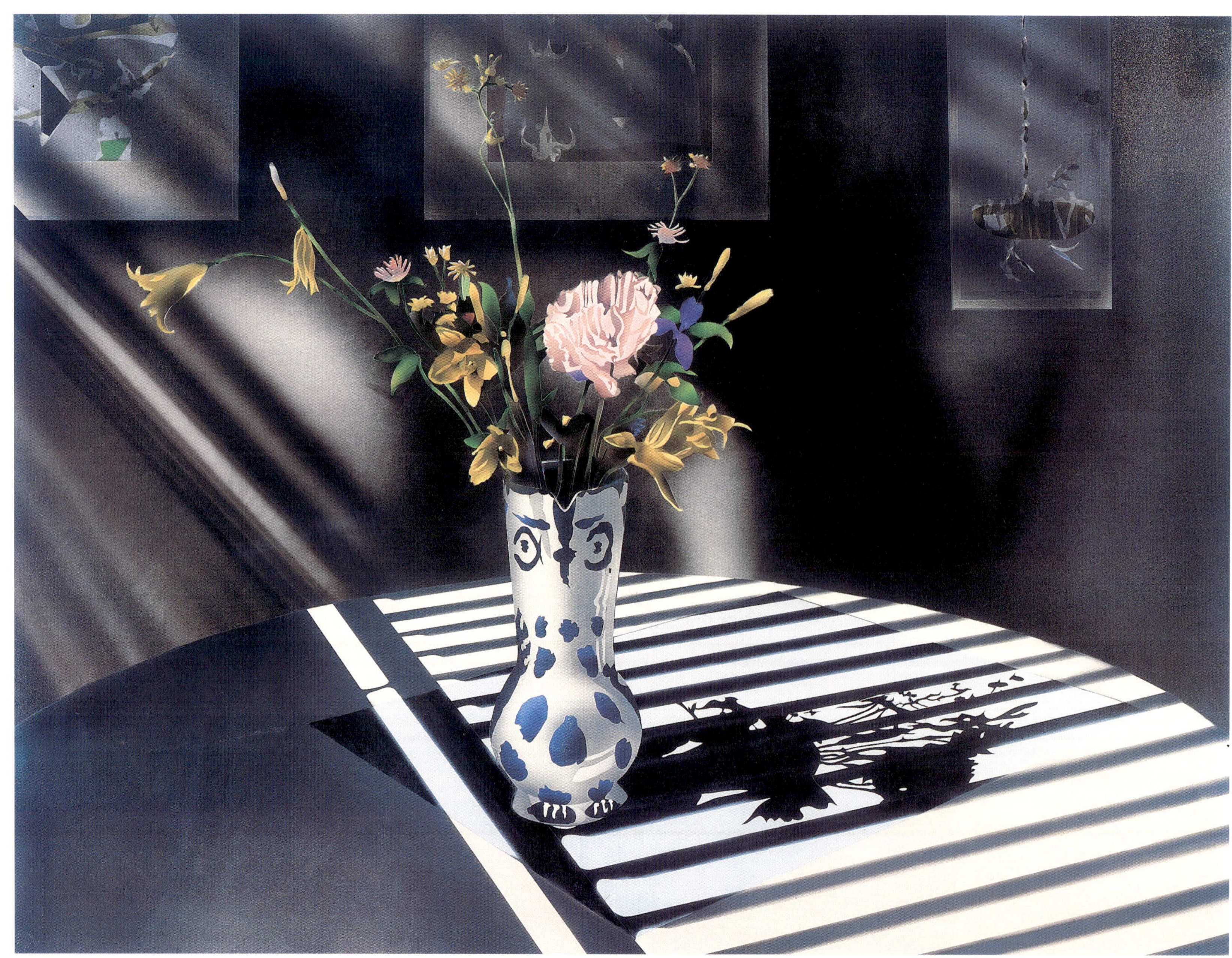

Pink Poppy in Blue Picasso Vase, 1981
Oil on Strathmore paper, 29 1/2 x 39 1/4 in.
Farnsworth Art Museum, Rockland, Maine
Gift of Mary-Leigh Call Smart

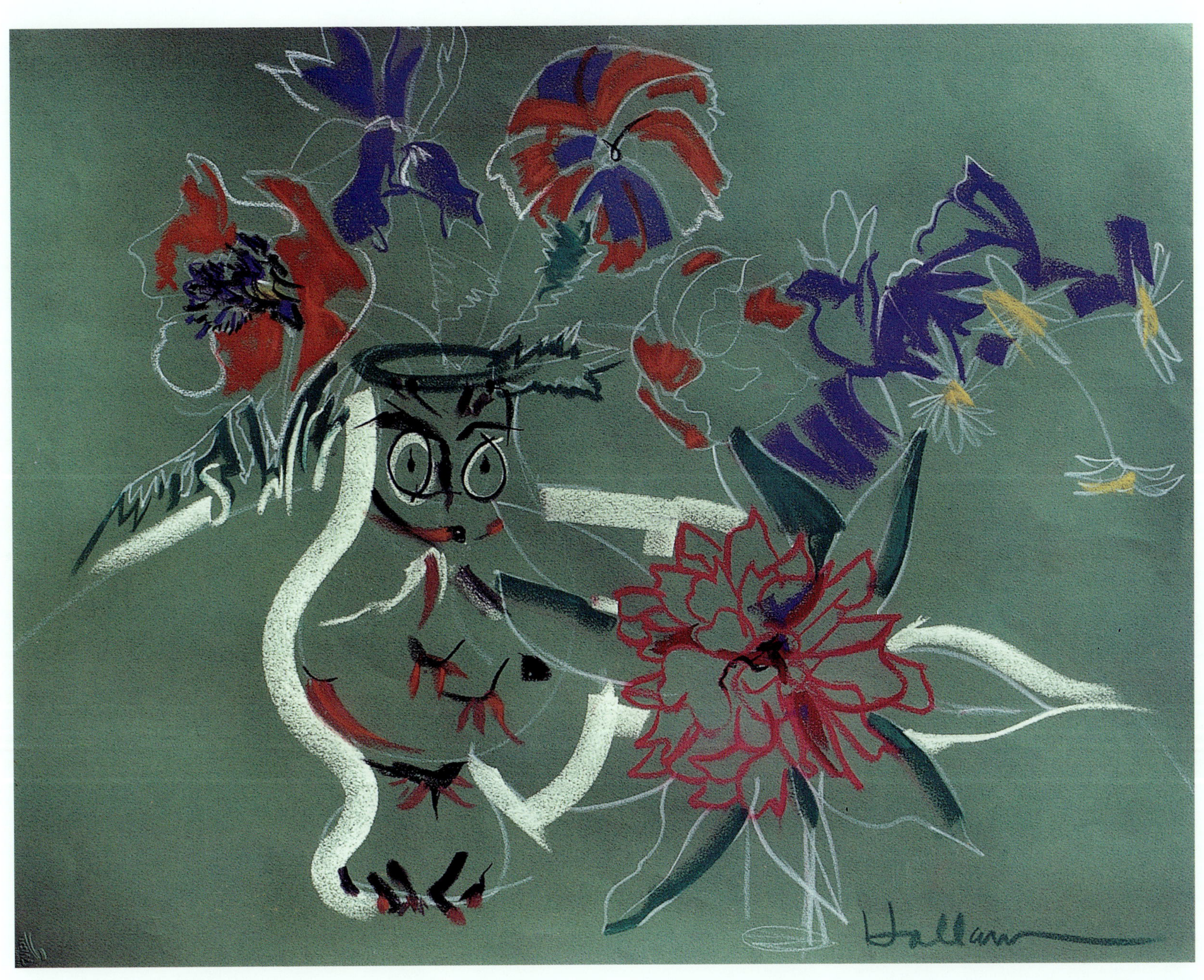

Oriental Poppies, Iris and Rhododendron in Picasso Vase, 1980
Pastel on green Canson Mi-Teintes paper, 19 3/4 x 25 5/8 in.
Collection of the artist

simple shapes, vases with Queen Anne's lace and nasturtiums, and made use of the late afternoon sun and the shadows it sent moving across the wall of her dining room.

The result was a series of delicate flower pieces, and an extraordinary display of shadow theater. The fine stems with their flat clusters of small white flowers make lovely lace-like traceries on the air and against the wall behind them. The palette consists of shades of pale gray. The titles of several of these pictures provide the exact time of the light during which they were painted: *Queen Anne's Shadow 6:15 P.M.*, *Queen Anne's Shadow 6:30 P.M.*, *Queen Anne's Shadow 7:00 P.M.*, etc. The composition of each of these images was essentially the same; it was the shadow configuration that changed, with the shifting of the late afternoon sun.

One piece from this series, *Queen Anne's Lace*, when shown at the Barn

Queen Anne's Shadow, 6:15 P.M., 1981
Acrylic on rag paper, 12 x 8 in.
Collection of Mrs. Leslie Davis Polk

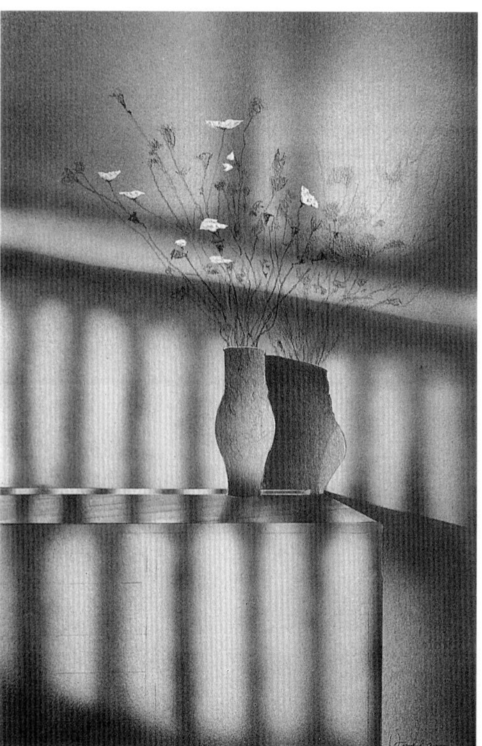

Queen Anne's Shadow, 6:30 P.M., 1981
Acrylic on rag paper, 12 x 8 in.
Collection of Mr. and Mrs. Lee Tanenbaum

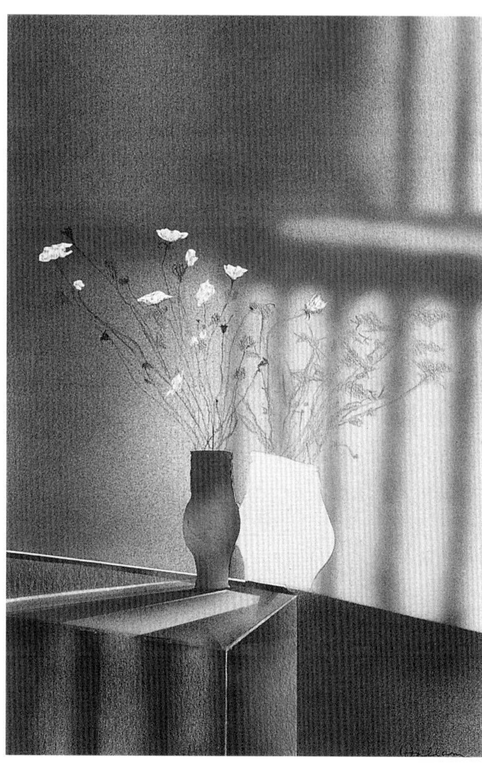

Queen Anne's Shadow, 7:00 P.M., 1981
Acrylic on rag paper, 12 x 8 in.
Collection of Mrs. Edythe Jean Haddaway

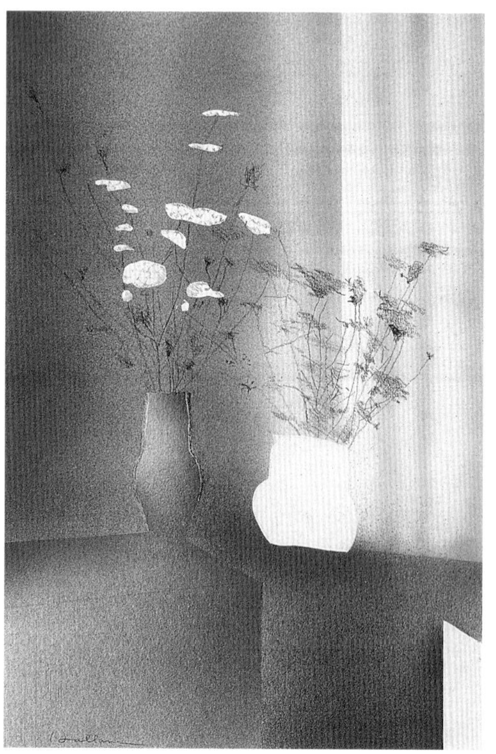

Gallery in Ogunquit in June 1981, caught the eye of *The Boston Globe* critic Robert Taylor. This acrylic, he reported, "shimmers—though it is done in a smooth matte brushwork style—with the phosphorescent silhouetted quality of objects placed on chemically treated paper by Man Ray in the '20s."

The comparison to Man Ray is very apt. This pioneering artist used airbrush in the years 1917-1920, and a number of his images from this period—pieces like *Untitled*, 1919—are direct ancestors of Hallam's *Queen Anne's Fan* and *Queen Anne's Lace*, 1981. They, too, used stencils to abstract effect.

Man Ray once likened his discovery of the airbrush to a "revelation—it was wonderful to be able to paint a picture without touching the canvas; this was a pure cerebral activity." Hallam derived equal pleasure and excitement from her mastery of this marvelous instrument of art.

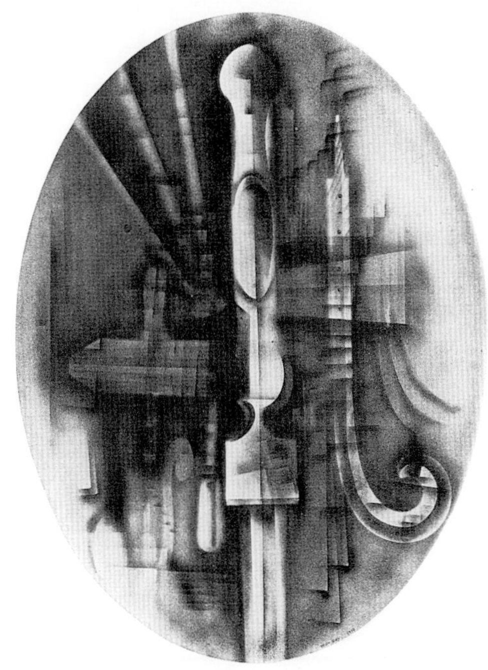

MAN RAY, *UNTITLED*, 1919
AIRBRUSH ON CARDBOARD, 22 1/2 X 28 3/4 IN.
COLLECTION OF LUCIANO ANSELMINO

QUEEN ANNE'S FAN, 1981
ACRYLIC ON RAG PAPER, 8 X 12 IN.
PRIVATE COLLECTION

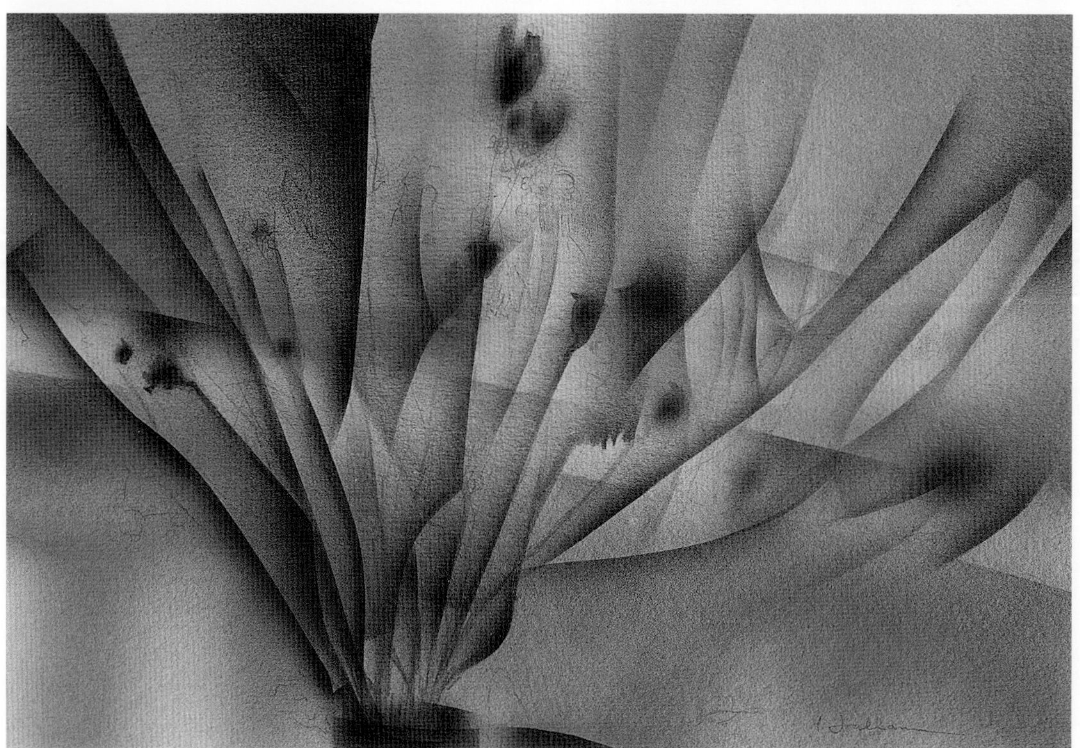

14

The Flower Paintings

"My great passions," Hallam has recently remarked, "are abstract design and sunlight." She traces these passions to an image from childhood: "On windy sunny days, apple tree branches threw their shadows all over the walls of my bedroom." The artist has never forgotten how glorious it was to sit in what she calls "this arena of moving abstract patterns."

Ever up to the challenge, Hallam soon tackled larger formats for her airbrush pictures; at the same time, she shifted from paper to gessoed linen. The first airbrush-on-canvas work, *May Bouquet*, 1982, measures 12 by 24 inches and was, in Hallam's estimation, "rather ambitious" as it contains a rendering of a spray of tiny lilies of the valley. The picture also marks the appearance of those remarkable effects of translucence that Hallam achieves in her flower paintings, where light comes through—suffuses, really—individual flower petals.

With *Rose Grass*, 1982, Hallam returned to the large scale she had ventured into in the 1960s with pieces like *Big Mussel*. Measuring 56 by 65 inches, this study of reddish grasses exemplifies the sense of perfection the artist brings to her airbrush work. Looking at a section of the tall, see-through glass beaker that serves as a vase, one wonders in awe how the artist managed to render so precisely the elaborate network of stems, like the cross-section of a conduit with its multicolored wires criss-crossing one another.

May Bouquet, 1982
Acrylic on Belgian linen, 12 x 24 in.
Collection of Timothy B. Ellis

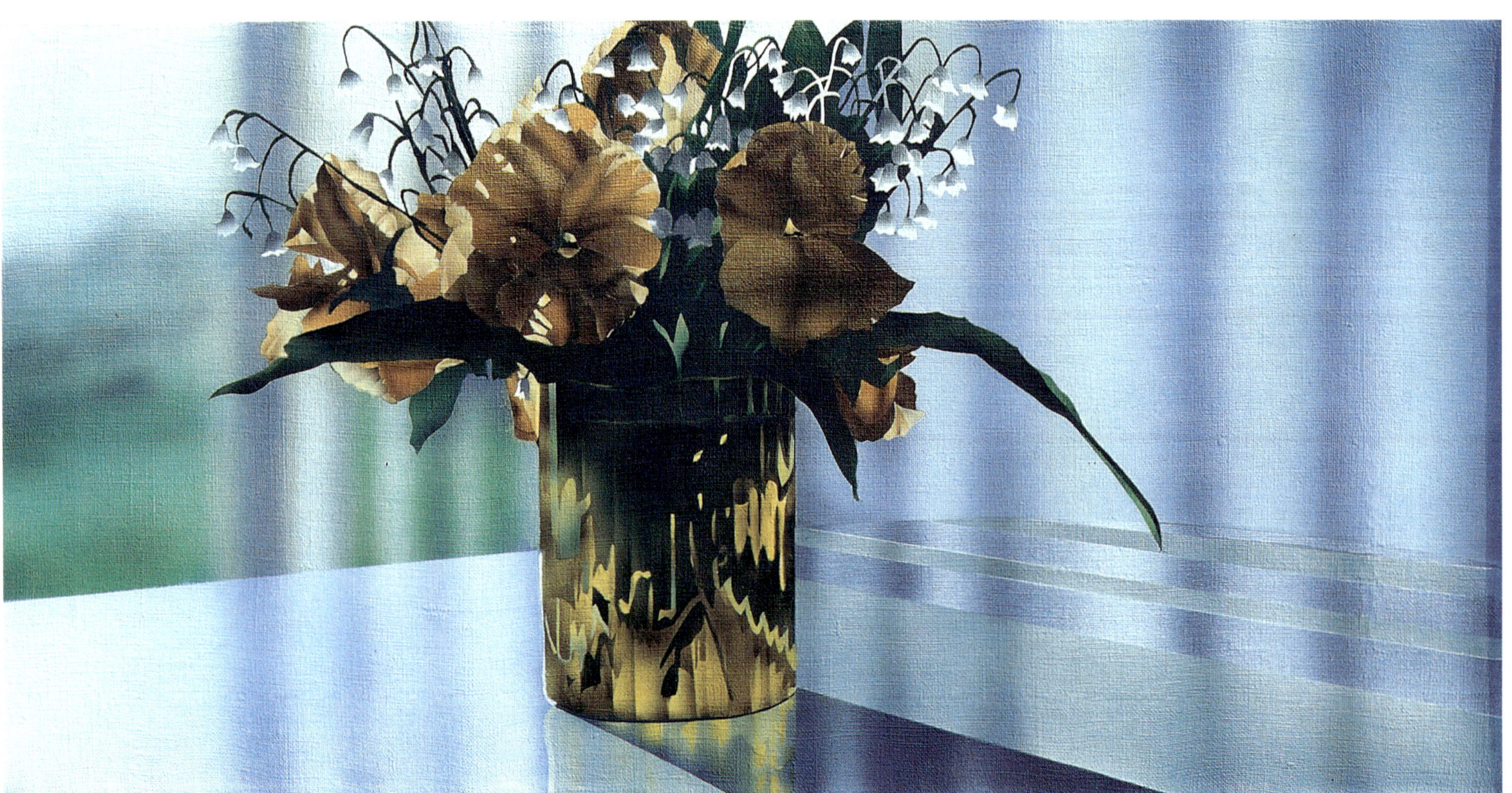

Rose Grass, 1982
Liquitex acrylic on liquitex gessoed Belgian linen, 56 x 65 in.
Addison Gallery of American Art
Phillips Academy, Andover, Massachusetts
Gift of Mary-Leigh Call Smart

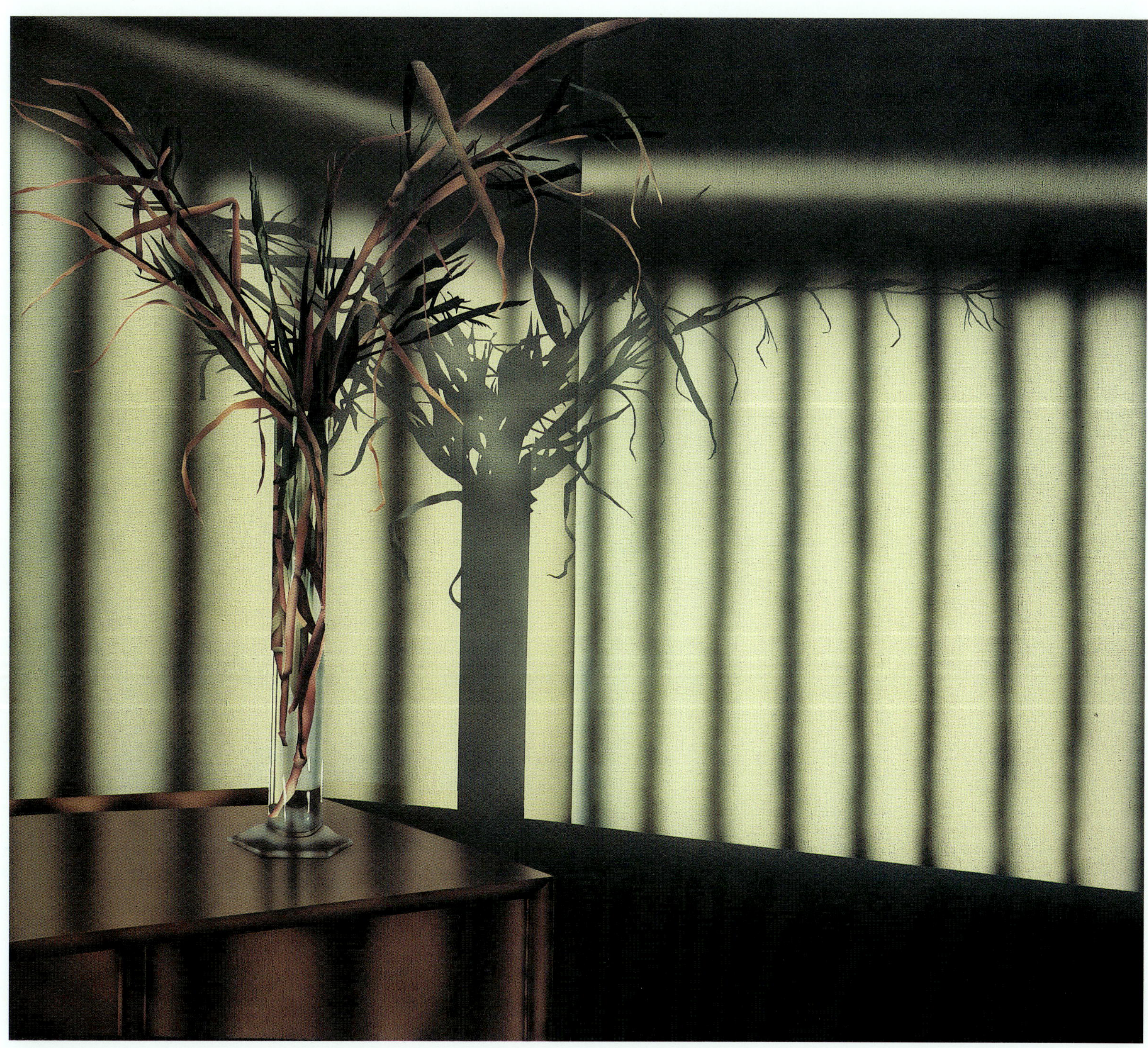

Part of the precision of these paintings derives from the procedure that Hallam developed to transfer a photographic image onto canvas. Choosing one of her photographs out of a boxful of candidates, she projects the image onto a canvas that has been covered with a translucent masking stencil called a frisket. She then traces the outline of the photographic image on the frisket with a felt pen.

Yet the photographic image simply serves as the foundation for the finished picture; the more Hallam works on the painting, the farther she moves away from the photograph, simplifying, abstracting elements of the real—creating her own rhythms, her own composition. (For a detailed description of the process, see Hallam's article "Painting Acrylics with an Airbrush" from *Watercolor 92* magazine, reprinted at the end of this book.)

Hallam has noted that, when she started using the airbrush, she almost felt ashamed about using photographs. "I never let my students use them; they were crutches and stifled imagination." When people came into her studio in York, Hallam would have the vases of flowers around, but never leave the photographs out to be seen.

Liberation from this embarrassment arrived when Hallam discovered Van Deren Coke's book, *The Painter and the Photograph*, 1964. There she read that artists had been using photographs 150 years ago. Suddenly, she felt a kindred spirit with a veritable host of artists, from Fantin-Latour to Ernst, who had used the photograph as a tool in making their art.

The perfectly square (50-by-50 inch) canvas *Mirrored Bouquet*, 1982, is a virtuoso piece of illusion. A vase of flowers is perfectly duplicated in the mirror it sits upon, as is its shadow, which recalls one of those symmetrical cut-outs created with scissors and a folded piece of paper.

The forms are equally evocative in *Late Shadow*, 1982. A small vase of flowers almost seems threatened by the profound shadows that surround it—the one in the foreground resembling a sharp-beaked creature. Here, again, the drama derives from a play of opposites: an arrangement of anemones and daisies juxtaposed with encroaching masses of darkness.

A similar sense of foreboding appears in *Goldenrod*, 1984, where the blinds cast shadows like the bars of a prison over the flower in its simple cruet holder. In this painting, Hallam resorted on one of few occasions to using a paintbrush in an airbrush floral piece, here to paint in the blossom. As the painting was being carried from her studio, a bee lighted on the goldenrod—a true and extraordinary tribute to Hallam's powers of verisimilitude!

In contrast to these two canvases, *Sherry Glass*, 1982, has an almost comic look. A drooping top of a single veronica might be the feather in a fool's cap. In this picture, the shadow of the bouquet falls toward the viewer—a neat compositional variation.

(OPPOSITE)

MIRRORED BOUQUET, 1982
ACRYLIC ON BELGIAN LINEN, 50 X 50 IN.
COLLECTION OF NANCY L. PAYSON

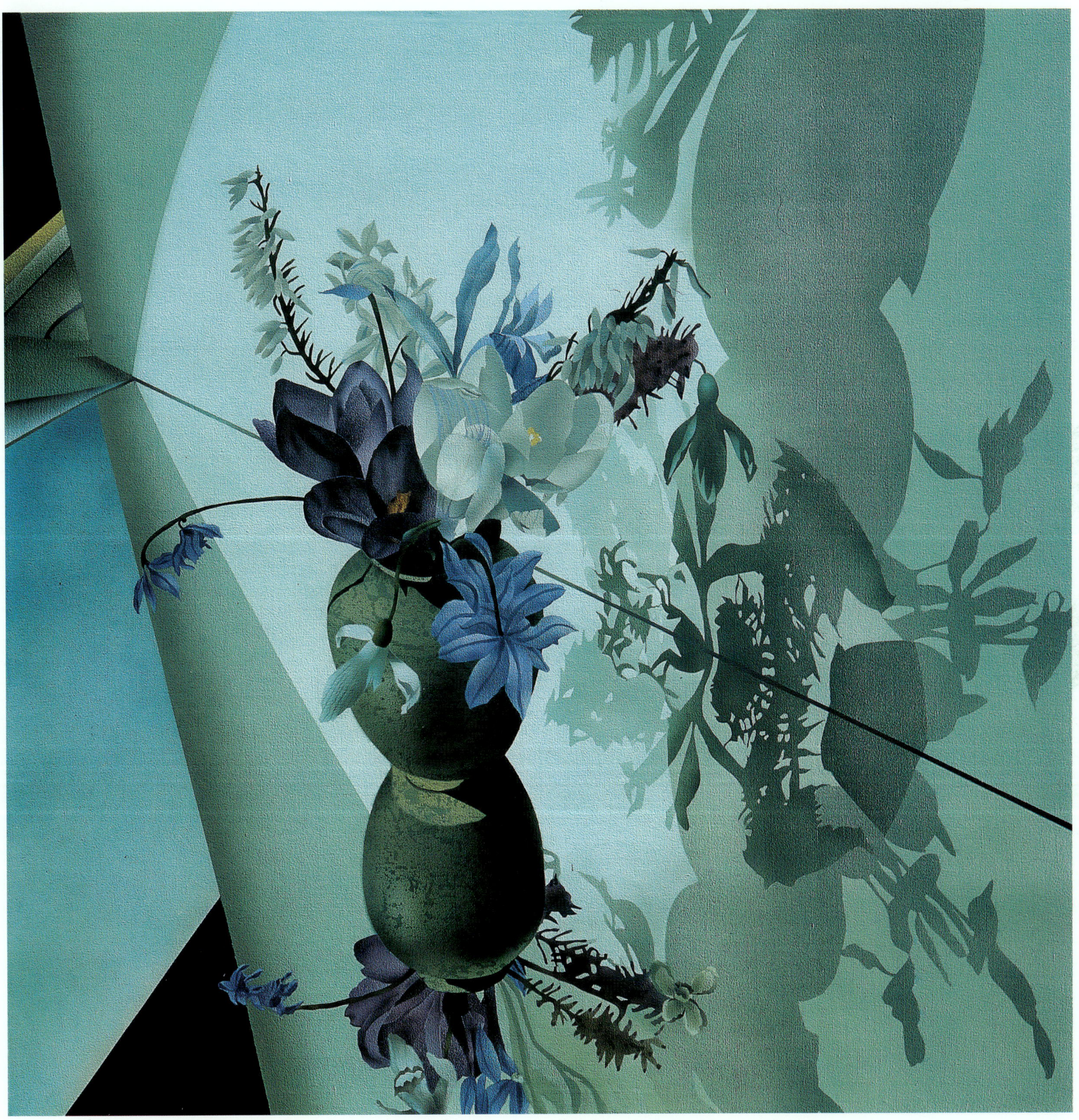

(OPPOSITE)

SHERRY GLASS, 1982
ACRYLIC ON BELGIAN LINEN, 24 X 38 IN.
COLLECTION OF CAROLYN BARTHOLF OXTOBY

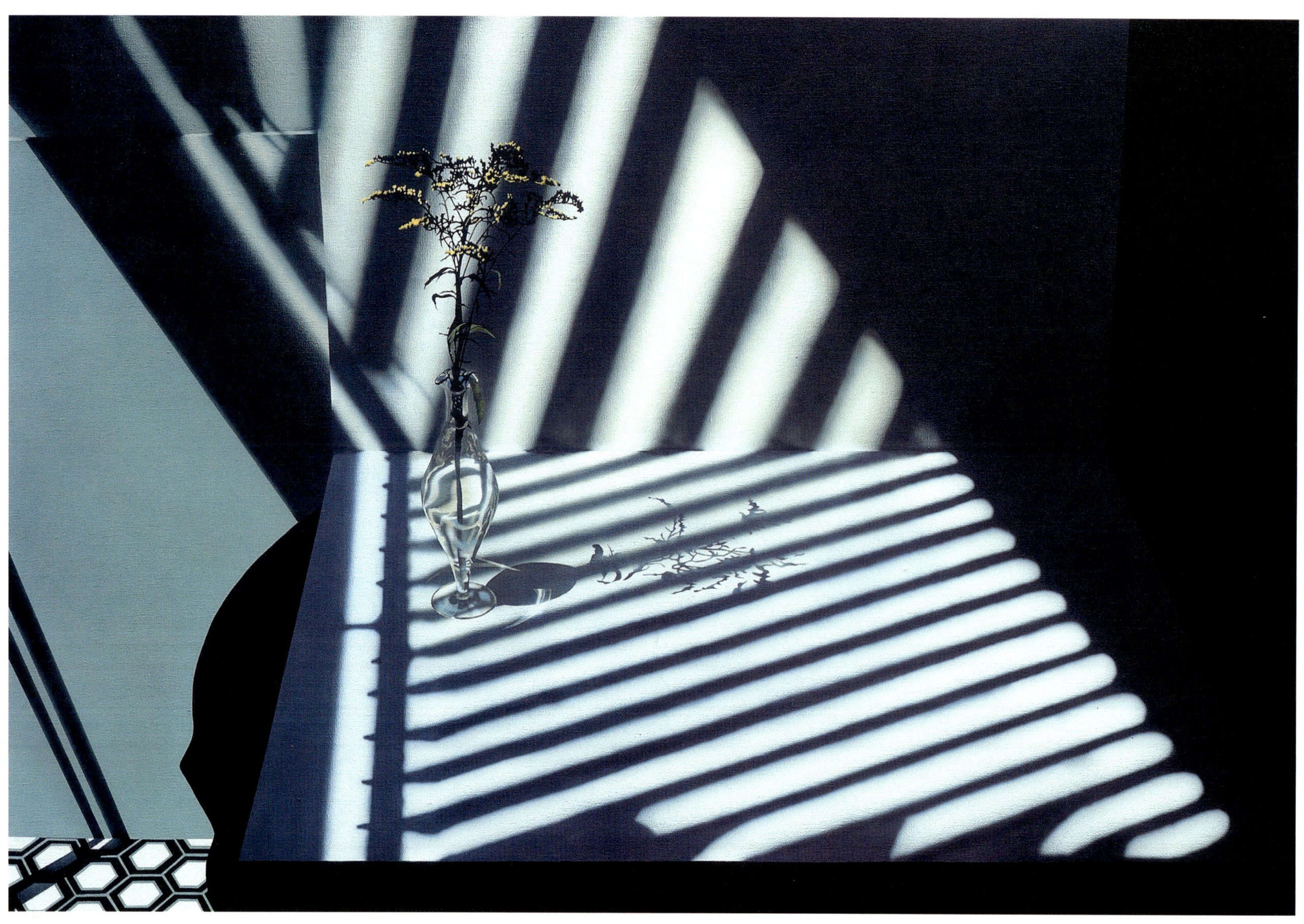

GOLDENROD, 1984
ACRYLIC ON BELGIAN LINEN, 64 X 96 IN.
COLLECTION OF MR. AND MRS. JOHANN GOUWS

(OPPOSITE)

LATE SHADOW, 1982
ACRYLIC ON BELGIAN LINEN, 48 X 72 IN.
COLLECTION OF THE ARTIST

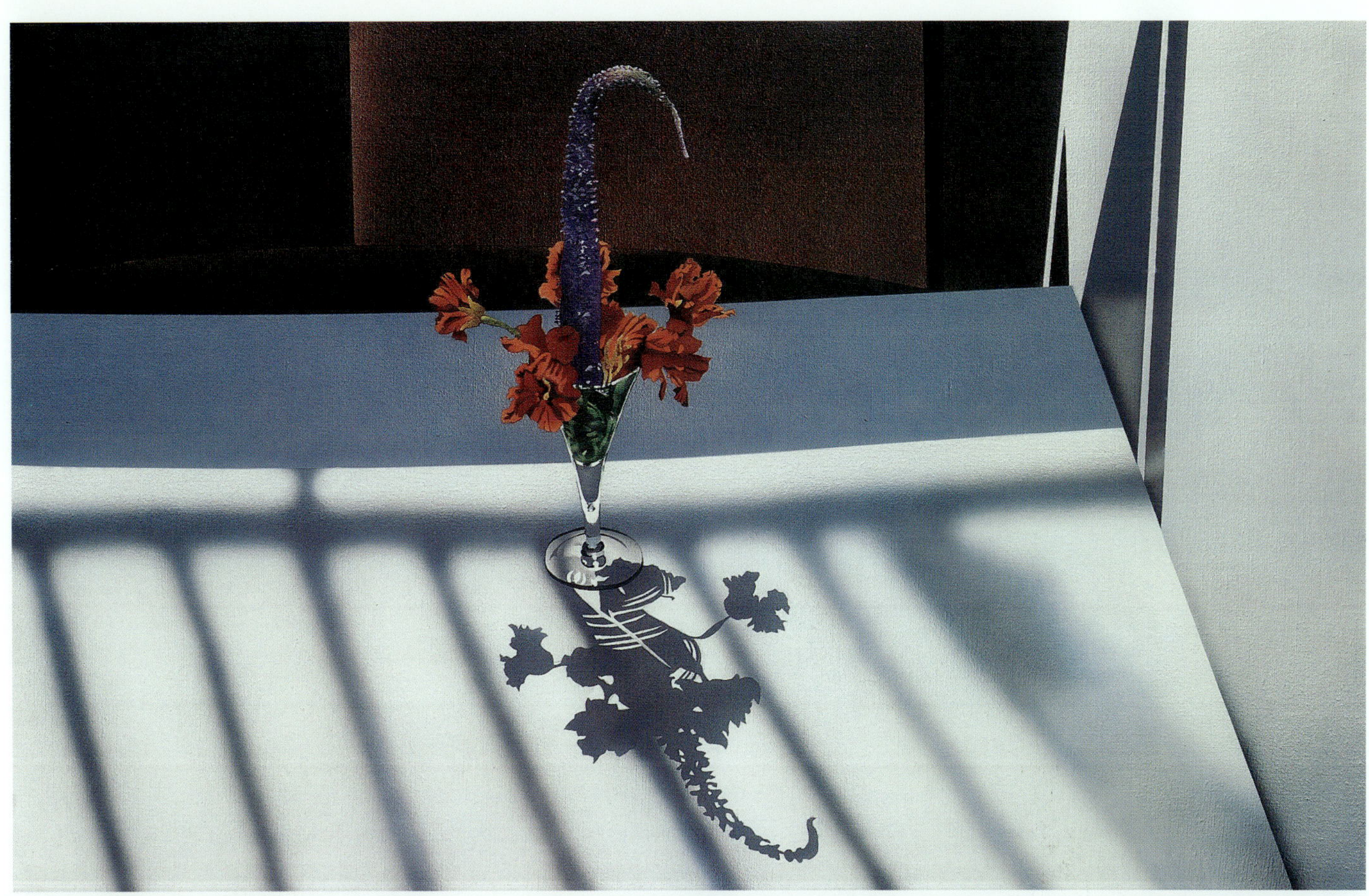

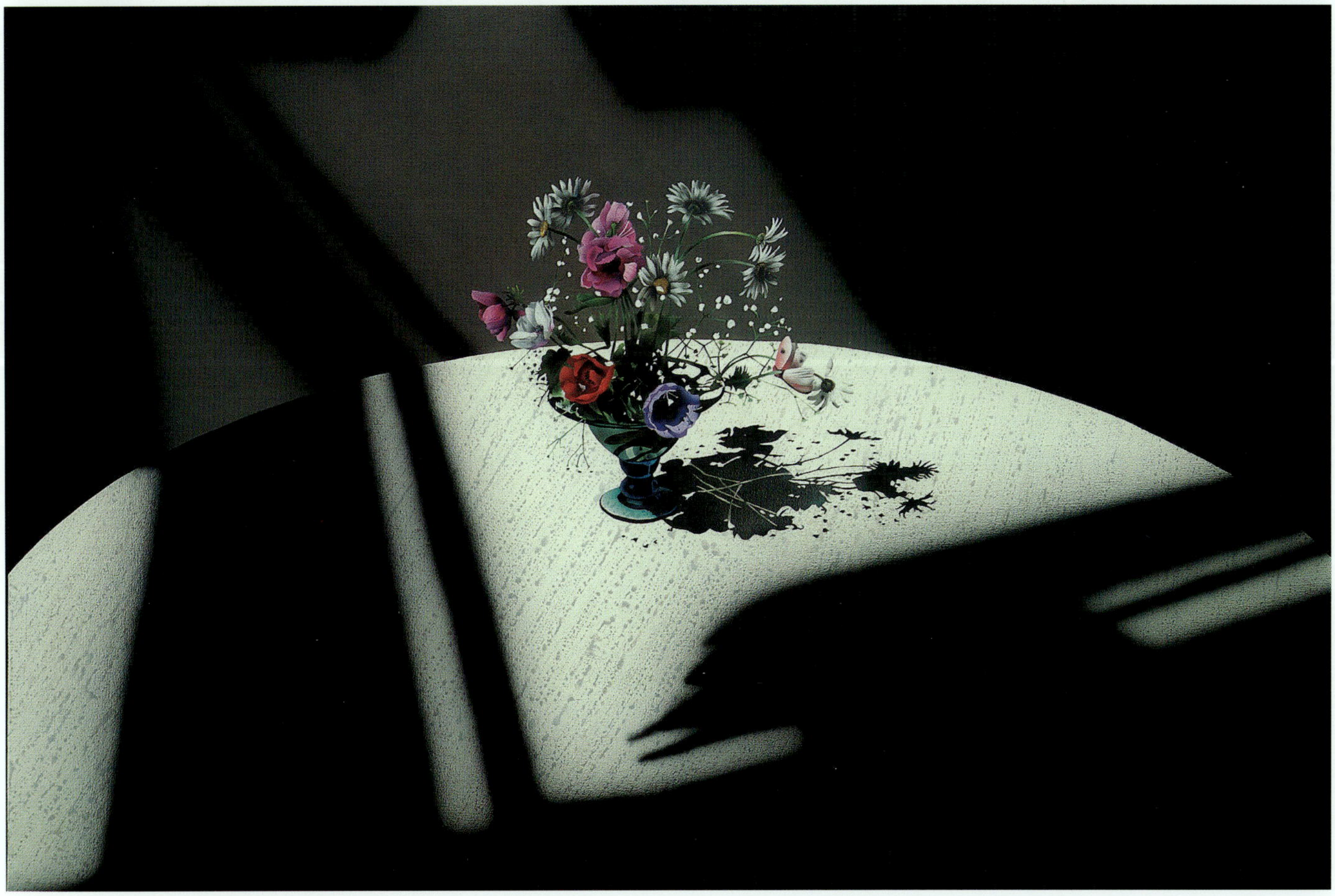

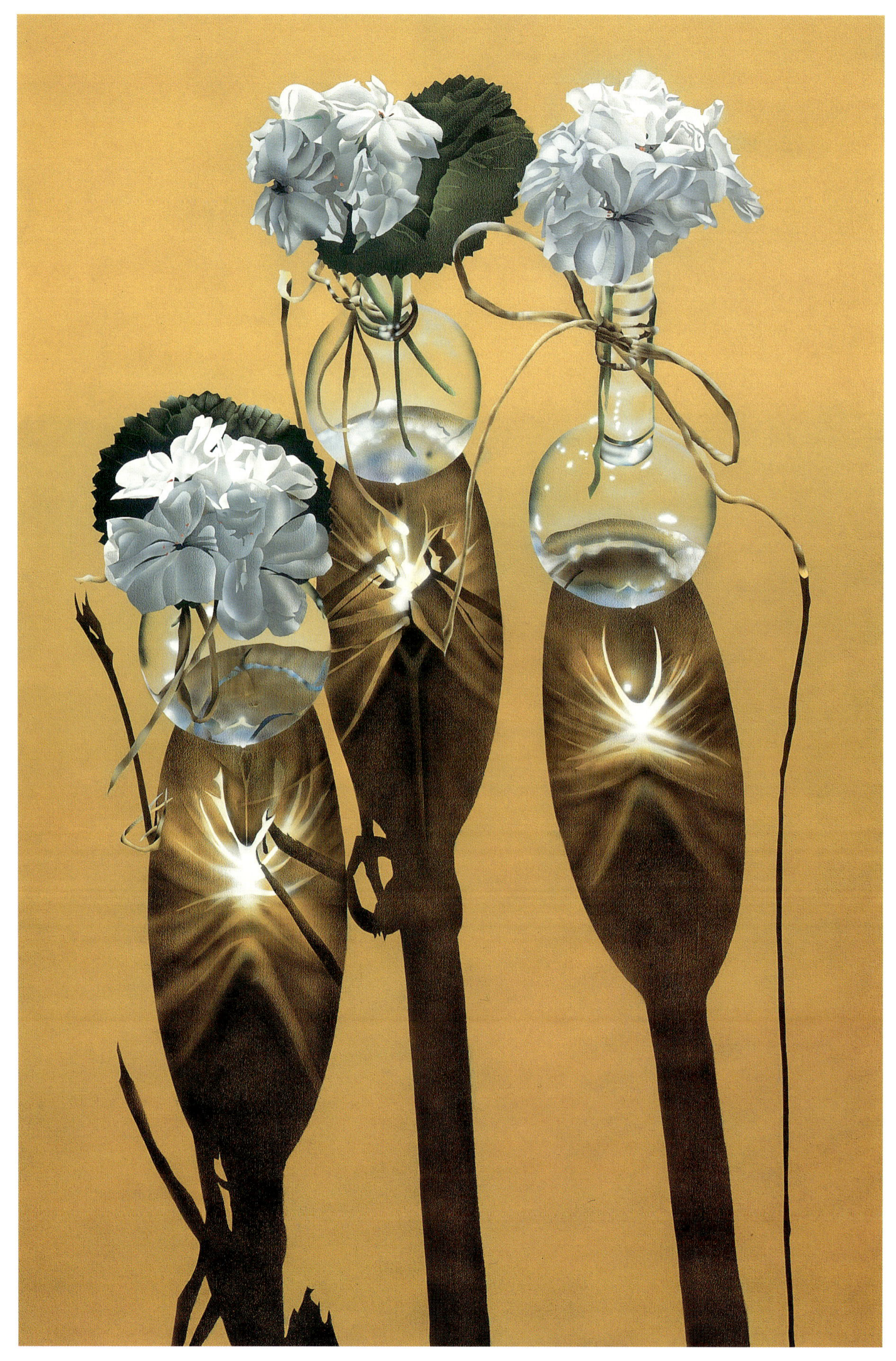

In his catalog essay for the exhibition *Aspects of Reality: Reflections by Beverly Hallam, Transformations by Abbott,* Pattison mounted at the Farnsworth Museum in 1984, Bartlett Hayes described the creation of the remarkable painting called *Sun Spots*, 1983. Hallam had placed three flasks of flowers on a shiny table before a sunlit window, he reports. "Suddenly a sunbeam fell directly on the flasks and was deflected into the cast shadows."

According to Hallam, this unusual phenomenon occurred "almost literally in a flash," and yet she managed to catch it with her camera and was able to reconstruct it in the painting. In its arrangement, *Sun Spots* represents

(OPPOSITE)
SUN SPOTS, 1983
ACRYLIC ON BELGIAN LINEN, 72 X 48 IN.
PRIVATE COLLECTION

HELEN ELIZABETH WITH FLAGS, 1984
ACRYLIC ON BELGIAN LINEN, 18 X 24 IN.
COLLECTION OF MRS. CAMERON BIEWEND

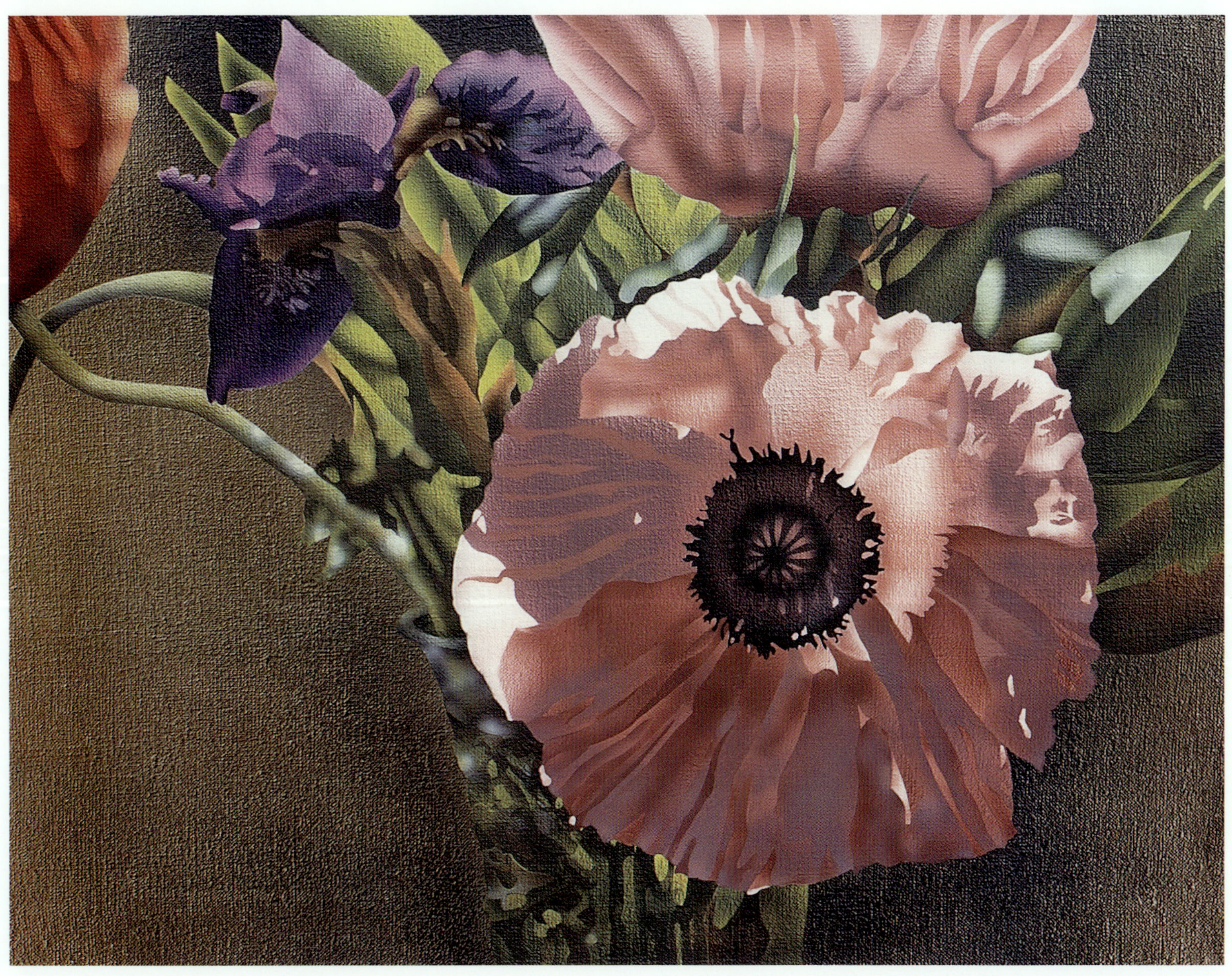

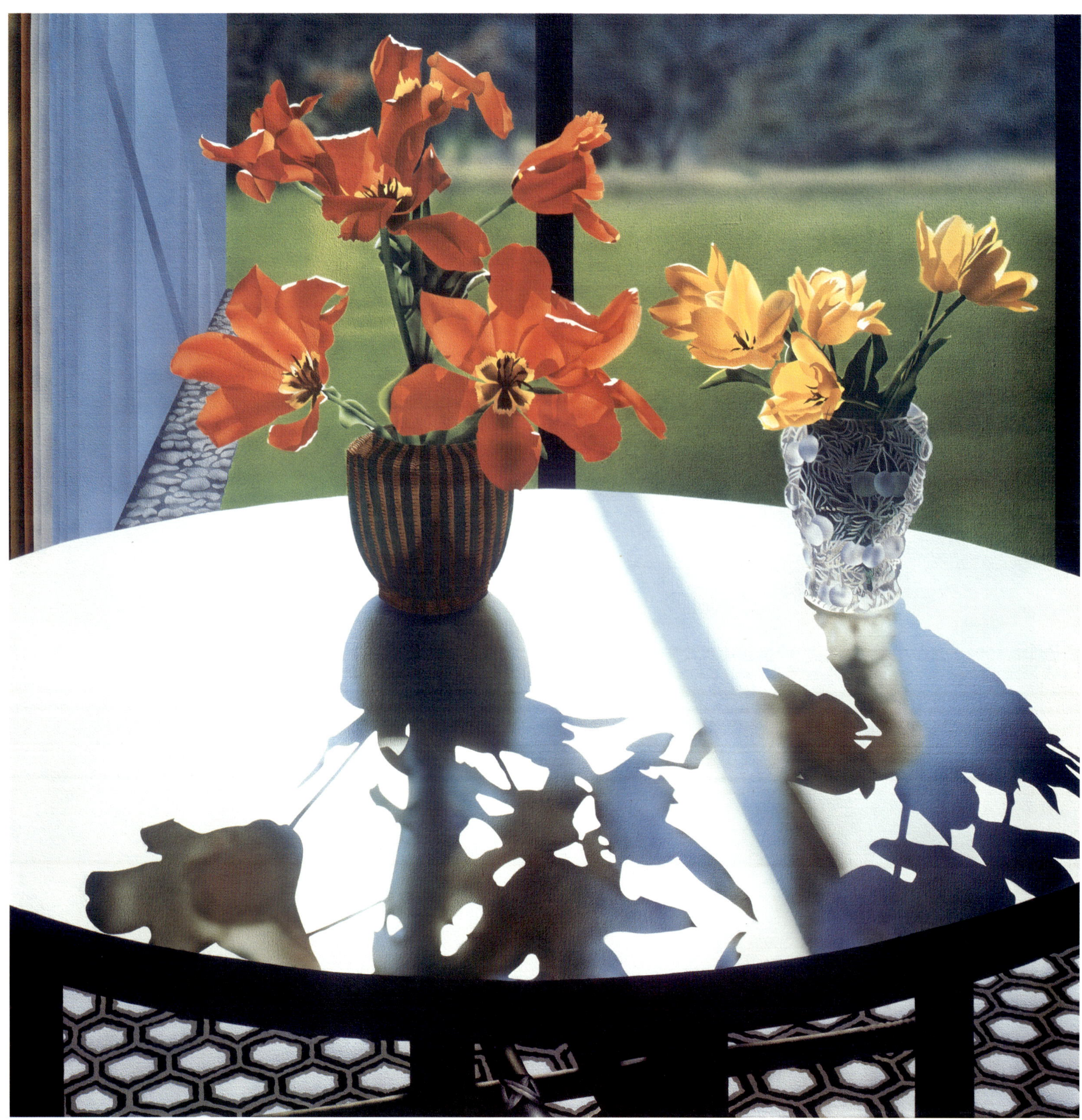

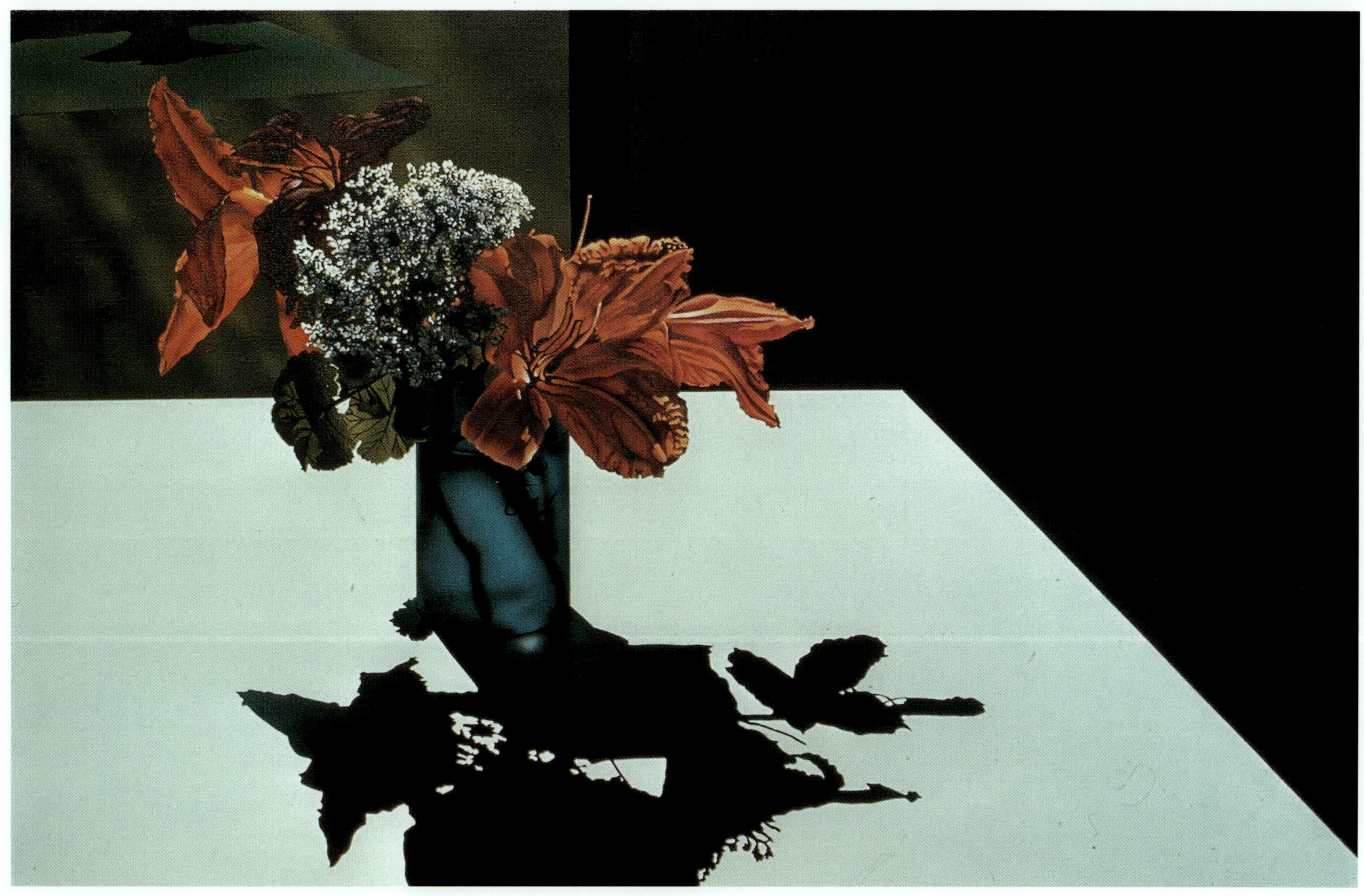

something of a balancing act. The torch-shaped shadows, lit from within by the sunspots, appear to hold up the glass vessels in air, against the neutral yellowish ground Hallam chose as a backdrop.

In *Emperors*, 1983, and *American Revolution*, 1983 (named for a black day lily in her garden), Hallam incorporates a bit of the outside landscape as seen through the window in her dining room, thereby connecting the flowers in their lovely holders with their original milieu. Any visitor to Hallam's home in York will recognize both the interior and exterior settings so carefully reproduced in these paintings.

The flowers are brought to the forefront in pieces like *Helen Elizabeth with Flags*, 1984, and *Nasturtium with Galax*, 1984. The blossoms appear to thrust outward, toward the viewer. The effect recalls some lines from Theodore

American Revolution, 1983
Acrylic on Belgian linen, 30 x 48 in.
Collection of Joan S. Harlow

(opposite)

Emperors, 1983
Acrylic on Belgian linen, 50 x 50 in.
Private collection

John Coffey, when he was curator at the Bowdoin College Museum of Art, singled out a photograph of flowers in a vase, which eventually led to this painting. He warned me that if I decided to paint it, placing it squarely in the center of the canvas would create a real challenge. This was all I needed to get fired up.

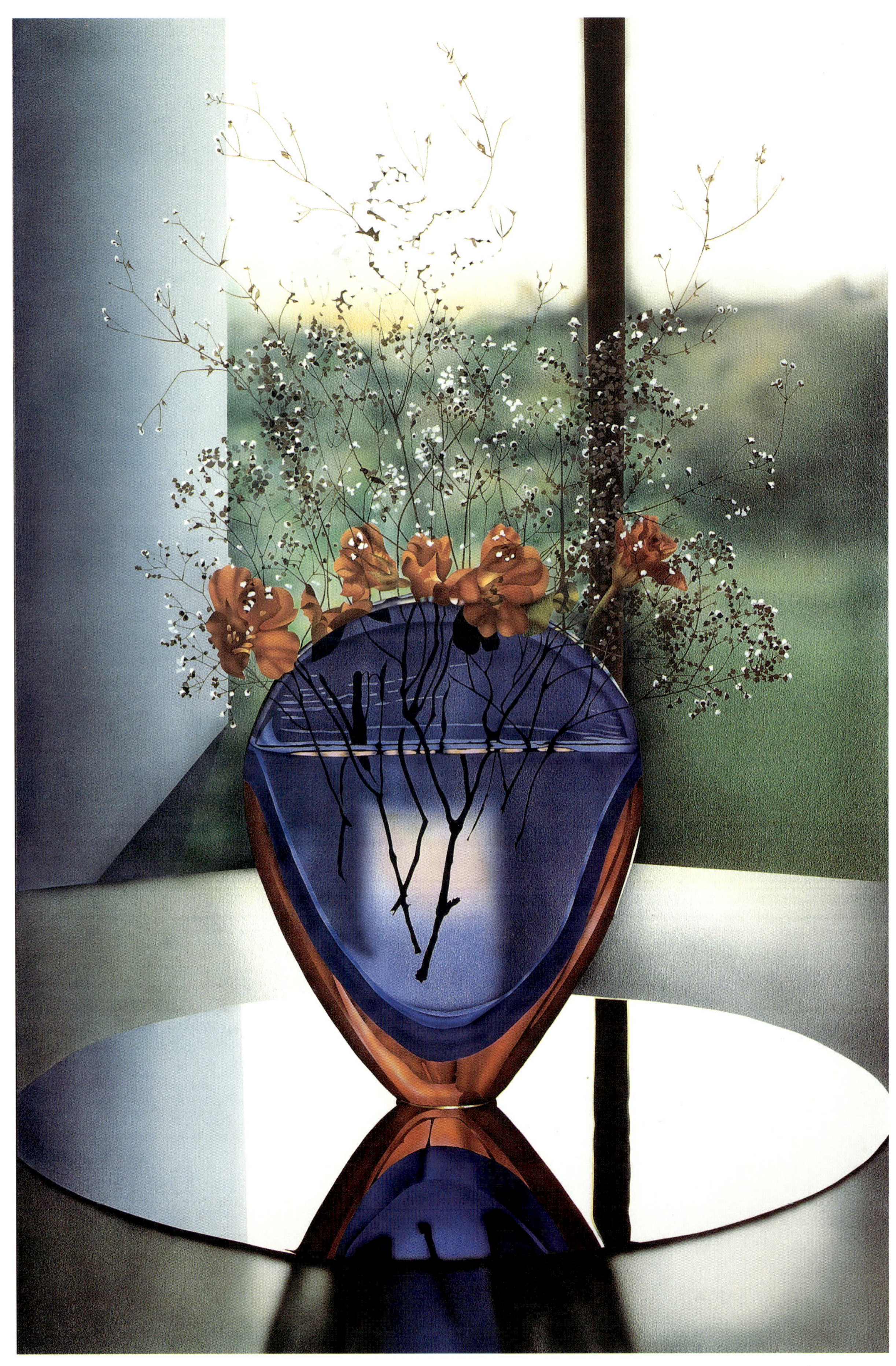

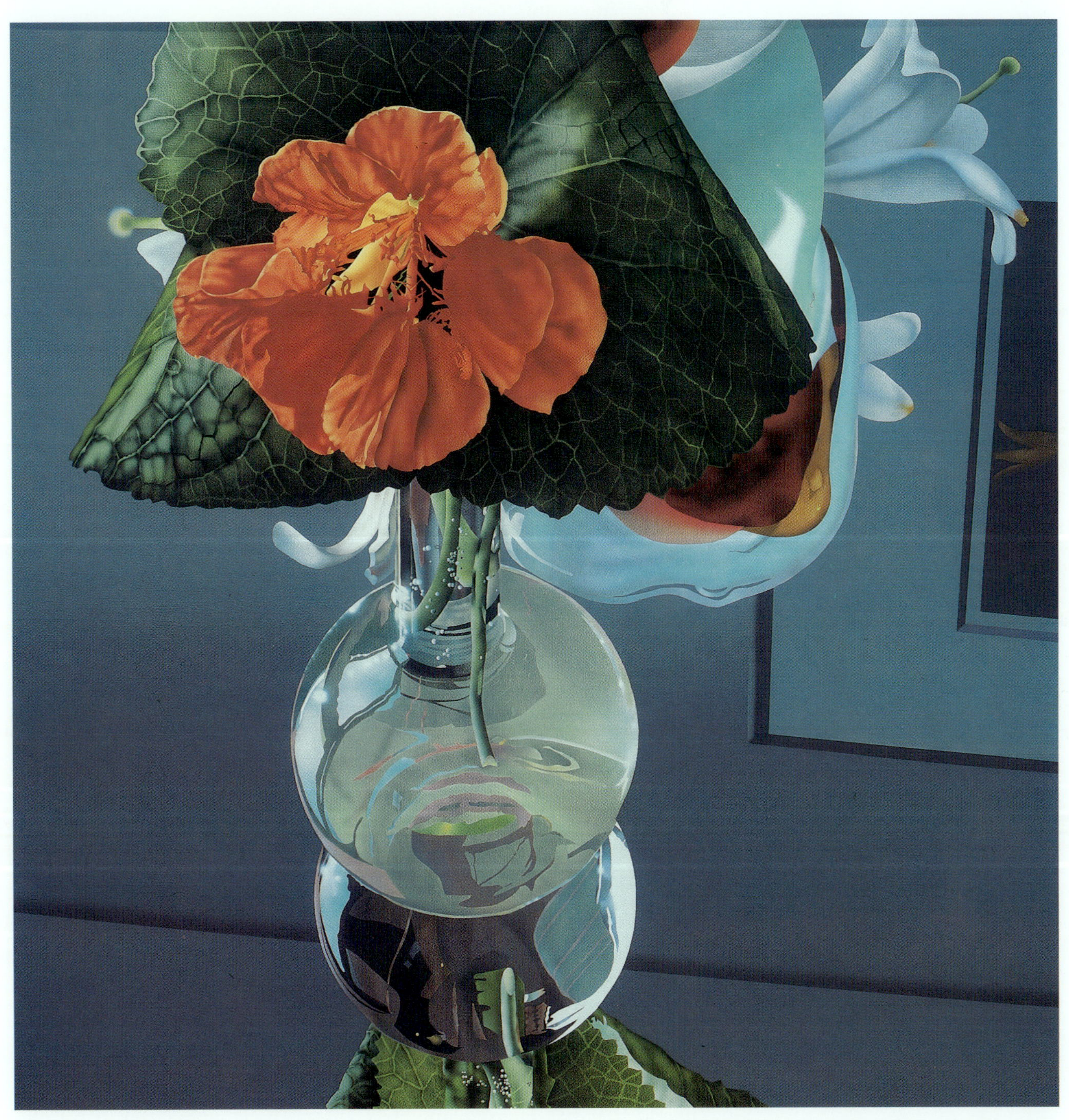

Nasturtium with Galax, 1984
Acrylic on gessoed Belgian linen, 72 x 72 in.
Fogg Art Museum, Harvard University Art Museums

(opposite)

Venetian Vase, 1984
Acrylic on Belgian linen, 72 x 48 in.
Private collection

Roethke's poem "Orchids," from his famous greenhouse sequence:

> They lean over the path,
> Adder-mouthed,
> Swaying close to the face,
> Coming out, soft and deceptive,
> Limp and damp, delicate as a young bird's tongue;
> Their fluttery fledgling lips
> Move slowly,
> Drawing in the warm air.

Hallam has linked her work with stage design and lighting at the Massachusetts College of Art to her ability to come up with dramatic set-ups for her floral pictures. "To bring out the beauty of my flowers," she has written, "I often place them center stage and let the late afternoon sun create shadows to fill up the compositions."

While not overly theatrical, *Madonnas*, 1984, reflects Hallam's skill at highlighting the beauty of a particular floral genus. Here, a simple black and white interior, accented by a variety of geometric elements, proves the perfect setting for the immaculate lilies. We are looking at a mirror on the wall, which reflects a vase of lilies placed on a mirror on a table. There is a purity in this presentation that conjures up the flower's namesake, the Madonna of the Annunciation.

Lilies are perhaps Hallam's favorite flower. One specific genus, the Canada lily, is the subject of canvases painted in 1984 and 1989. Also called the meadow lily, these plants have spiked leaves and a sharply defined blossom that tends to trumpet downward. Nearly the entire canvas consists of the shadow of the bouquet. One stem of flowers was placed over the shadow on the wall—a whimsical trick.

As its title suggests, *Venetian Vase*, 1984, focuses not on the flowers—here, minute baby's breath and nasturtiums—but rather on the container. Made of blue Murano glass, the vessel seems liquid in its transparency.

Critics have resorted to the word "magic" to describe what Hallam achieves in her floral pictures. In writing about this work, the artist herself looks back on her teenage days when she performed acts of prestidigitation before a captive audience under the hair dryers in her mother's beauty salon. "Creating abstracted 'realism,'" says Hallam, "is my grown-up magic."

Two paintings from 1985, *Parrots* and *Orange Prince*, pull off the kind of magic that has elicited universal amazement. The latter, a 6-foot-square painting, focuses on wilted pansies called orange prince. They are combined with lily of the valley leaves. The viewer is deceived by the gigantic scale, which makes the flowers look exotic and tropical. The container

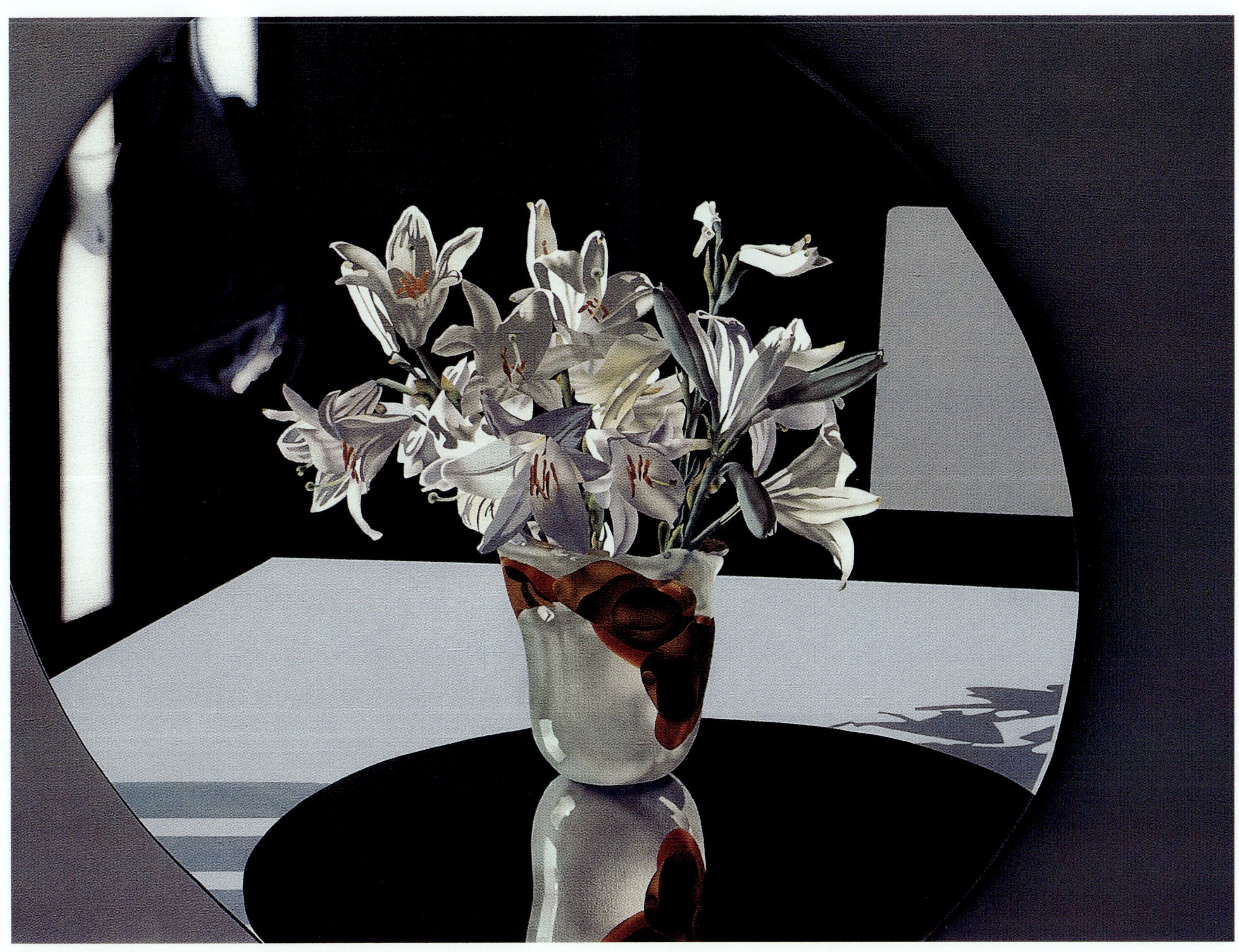

Madonnas, 1984
Acrylic on Belgian linen, 40 x 54 in.
Private collection

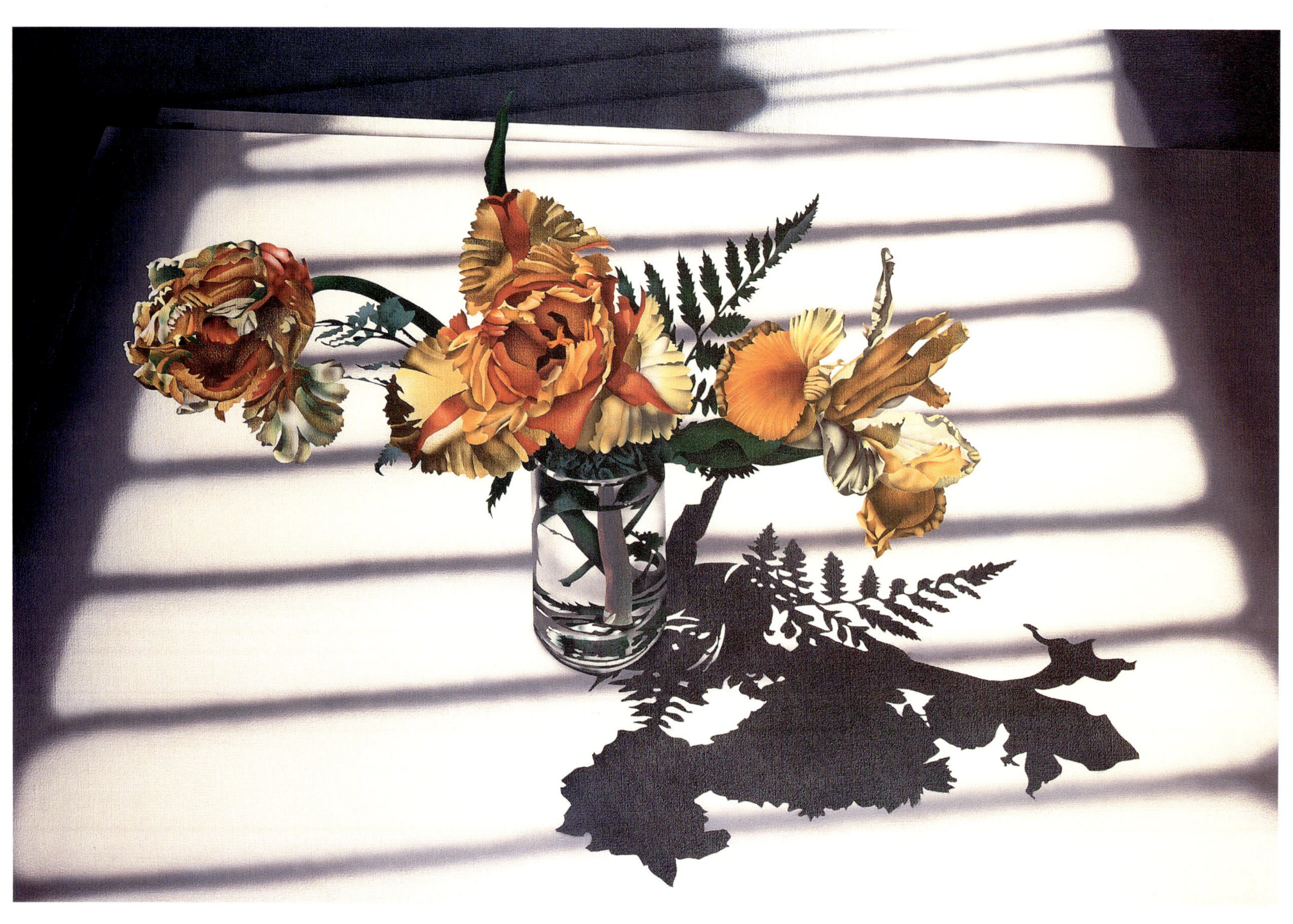

Parrots, 1985
Acrylic on Belgian linen, 30 x 44 in.
Private collection

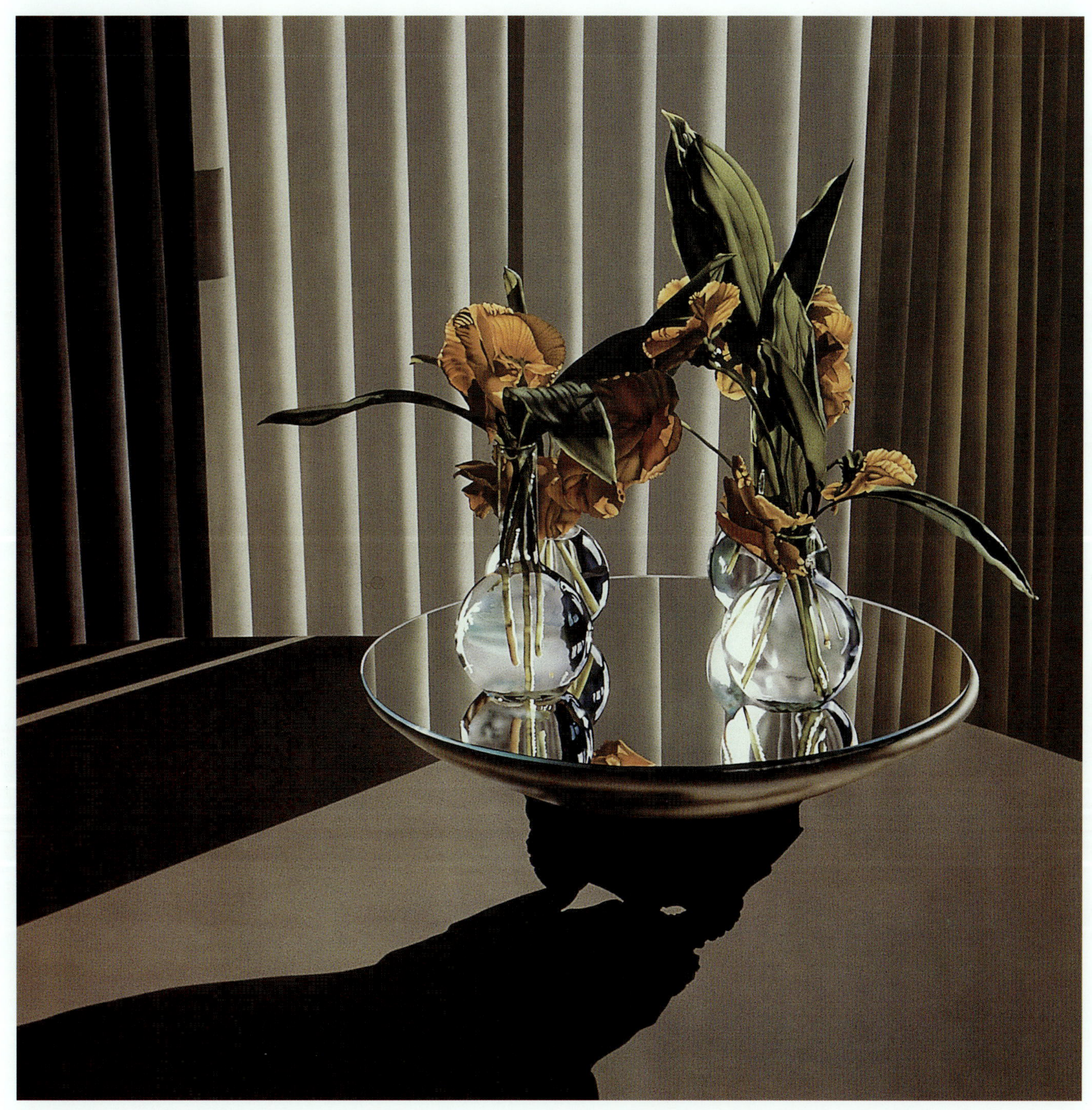

Orange Prince, 1985
Acrylic on Belgian linen, 72 x 72 in.
Farnsworth Art Museum, Rockland, Maine
Gift of the artist

Tulips on Carpet, 1986
Acrylic on Belgian linen, 48 x 72 in.
Private collection

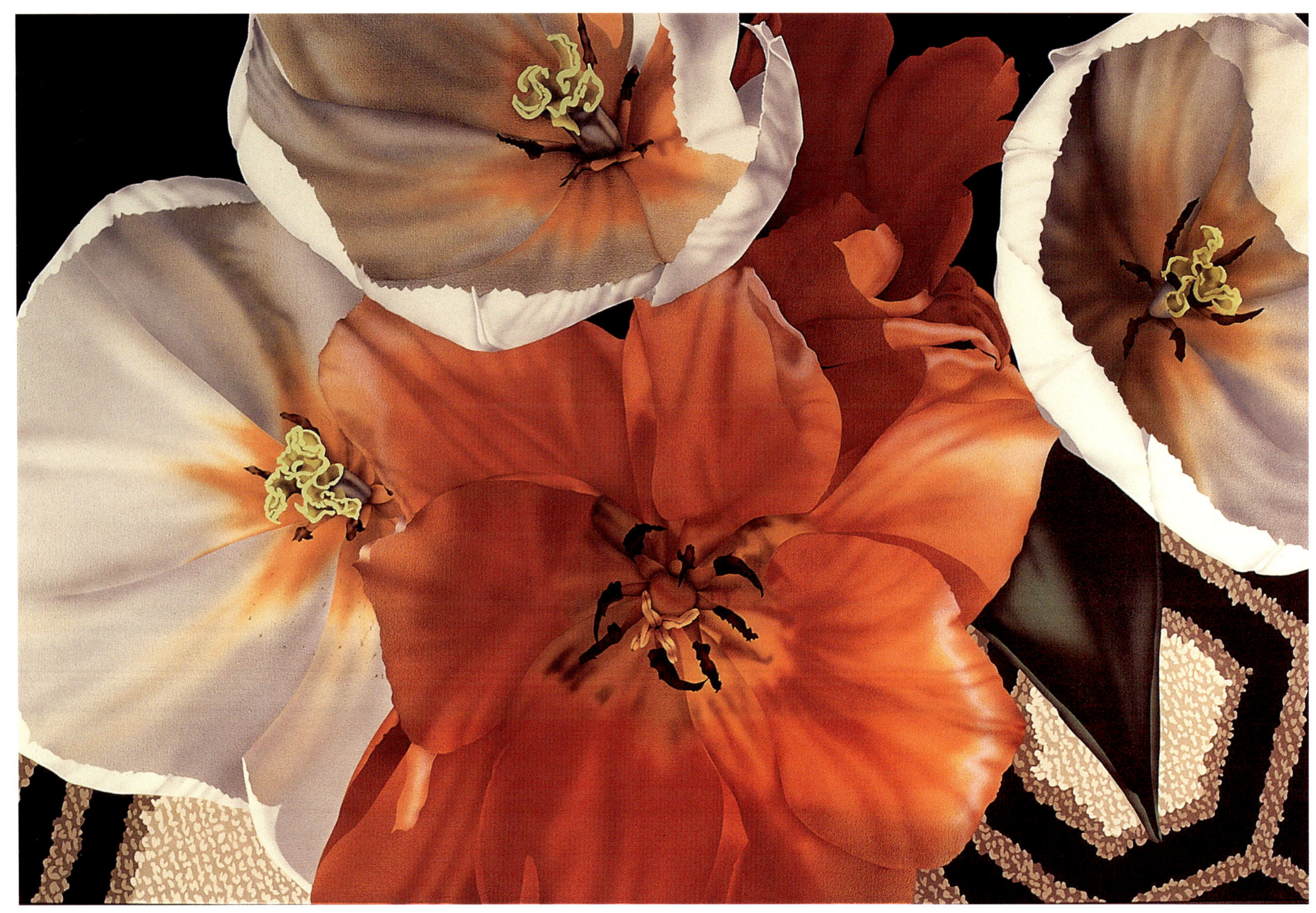

sits on an 11-inch-round elevated mirror that appears to be a large glass-topped table.

How does the artist manage to reproduce the many folds of the flowers that figure in the lovely sprawling bouquet in *Parrots* or the subtle shades of pink in the petals in *Stargazer,* 1984? And how, people have asked her, does she make the reflections look so real in the glass flasks in *Orange Prince?* To the last question, Hallam responds that she simply doesn't think about what the objects are: "I just paint exactly what I see, two forms with geometric shapes, colors and gradations within them. Like a miracle they end up looking like glass."

Elsewhere, in a 1986 interview with Robert Taylor of *The Boston Globe,* Hallam stated, "I don't like a fussy look; my canvases should have the qualities of an enlarged photograph." *Tulips on Carpet,* 1986, among Hallam's greatest and, in a certain manner, her most modern floral picture, bears out this concept. She placed the vase on the carpet and, looking straight down, brought the blossoms right up to the viewfinder—so close, in fact, that the flowers are cropped at the edges of the canvas. The magnified geometric fragments of the hooked carpet act as a ground for the gargantuan blossoms.

Looking at a detail of this painting—the center of the red-orange tulip in the middle of the canvas—one wonders at the precision of Hallam's rendering. This configuration of stamen and pistil resembles a spider-like creature, pinned to the velvety petals.

Hallam credits the airbrush for some of the spectacular effects she achieves in her paintings. "With an airbrush," she told Taylor, "I can study effects such as a light source through petals." In *Thalia with Tulips,* 1986, a group of blossoms, lit from behind, become a complex arrangement of light and shadows. One is not entirely sure where flower begins and shadow ends; the interweaving of elements is exact yet beguiling.

Measuring 5 feet 4 inches by 8 feet, this rendering of fosteria tulips and narcissus, Hallam reports, took her approximately 250 hours to complete. "I get great satisfaction out of planting, fertilizing, cutting, arranging, photographing, painting, and hanging flowers," she has said, but she also acknowledges the labor involved. "Everything is exciting except actually painting [the pictures], and that's hard work. I once read that the only time success comes before work is in the dictionary."

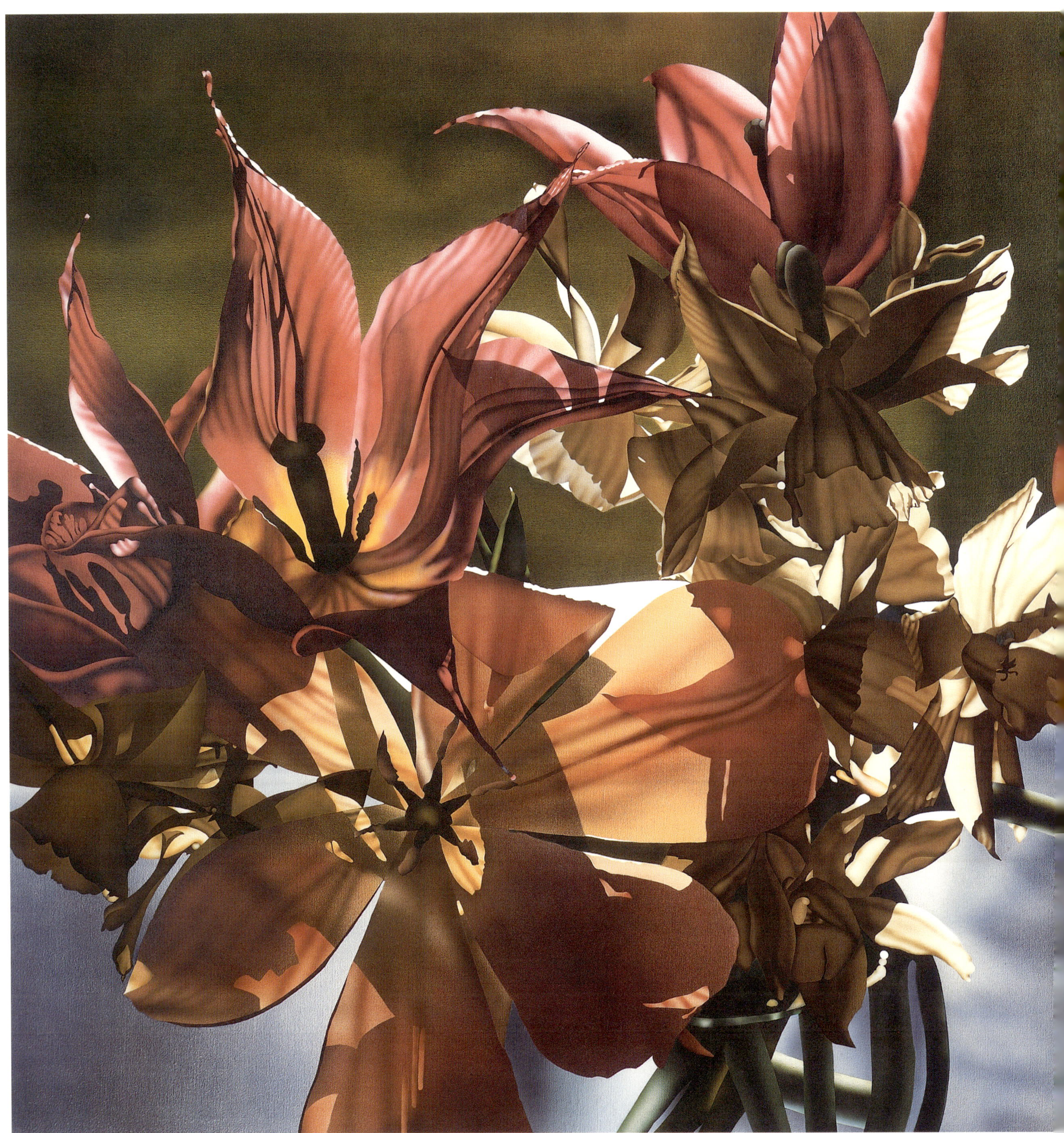

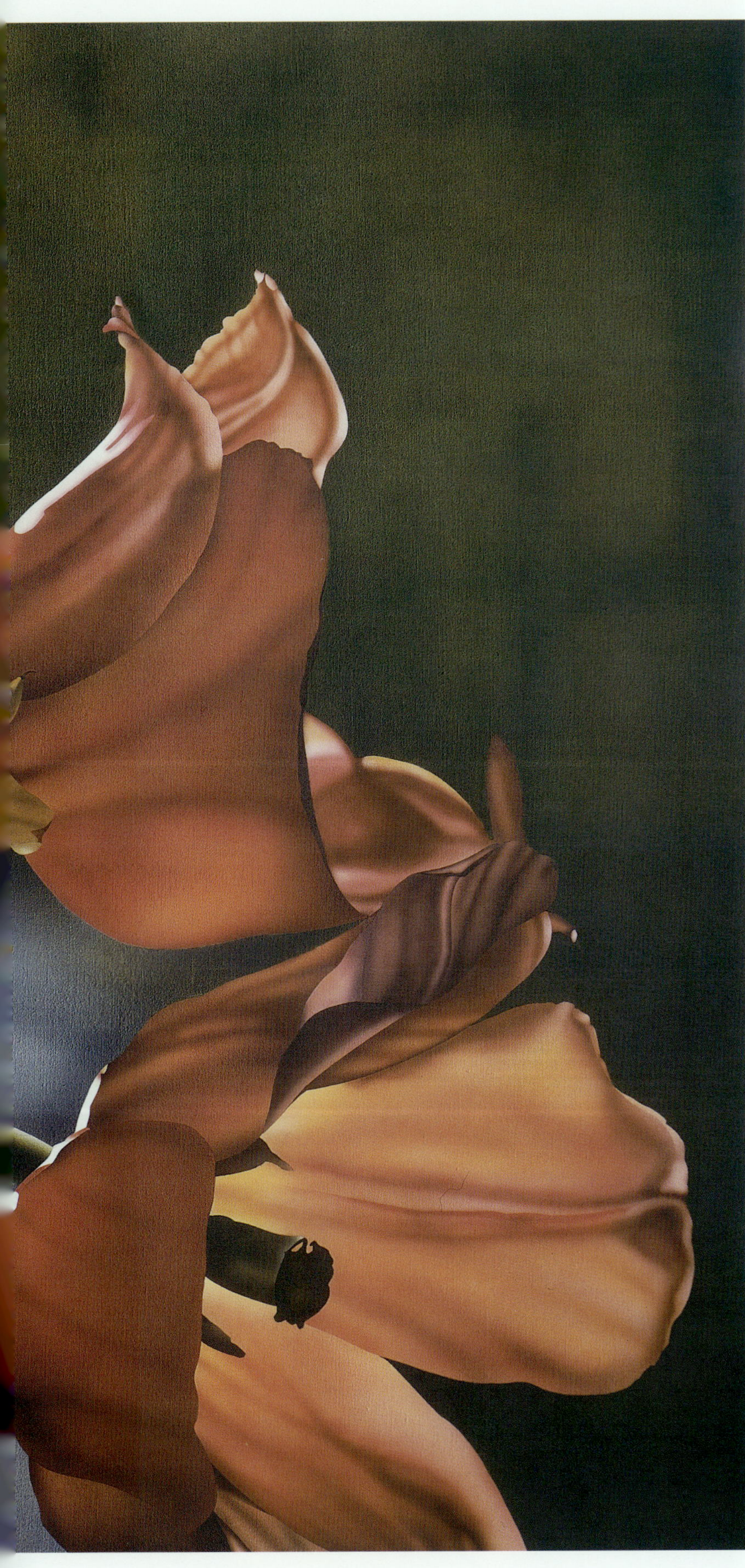

Thalia with Tulips, 1986
Acrylic on Belgian linen, 64 x 96 in.
Collection of Mr. and Mrs. Dana S. Russell

15

More Flowers—and the Future

> This extraordinary body of images, nasturtiums, poppies, Japanese irises, freesias and other palpable flowers, confronts a reality that is in fact comprised of reflections, and that turns out to be magical rather than photographic. Beverly Hallam's blossoms glow in a painted vase, while outside the studio the seascape is soundless except for mewling gulls and the breeze in the ruffled aisles of day lilies.
>
> Robert Taylor, *The Boston Globe*, 1986

Cascade, 1986
Acrylic on Haye Mill paper, 30 5/8 x 22 1/4 in.
Collection of Graham W. Cookson

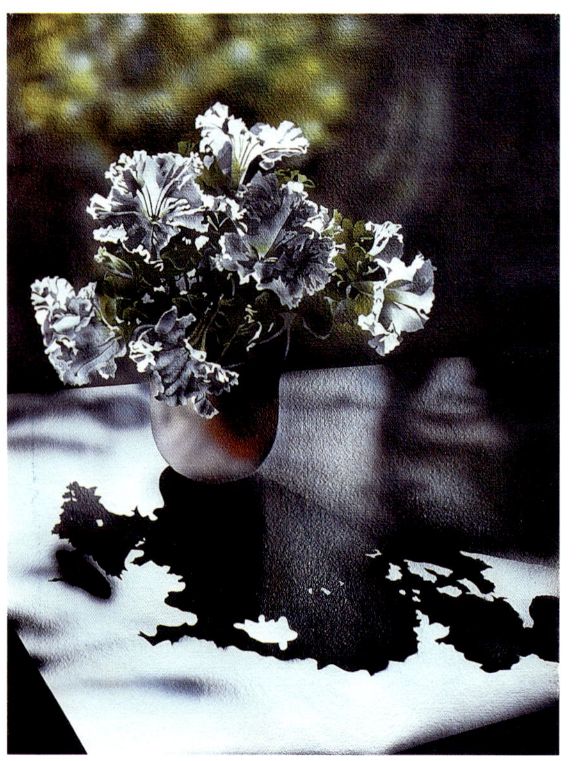

As one speaks of perfect pitch, so one might refer to perfect scale when considering Hallam's flower paintings. All these pictures, great and small, seem perfectly measured. One arrangement may call for the monumental, another, for a more intimate treatment. In the latter category, two 1986 pictures—*Cascade*, measuring 31 by 22 1/4 inches, and *Stonecrop Bouquet in Lusterware*, at 19 1/2 by 19 3/4 inches—are the finest of the smaller florals. The latter, combining airbrush acrylic and pastel on paper, is a personal favorite of the artist's.

Hallam admits to cleaning up the motif before working with it. "Good as nature is," she once told an interviewer, "it's often jungled up." On the other hand, a piece like *Birds of Paradise*, 1987, testifies to Hallam's uncanny ability to represent a jungle-like array of flowers and garnishes, here placed in a mottled glass vase.

The stylized, streamlined heads of the birds of paradise flowers anchor the abundant bouquet against a richly complex background—which is actually a woodland scene painted by Gary Buch. With its daunting range of shapes and colors, this canvas represents a mighty feat of painting. "I was attracted to this combination," Hallam relates, "because the bouquet was in camouflage in front of the background."

Here, as elsewhere, the out-of-focus background serves to accentuate the individual elements of the frontal floral array. Writing of this painting in the *Maine Times*, critic Edgar Allen Beem referred to photorealism. "The painting is photorealist," he wrote, "principally because the focus and depth of field are those of the camera, not the human eye."

As much as critics would like to include Hallam in the photorealist category, in general the artist defies such labels. In Beem's profile, she is quoted as saying, "I'm not really a photorealist; I'm not that painstaking. I don't know what I am, but I've never gone with the tide."

In the same article, several contemporary American flower painters are mentioned, including Carolyn Brady, who also works in Maine (on Vinalhaven), and Audrey Flack. In Hallam's opinion, some of this work "looks sprayed," an impression she says she tries to avoid in her own work. "I like variation more than having everything look soft."

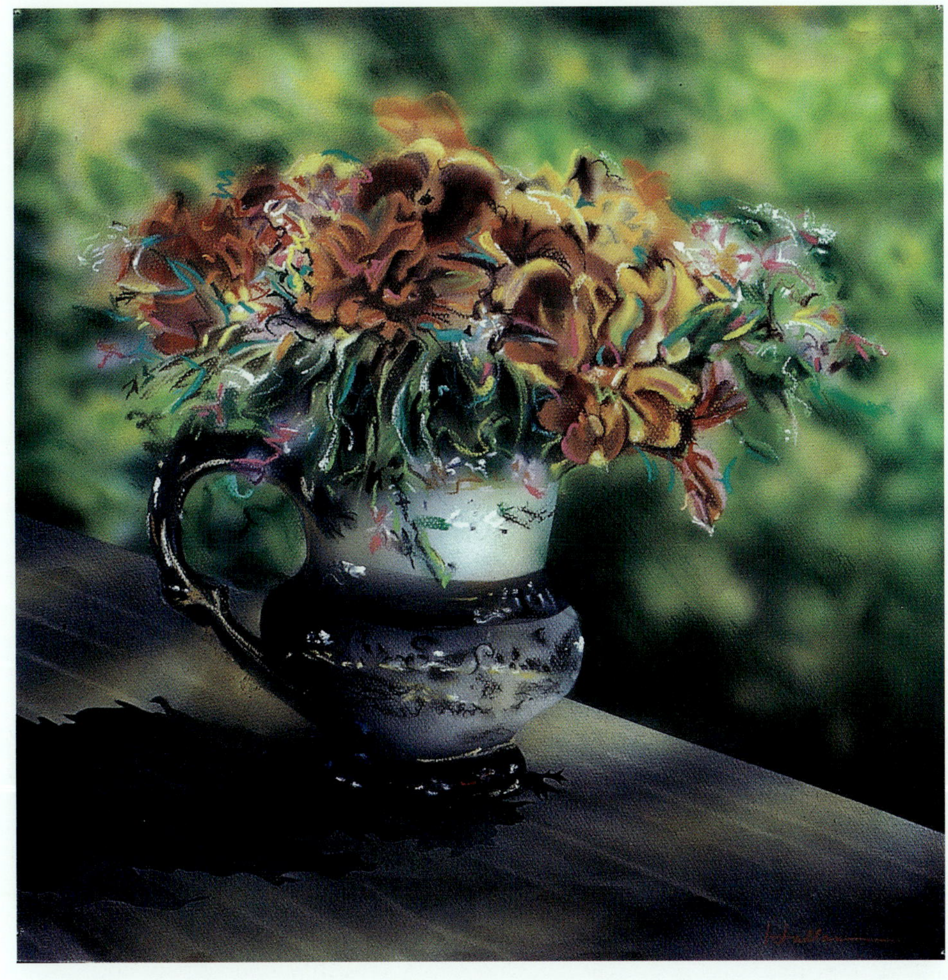

Stonecrop Bouquet in Lusterware, 1986
Acrylic and pastel on paper, 19 1/2 x 19 3/4 in.
Collection of the artist

Hallam thinks of herself as a flower painter, not, she will strongly attest, as a still-life artist. "I used only one object in my paintings other than bouquets during my airbrush period," she has written, "and that was a paperweight." Even in this painting, *Paperweight*, 1987, the still-life object, which Hallam found in a Paris flea market in 1961, has a floral appearance—the central swirling pattern might be a small bouquet embedded in the round glass. The paperweight shares the tabletop with small campanula set in a turquoise tumbler, the two of them raked by strong vertical shadows cast by window blinds.

The single flower in *Hibiscus*, 1987, afloat in a short crystal glass, seems to hover in its airbrushed space. As Rose Safran noted in a review of Hallam's show at Midtown-Payson Galleries in 1988, this diminutive painting packs "a powerful punch with a single vividly orange blossom, nicely staged to the side with a darkened background emphasizing its brilliance."

"Some blossoms," Hallam has written, "like to be left alone; others enjoy being crammed together; then there are quiet ones, cockies, and

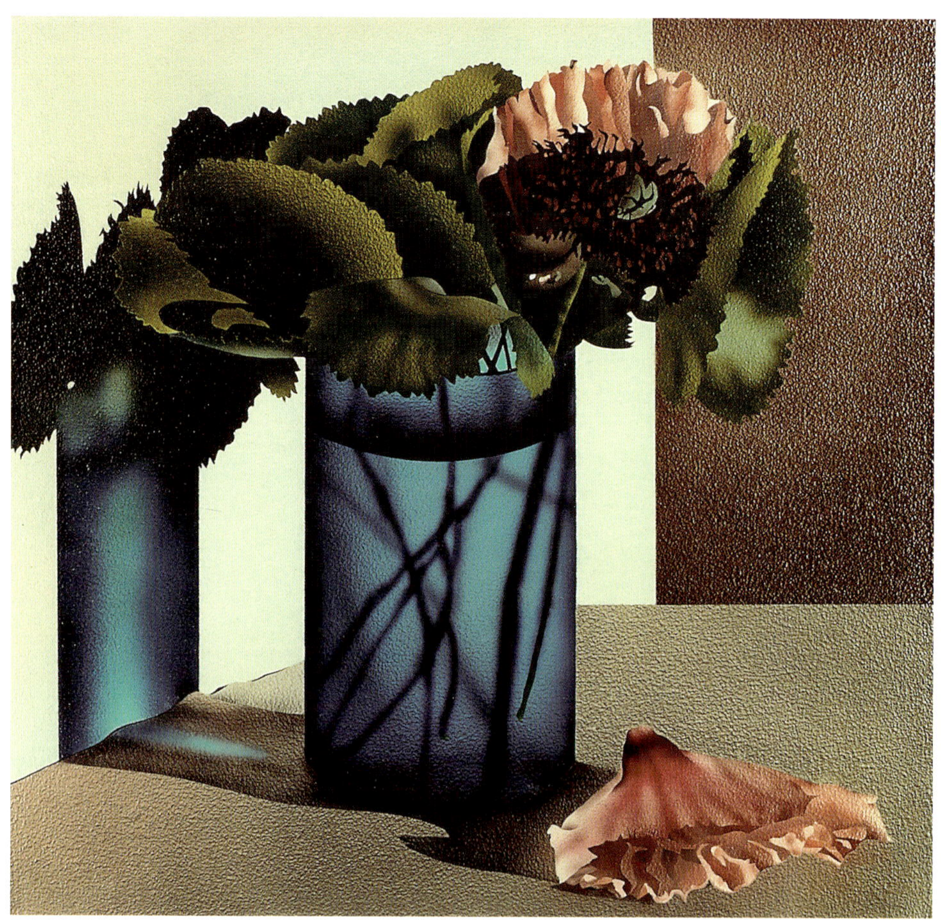

Fallen Petal, 1990
Liquitex gesso and acrylic on Belgian linen
19 x 20 1/4 in.
Portland Museum of Art, Maine
Bequest of Elizabeth B. Noyce

loudmouths." The lily pictured in *Golden Splendor*, 1987, might fall within that last category: looming into the foreground, it almost seems to be trumpeting its magnificence.

The word "distort" has been used more than once in describing what Hallam does with flowers. She can bring out the grandiose in one flower, highlight the fragility in another, and heighten the sensuousness of a third.

A certain distortion comes into play in *Bouquet Shadow*, 1988, especially in the patterns of transfigured light in the body of the vase. Here, the shadow is the focus of the artist's eye, the bouquet itself only partly in view in the upper left-hand corner.

Egyptian Onions, 1988, stands out from the rest of Hallam's floral work. In place of the large blossoms, we have three elongated stems of onions that take graceful stances against a white wall broken up by the shadows of vertical blinds. How beautiful and simple are these slightly curving shapes breaking across the hard-edge pattern of light and dark. The effect is breathtaking. Again, Hallam chooses the perfect 50-by-50-inch dimensions as the framework for her theater.

(opposite)

Paperweight, 1987
Acrylic on Belgian linen, 72 x 48 in.
National Museum of Women in the Arts

Over the fifteen years that Hallam has worked on her airbrushed floral

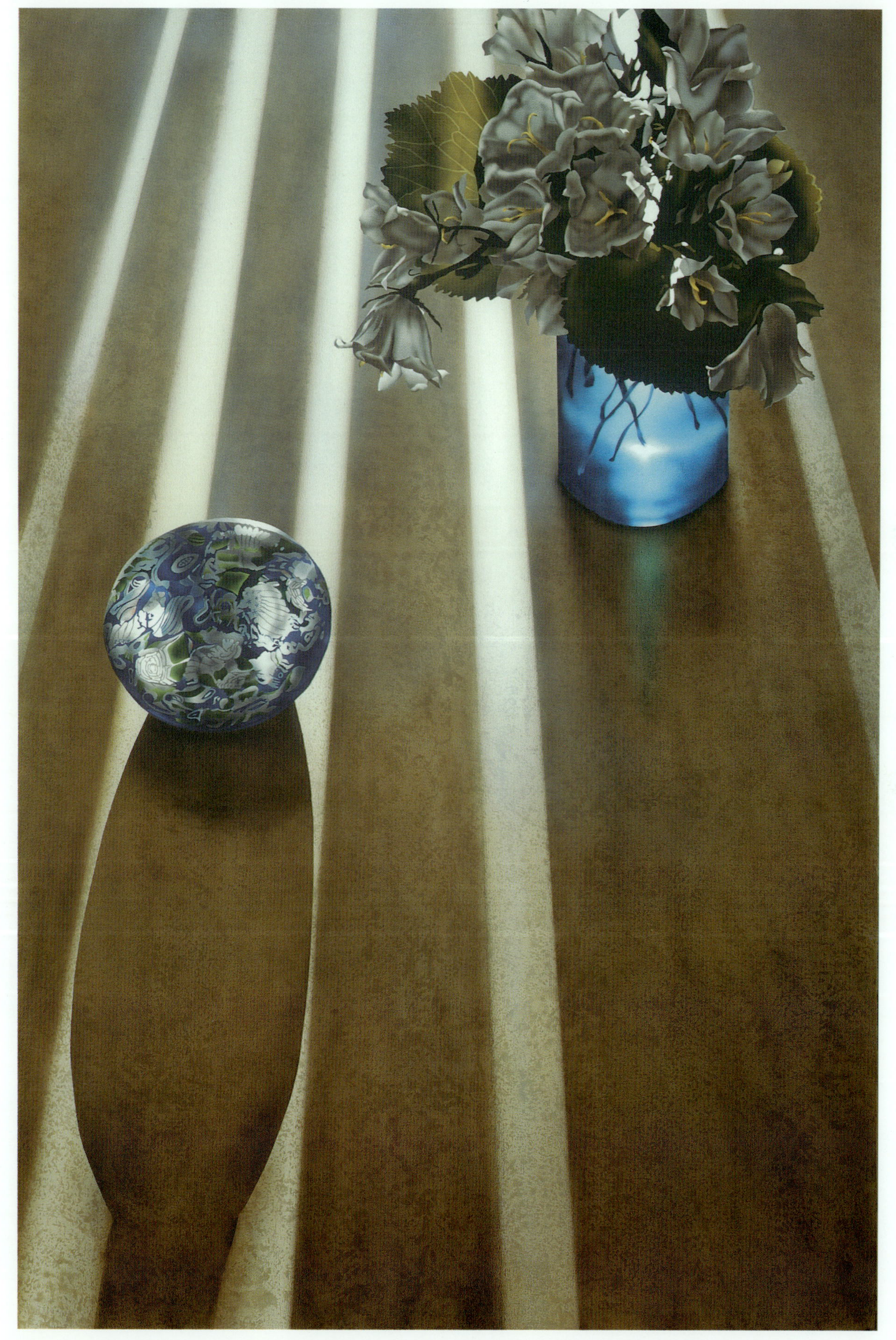

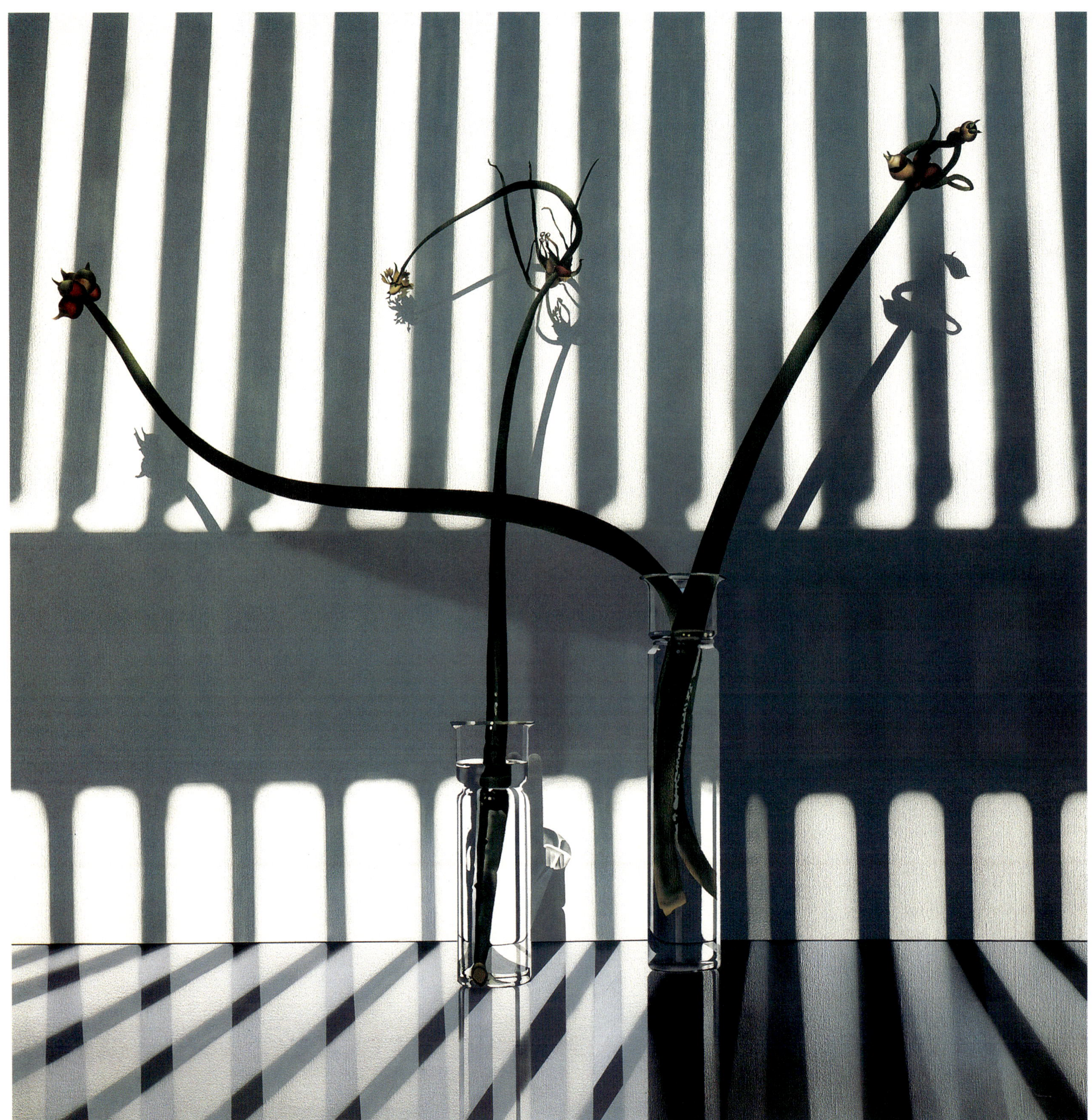

pictures, she has established a repertoire of subjects. At times, she will return to a favorite arrangement, as in the 1988 *Queen Anne's Lace in John Natale's Raku* or the 1989 *Nasturtiums in a Circle,* a descendant of the marvelous *Nasturtium with Galax* of 1984.

These are not repetitions by any means—Hallam would not consciously try to make things easier for herself and simply redo a subject. Rather, the challenge of orchestrating complex new compositions and palettes remains constant, as witness the formidable rendering of the v-shaped glass vase in *Nasturtiums in a Circle.*

As Hallam herself avers, she has never had a fixed palette. Although she has distinct favorites—"I like Schiaparelli pink and lemon yellow; they're happy colors," she once noted—her approach is quite free. She has always believed that the way to learn about color is to "splash around," using all kinds of tools, papers, etc.

In speaking of a particular drab green she mixed up during her monotype period, Hallam wryly observes that, in Maine, green sells better than yellow, while in Chicago, yellow sells better than green. She thinks that weather has something to do with it. She has also observed that men and children tend to love the color red.

In the flower paintings, Hallam used the Pantone Matching System and has tried to remain as true to the actual colors as possible, going so far as to wrap the petals in Saran Wrap at the end of the day and put them in the freezer to maintain their color. In addition, she keeps swatches of color and mixing notes in her workbooks for future reference. She has kept these color annotations for every painting she has done for the past 15 years or so.

Even as she paints variations on a theme, Hallam seeks new ways of presenting the flower, as in *Fallen Petal,* 1990. Here, a single petal lying on the table below its bouquet lends the picture a sense of impending loss: the arrangement will eventually fade and fall apart.

From time to time, Hallam will also expand her floral inventory. *Amaryllis,* 1990, is a small but spectacular study of the belladonna lily. Once again, the soft focus of the background lends this picture that quality of photo-realism—not to mention the fact that the painter has reproduced this radiant and forthright lily with preternatural clarity.

In 1990–1991, Hallam interrupted her work in order to make the documentary *Beverly Hallam: The Flower Paintings,* and to visit museums on the tour of her show of the same name. The exhibition, organized by the Evansville (Indiana) Museum of Arts and Science where it started, made stops at the Sheldon Swope Art Museum in Terre Haute, Indiana; the Art Museum of Southeast Texas in Beaumont; the Bergen Museum of Art and Science in Paramus, New Jersey; and the Polk Museum of Art in Lakeland, Florida.

(OPPOSITE)

EGYPTIAN ONIONS, 1988
ACRYLIC ON BELGIAN LINEN, 50 X 50 IN.
COLLECTION OF MARY-LEIGH CALL SMART.

In the video, which was filmed on location in Hallam's studio by Calvin Kimbrough, the first thing the artist talks about, quite fittingly, is light and the vital role it has played in her latest work. She goes on to provide an abbreviated resume of her career, making reference to the "[Thomas Hart] Benton-like" early work, the semi-abstract acrylics, the monotypes, and, finally, the airbrush work.

The heart of the film is devoted to Hallam's flower paintings, how she came to paint them, and the excitement and pleasure she derives from creating them—and growing the flowers that appear in them. As is her way, Hallam details the painstaking preparation that goes into each picture, from the initial photographing of the subject, through the mixing and matching of paints, to the cutting of the stencil and the spraying.

Working blossom by blossom, section by section, Hallam explains that she doesn't really see the whole canvas until the very end. Removing the frisket at that point, she says, is "like taking the wrapping off after cosmetic surgery."

"Flowers are kind of like personalities to me," Hallam says. She seeks to bring out their characters in her canvases. She would be less obvious in her depictions if she could be, and thereby bring more mystery to her floral portraits. At the same time, she repledges her allegiance to the abstract, pointing out, for example, how essentially nonrepresentational the shadows are in her pictures.

"A bouquet of flowers is nothing more than a bunch of abstract shapes joined together," Hallam reasserts in a 1995 article in *Art Masters*. "When I

Hibiscus, 1987
Acrylic on Belgian linen, 18 x 27 in.
Collection of Mrs. Julius H. Appleton

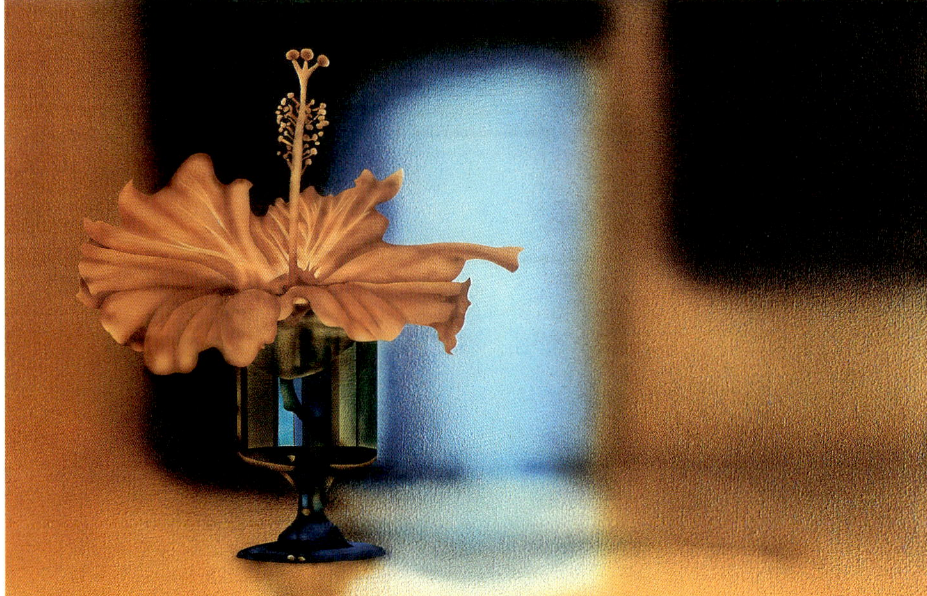

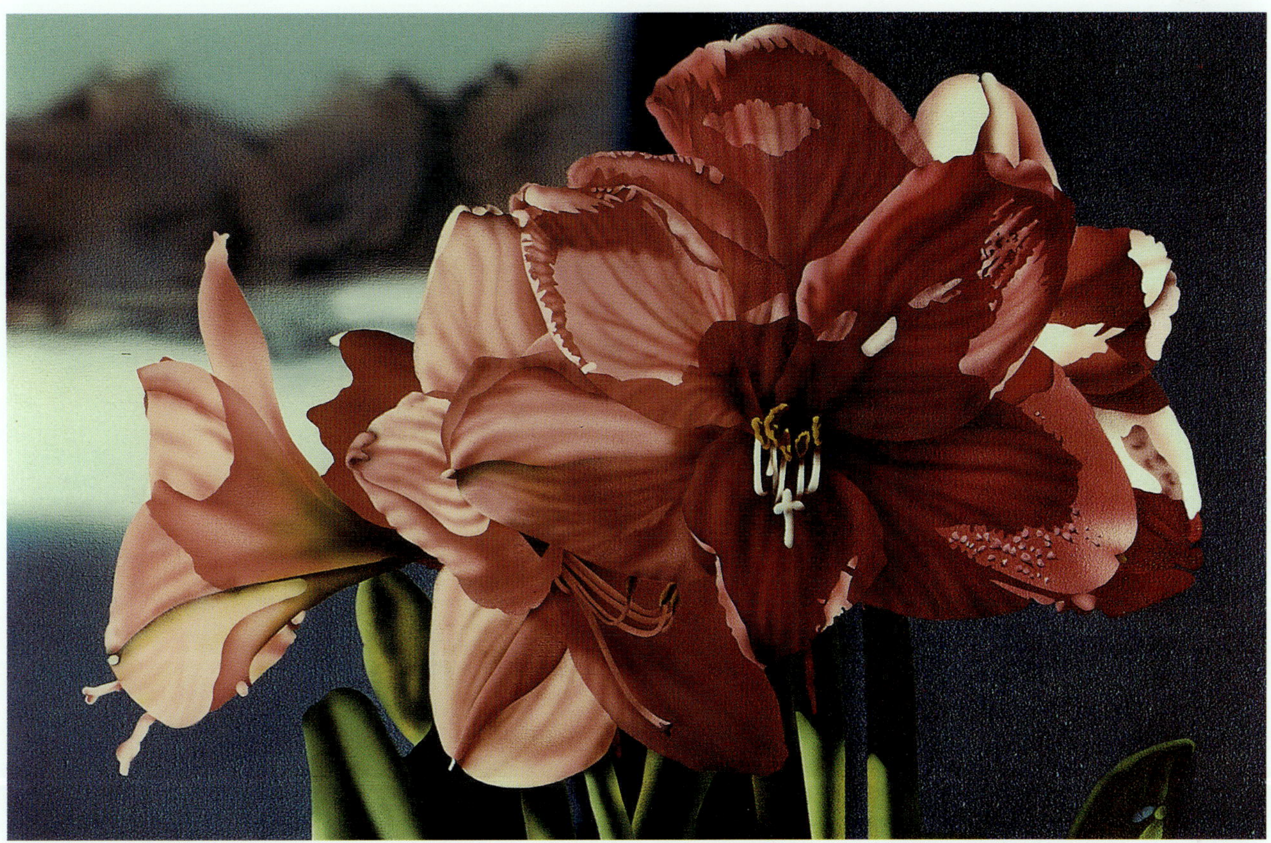

Amaryllis, 1990
Acrylic on Belgian linen, 22 x 34 in.
Collection of Mr. and Mrs. Kennedy Buell

paint a picture of still-life objects, I concern myself with one shape hitting another," she notes, "and I think abstractly the whole time. Everything realistic is abstract."

Hallam also reiterates her love of the camera. In fact, her first thought at the time she became enamored of the flower arrangements was that she would simply enlarge the photographs of them, to attain the larger-than-life effects she desired. Yet blowing up the prints to enormous size did not prove satisfactory.

The video also proves enlightening regarding the visual effects Hallam did *not* wish to achieve in her flower paintings. At one point she notes that the flowers should not appear to "pop off" the canvas. She also wished to avoid a Rubens look in her blossoms, feeling that too much voluptuousness would cheapen the look of the airbrushed flowers.

"Design is my big thing," Hallam states toward the end of the film, recalling that earlier in life she had almost become a fabric designer. The background shapes in her paintings should be, she says, as interesting as the featured objects. The procedure requires problem solving and technical considerations; Hallam purposely chooses more difficult tasks, thriving

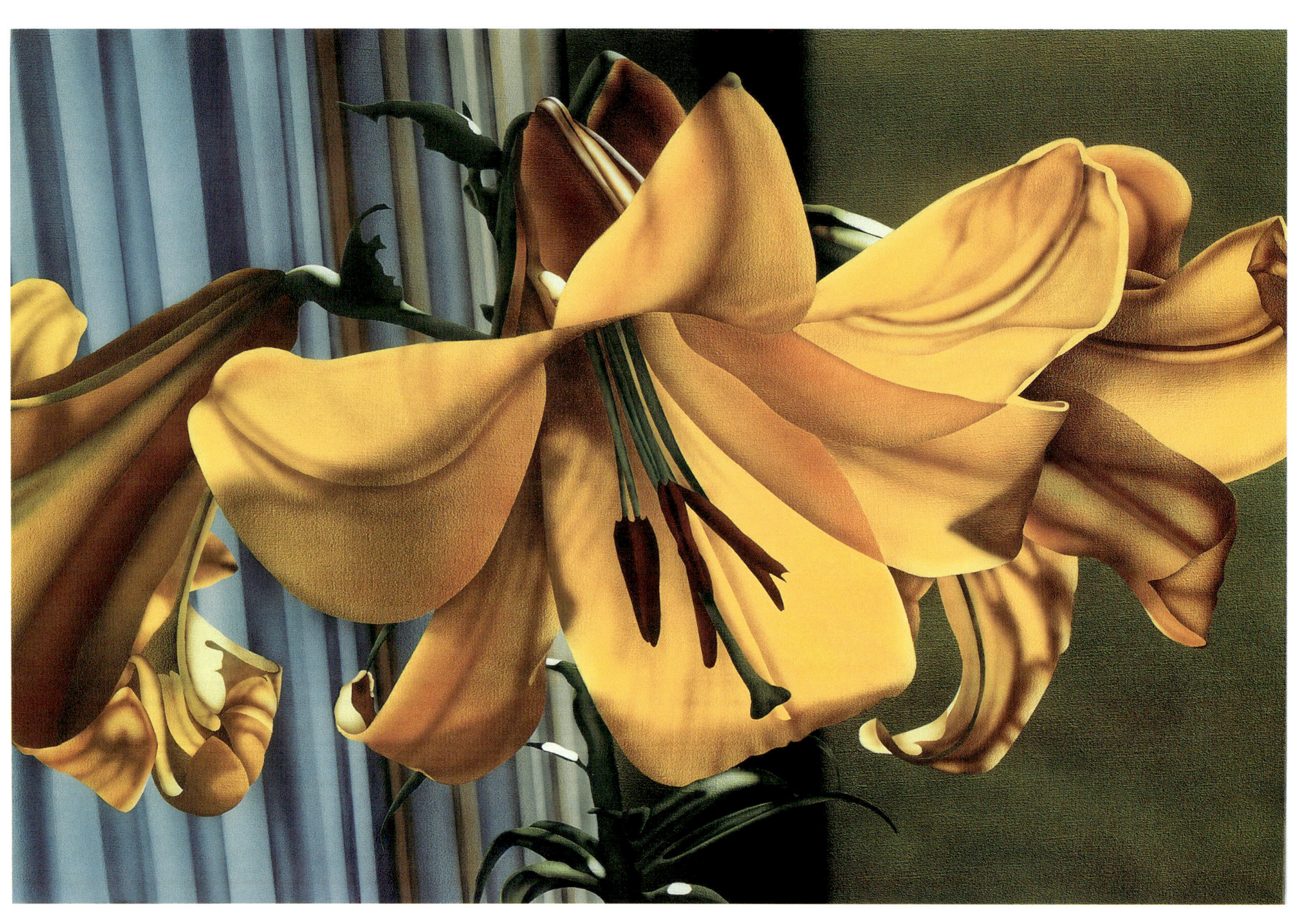

Golden Splendor, 1987
Acrylic on Belgian linen, 36 x 54 in.
Collection of the artist

on challenge and what she terms the "learning process."

The film also highlights the modesty of this brilliant, vital artist as she almost nonchalantly creates her extraordinary canvases. One comes away from this encounter with a sense of awe and wonder that, in her early 70s, Hallam displays the kind of energy and drive worthy of someone half her age. One returns to earlier descriptions—medicine man, magician—even as one comes up with new ones: maker of miracles, master.

In 1992, on a 5-by-8-foot canvas, Hallam completed one of her most ambitious and beautiful flower paintings, *Double Feature,* that stars the delightful Picasso bird vase she has painted time and again. She has also returned to favorite flowers—lilies, poppies, birds of paradise, Queen Anne's lace, tulips, and irises—rendering them in smaller formats using a variety of mediums, including acrylic, black ink, and graphite.

At the same time, Hallam has retreated, in a manner of speaking, from the labor-intensive monumental work, as presaged in her From the Garden series of 1989. She created several exquisite and miniature paintings using the airbrush with acrylic over black-and-white photographs. In abstract terms, the five pieces record the passing of the flower garden, from "first frost" through "last gathering" to "final bloom."

Another hint that Hallam might once again shift aesthetic gears came in an interview published in the Beaumont (Texas) *Enterprise* in September 1990. There the artist remarked that she imagined that her work might evolve into something "more subtle and not so factual in the final result."

In more recent times, Hallam has been straightforward in expressing her need to move on. "I've been on this trek for 15 years now," she says in reference to her airbrush flower painting period. She notes that her eyes and sinuses now bother her; she blames the condition on the fine mist of pigment that hangs in the air after spraying all day. During the last talk she gave, she found herself swigging lemon juice to clear her throat.

Hallam has always worn a heavy-duty Niosh respirator mask, and her studio is large, with a high ceiling, yet these factors make little difference when she is working on large pieces. For a while, she worked on paper and tried to reduce her use of the airbrush by combining it with pastel and other mediums, but it has now gotten to the point where she feels she should give it up completely for the sake of her well-being. "I will miss the surface intrigue created by spraying the canvas," she says. "Brushes will never achieve that."

Hallam is fully aware of the consequences of such a move. "Naturally, it's risky business to take all the components that I've developed over the past years and shift them around, but I've got to do it. I've mastered what I set out to do," she asserts, "and now I'm ready to discover some new, exciting

Birds of Paradise, 1987
Acrylic on Belgian linen, 50 x 50 in.
Collection of Roger H. Howland

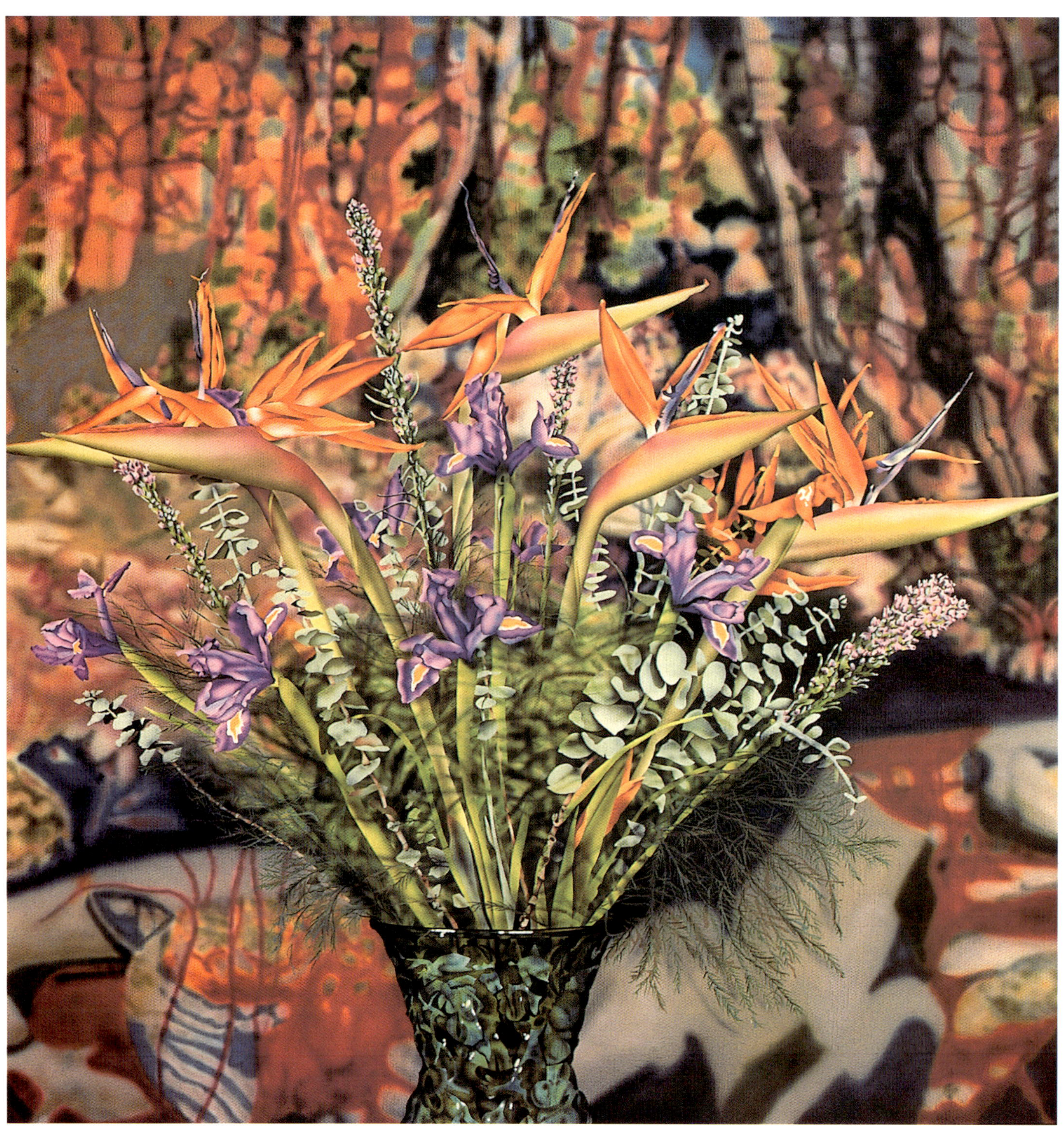

images. I'll have choices to make. It's always difficult, but that's progress. The way it is. The way it has to be. The answer. The pattern that I've always followed." Flowers still have a hold on her, and she wants to investigate certain floral variations.

Elsewhere, Hallam has written with passion of the artist's need to evolve. "An artist should push, change," she explains, "not be afraid to get out of his rut—off his track—and make a mistake or two." Such evolution should be his privilege, she notes. "He owes it to himself. If he keeps painting the same way he will go to the grave never knowing his potential. It's a waste," she concludes.

Casting an eye over the contemporary art scene, Hallam says, "I'm not opposed to the bleak and political art that's in vogue today. Yet I think there's plenty of room in the art world for beautiful imagery, too. In an age like this," she continues, "it's nice to have something that buoys up one's visual sensitivity and spirit." She points to Andy Goldsworthy, a British

Nasturtiums in a Circle, 1989
Acrylic on Belgian linen, 34 x 52 in.
Collection of Mr. and Mrs. David L. Linney

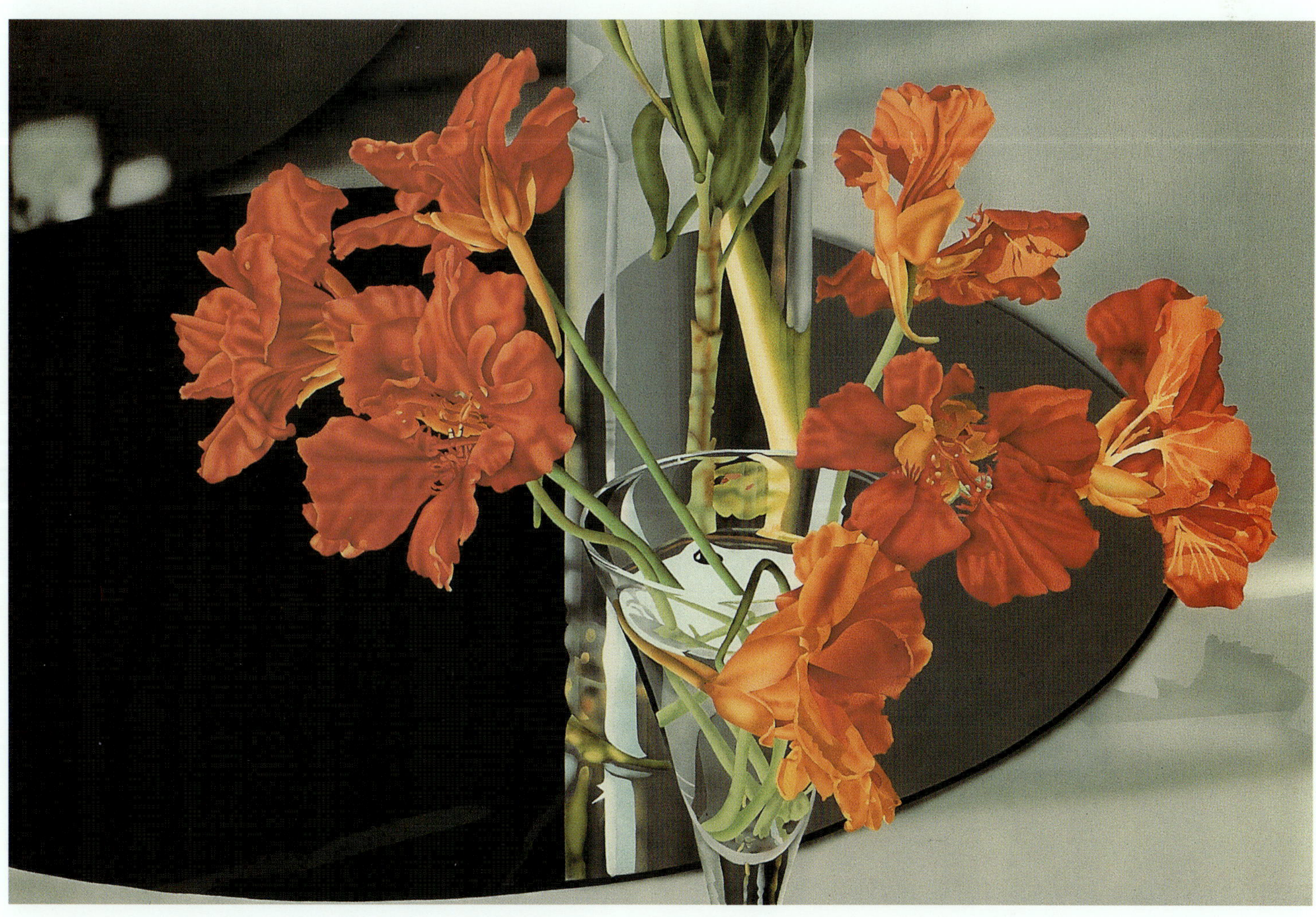

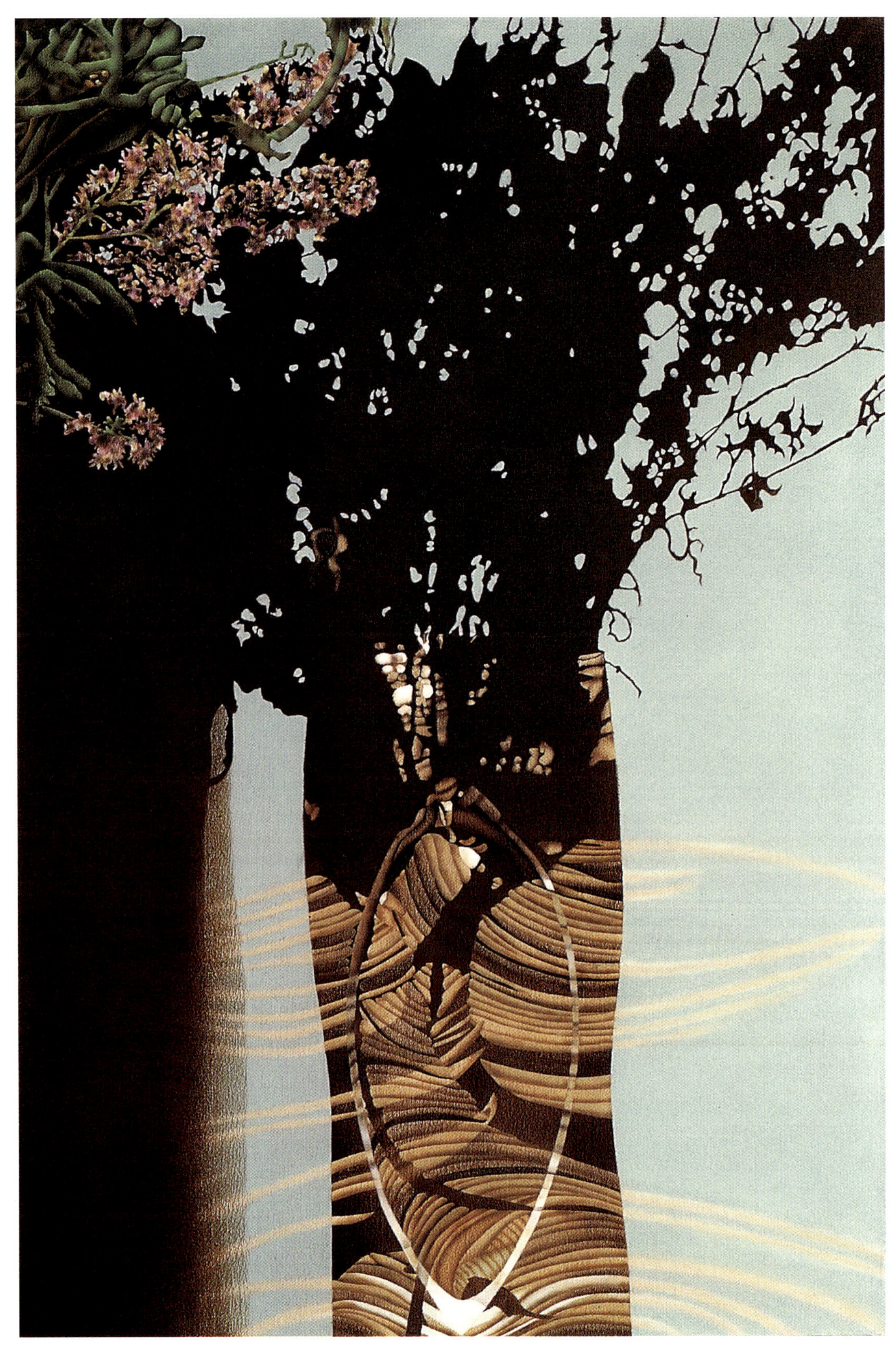

Bouquet Shadow, 1988
Acrylic on Belgian linen, 38 x 26 in.
Collection of Heather L. Payson

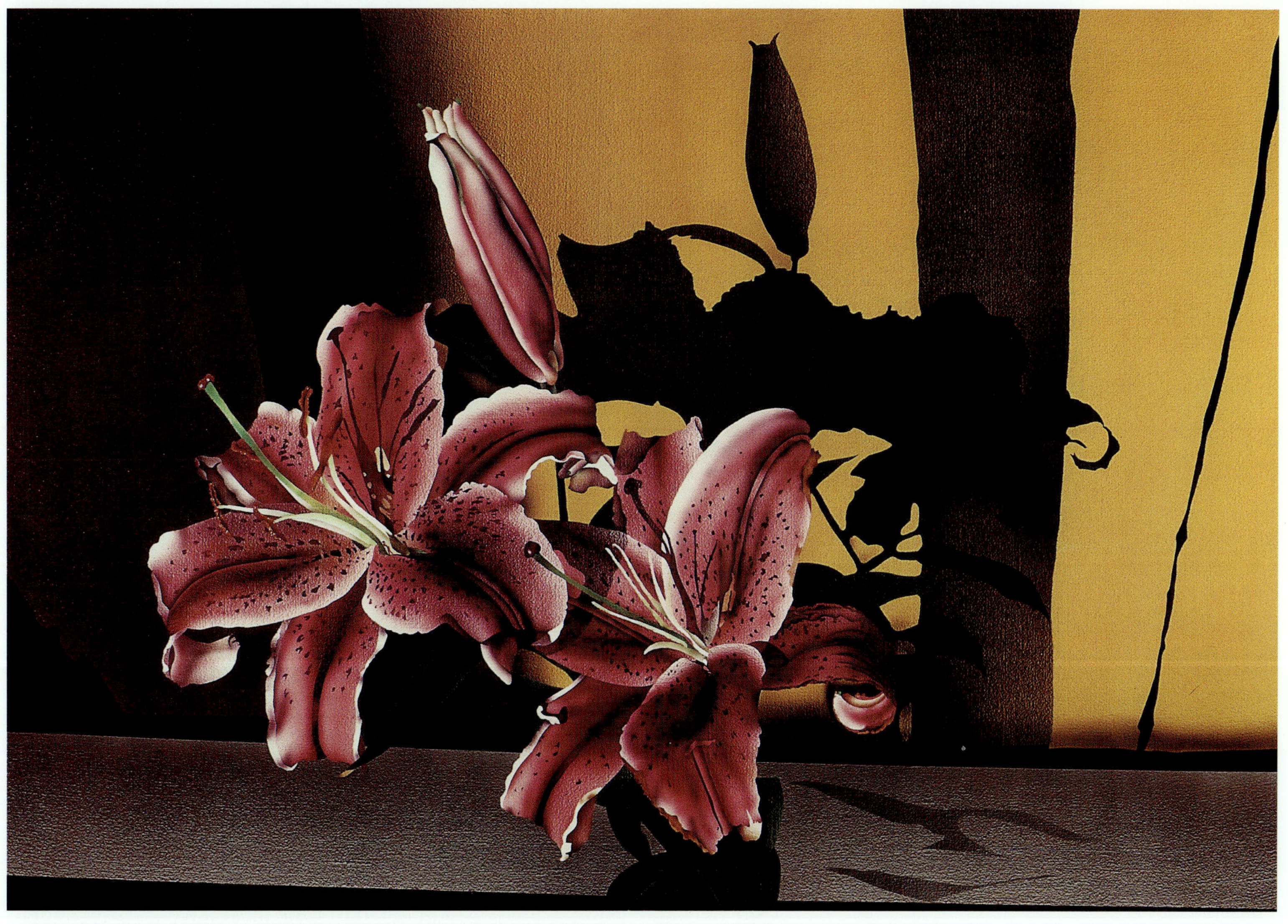

Stargazer, 1984
Acrylic on Belgian linen, 30 x 40 in.
Collection of Mrs. Cameron Biewend

artist: "If I ever have a second chance to live, I'll choose to be him," she remarks. "He's a *true* magician, with a great sense of scale. His work is imaginative—amazing and beautiful, using God-given materials."

A wide range of artists find themselves on Hallam's favorite list. Some are constants and others change as time goes by: Pierre Alechinsky, John Van Alstine, Louise Bourgeois, Helen Frankenthaler, Julio Larraz, Joseph Raffael, Lucas Samaras, Wayne Thiebaud, Donald Roller Wilson—the roster is long and very much up to the minute. She also likes the drawings of Christo, Jim Dine, and David Hockney.

An avid reader, she keeps tuned to the art world through books, journals, and magazines. *Interview* and *W* are a constant pleasure. She admires the clothes designed by Hanne Mori and the Missoni family and respects

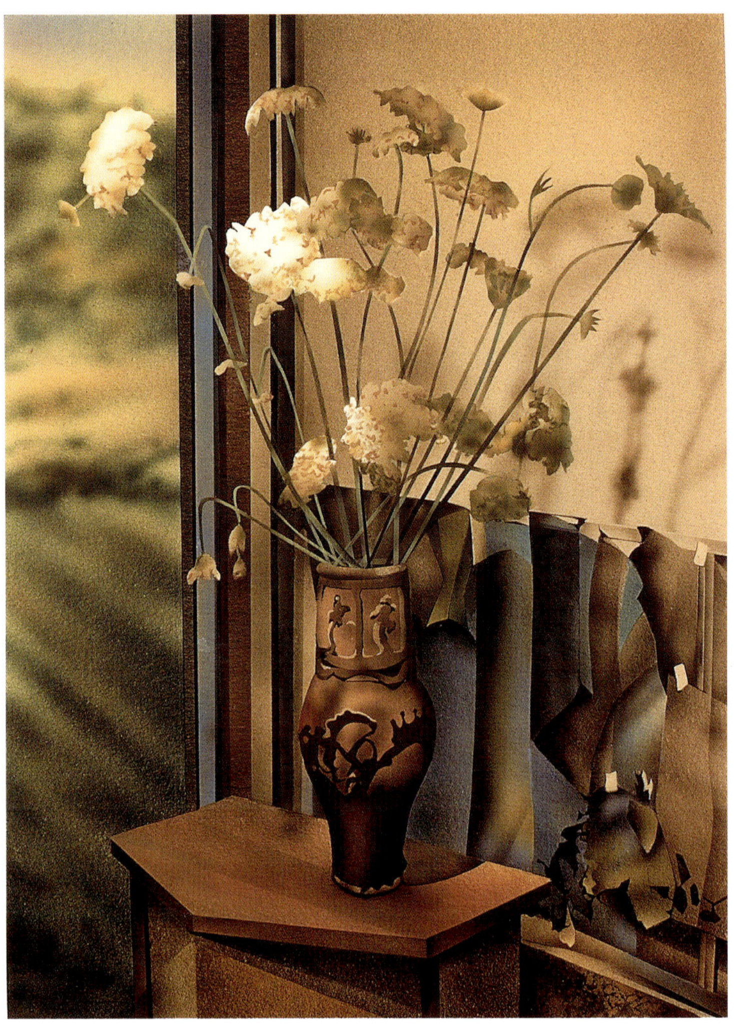

Queen Anne's Lace in John Natale's Raku, 1988
Acrylic on canvas, 11 3/4 x 7 7/8 in.
Collection of the artist

the aims and philosophy of designers like Karl Lagerfeld and Ralph Lauren. She likes something Lauren said in *W*, that "One must have a sense of identity and believe who you are and don't look at the other guy." And she shares Lagerfeld's feeling that an artist should not have "only one style and stick to it for the rest of your days."

Exhibitions of Hallam's work, both group and solo, multiply each year, as do the number of new public and private collections that have acquired her work. She has also received her share of honors: In 1990, she was given a prestigious Deborah Morton Award from Westbrook College in Portland, which honors Maine women who have achieved distinction for their civic, humanitarian, or cultural leadership. In 1993, Hallam won the Artistic Achievement Award for airbrush from *American Artist* magazine.

And yet, as Hallam has written, being a painter, for her, is something of a lonely affair. "A writer gets fan mail," she notes with some envy. A few people do write to her after a big opening, but not many. "So after my

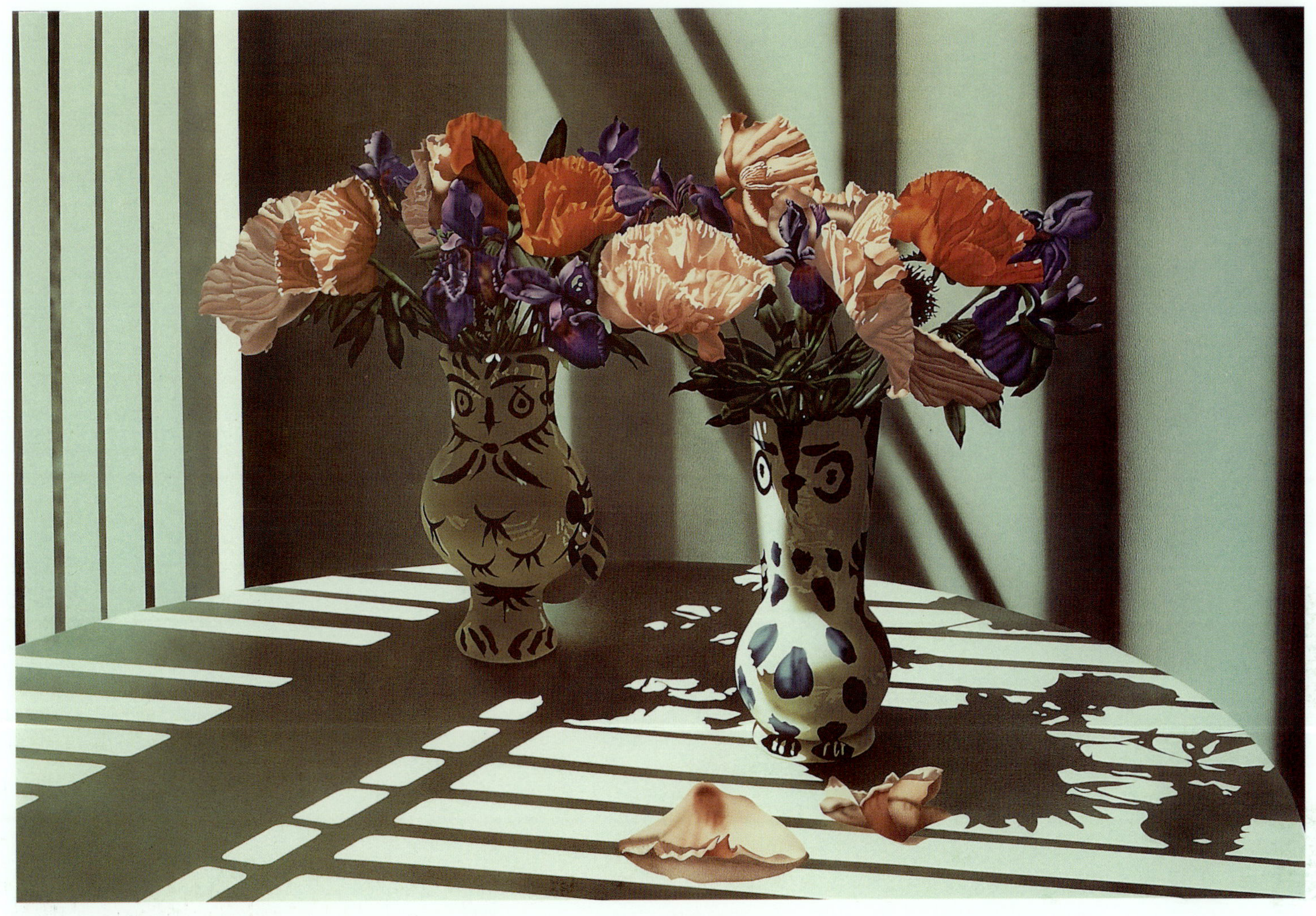

Double Feature, 1992
Acrylic on Belgian linen, 64 x 96 in.
Collection of Mrs. Stephen Carner

babies leave the studio," she states with a half-smile, "I seldom hear how they grow...on people."

Hallam's work has grown on just about everyone who has come into contact with it. The artist's perseverance is remarkable. "It's my nature to see things through to completion," she has said. "Mistakes are golden; they bring about decisions. This is what creativity is all about." And determination and an unerring eye for art. Perhaps Matisse sums it up best, in a passage dear to Hallam:

> The artist should call forth all of his energy, his sincerity, and the greatest possible modesty in order to push aside during his work the old clichés that come so readily to his hand and can suffocate the small flower which itself never turns out as one expected.

APPENDIX I:

"Painting Acrylics with an Airbrush," *Watercolor 92*
by Beverly Hallam

Despite what you may think after seeing my paintings in this article, I am actually a very spontaneous person who, nevertheless, finds the patience required to create highly detailed paintings. I am also mechanically inclined, so I am quite comfortable using an air compressor. (An air compressor provides the stream of air needed to spray a mist of paint onto canvas.)

Airbrushing is very hard work and my particular method is tedious and time-consuming but, after 12 years of using the technique, I guess I have to say I am mesmerized by the results. I always aim to please myself first and then hope my sense of pleasure in creating a painting will be contagious.

I remember the exact moment when I got hooked on the airbrush. I was using gelatin rollers to paint hard-edged flowers and I wanted to make a few fuzzy clouds in the background of the picture. I dug out a Thayer & Chandler airbrush someone had given me and started reading the directions that came with it. I then bought a can of compressed air and an adapter. In no time at all, I had zipped those clouds into the painting, and I found I just couldn't put the airbrush down. I painted a bouquet of flowers on a small sheet of paper, then moved on to a larger sheet of paper, and finally wound up working on a stretched piece of 5'-x-8' canvas.

People often ask me how long it takes to paint a picture, and my answer is that it all depends on the size of the painting and the complexity of the design. A 5'-x-8' canvas, for example, requires approximately 250 hours to complete. The actual process of applying paint with an airbrush takes only a few seconds or minutes, but that action is usually preceded by the preparation of stencils which eats up hours of time.

Here's how I create paintings using acrylic paint on paper and canvas: I begin by picking flowers in my garden and arranging them in my studio. I don't like them to look fussed over, so I follow Renoir's procedures which he described to Matisse: "When I have arranged a bouquet in order to paint it, I go round to the side I have not looked at."

Almost all the flowers that appear in my paintings have

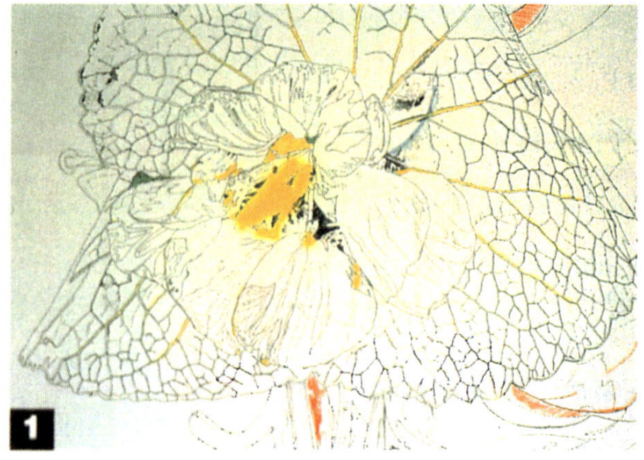

1 I began by covering the gessoed canvas with a sheet of translucent masking film, called frisket. My photograph was projected onto this. I outlined the details with a waterproof felt-tipped pen.

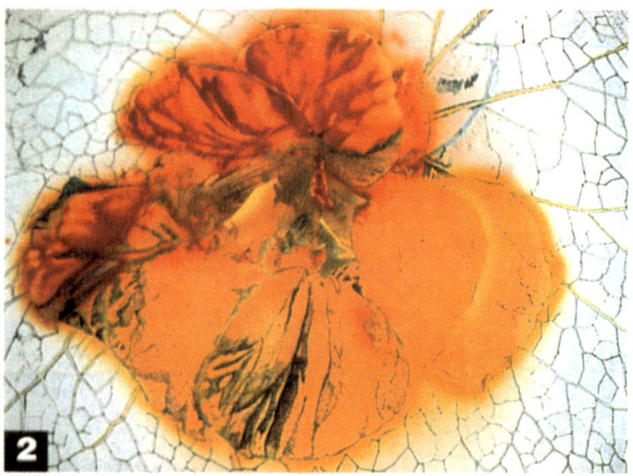

2 I cut away large areas of the frisket and sprayed the lightest color first. After the paint had dried, I put the frisket back in place so I could cut the outlines of the smaller shapes from the same piece of frisket. I worked from light to dark.

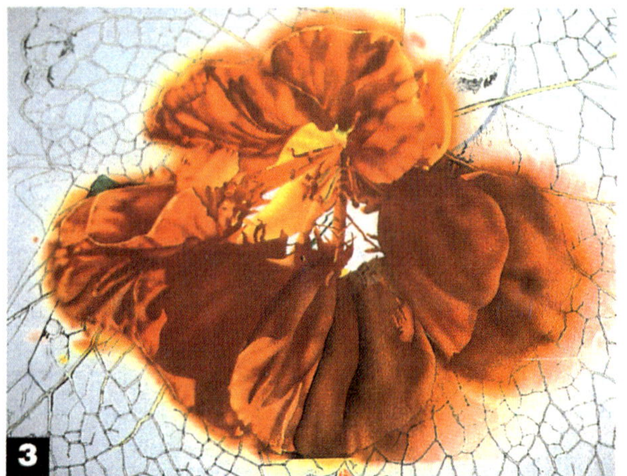

3 After completing the entire blossom, I covered it with frisket, leaving the white center exposed so it could be sprayed black. Then I covered the center before spraying the leaf.

been arranged on the round dining room table in my home in Maine. The table is placed near a window with vertical blinds. Those blinds have played a major role in throwing drama into the scenes in my paintings, such as *Parrots*.

I set up my camera in the late afternoon and wait for the action of the sunlight to begin. As soon as the low-angled light hits the bouquet, I become a whirling dervish, shifting blinds, flowers, and camera in a frantic effort to catch the sun filtering through the petals and to establish the fast-moving, intricate shadows on the table. I sometimes add one or two circular, 12″ mirrors to the arrangement. In *Madonnas*, the mirror on the wall reflects the mirror on the table with a vase of lilies on it.

I use either a Nikon or a Rollei camera to take these photographs, frame the composition in the viewfinder in the same way that the composition will appear in the painting. I never crop the photographs once they are taken. I take anywhere from 10 to 24 shots from different angles and distances, depending on the complexity of the arrangement. From these images, I select one that I will make into an 8″-x-12″ C-print. (I tried using Cibachrome prints but found the color too saturated.)

I throw the C-print into a box labeled "Possibilities," and I wait at least a year before using it as the basis of a painting. In fact, I may never use it. I have to be certain that the image will wear well over the course of time, so I am constantly adding more pictures to the box than I am taking out. At this moment, there are probably over 30 eligible candidates sitting in there waiting to come alive.

When I'm ready to start a new painting, I open the box and find that one of the photographs will always spark my interest. The image may affect me because of my mood, or because it seems right for the scale of painting I have in mind. I find that scale has a great deal to do with the success or failure of a painting. For example, *Nasturtium with Galax* is actually a blossom with a single leaf in a six-inch-high pharmaceutical flask. The mirror on which it sits reflects the arrangement and its surroundings. I chose to make this painting 6′ by 6′ for a dramatic effect. In the painting, the image of the nasturtium is 29 inches wide.

I cover the paper or gessoed canvas with a sheet of translucent masking film, called frisket, which adheres to the surface.

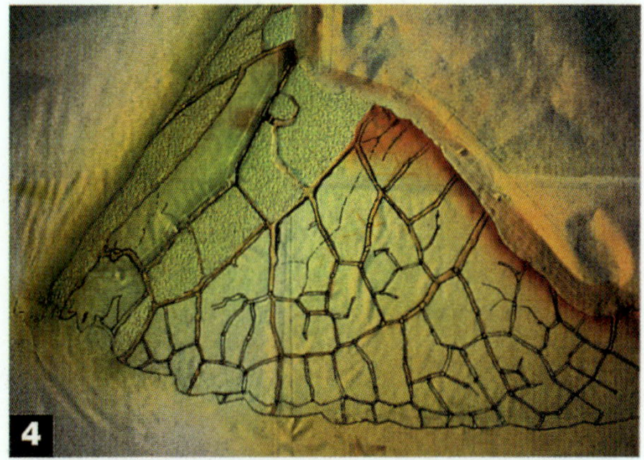

With the large Paasche AUF airbrush, I sprayed the entire leaf with an undercoating of pale green. I repositioned the frisket, cutting around the veins of the leaf and removing the sections between them. The veins remained covered with frisket, resembling a lacy network.

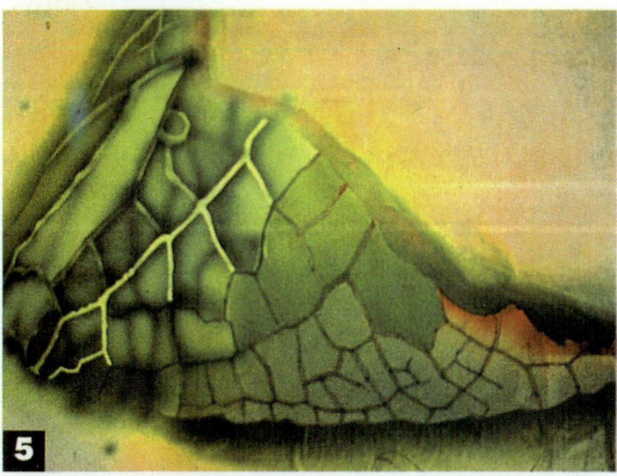

Using the smaller Paasche VL airbrush, I sprayed darker greens to get a three-dimensional effect within each section. When the frisket was removed from the veins, they appeared pale green. I then sprayed some dark green over the entire leaf to blend in the veins.

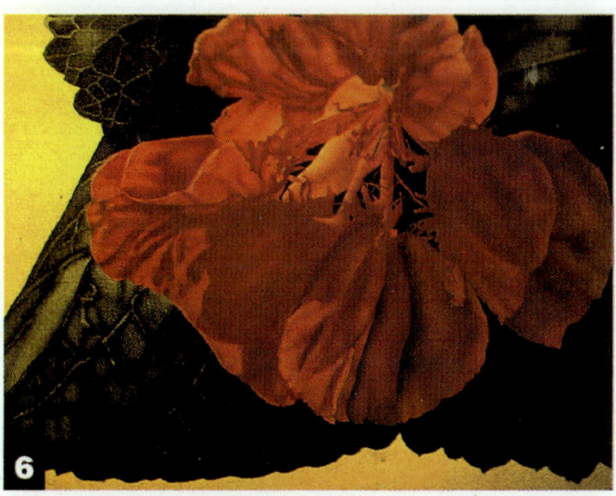

Next, I cut a large mask and covered the whole nasturtium blossom and galax leaf before I proceeded to spray the glass flask and the background shapes.

I project my photograph directly onto the film and trace the outlines of the image with a black waterproof felt-tipped pen. (A grid system can also be used to enlarge and transfer the image, but that procedure is more time-consuming.) Later, I carefully erase lines that have been distorted by the projection system, using a Q-Tip dipped in alcohol to dissolve the pen's ink. I redraw some lines and eliminate others because nature must be simplified. Rhythms have to be established, new shapes have to be invented, and bits and pieces must be created so there is variety in the shapes and sizes within the painting. Murky sections of the photographic image often have to be clarified.

Designing background elements in my paintings is just as difficult as establishing the central image. To me, the entire picture is a big abstraction that has to be adjusted for purely compositional reasons. I don't really consider myself a Photo-Realist painter, because I abbreviate and alter the photographic image much more substantially than artists whose work fits the definition of that style.

I carefully analyze the colors in my photograph and mix samples of acrylic color to match each chroma and value as closely as possible, and then I put swatches of each color in a notebook next to notations of the mixing data. I then prepare sufficient amounts of each color, using either Liquitex acrylic jar colors or Golden acrylic thinner colors. That paint is then strained and stored in airtight film canisters.

Next, I carefully plan the sequence in which each area of the painting will be painted and make notations of that working order in the same notebook. Even though I approach each new painting differently, the notes about my procedures and the hours I have spent creating a painting prove valuable. George Rickey, a sculptor friend of mine, says: "My wife always reminds me that it will take longer than I think. Luckily, I think it will be shorter or I wouldn't start."

When I am ready to start spraying the paint with an airbrush, I set my glasses down on my nose to make room for a pair of special magnifying lenses, and I strap a heavy-duty Niosh respirator over my face. Although the binder in the acrylic that I use is nontoxic, the pigments that remain in the air are toxic.

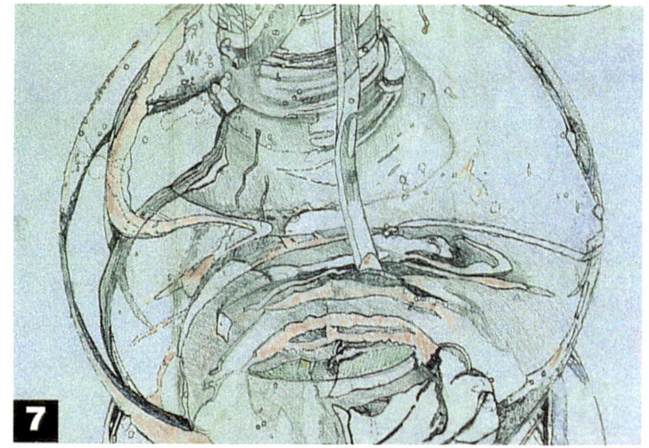

7 **Here is the frisket drawing of the flask of water and the leaf stem before it was cut and sprayed, using the same procedure. I invented many lines that were murky in the photograph.**

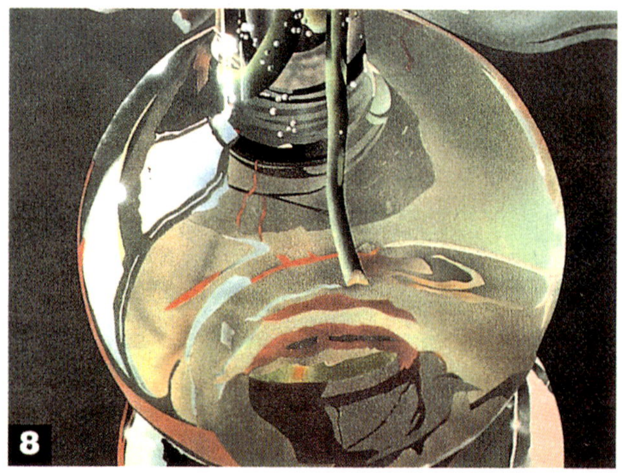

8 **I observed the abstract shapes very carefully. I altered the darks, but left all the whites exactly as I saw them.**

I use a Dayton Speedaire compressor, which stores 100 pounds of air pressure, and a Paasche VL airbrush. The airbrush itself resembles a fountain pen that has a little cup hitched to the side for holding paint. When the finger lever on top is depressed, air comes out; when it is pulled back, paint comes out. While spraying paint, I must keep the airbrush in motion so that puddles will not form. I have to control the consistency of the paint because if it's too thick, the airbrush will sputter and spray unevenly; if it's too thin, the paint will simply run down the picture.

I cut the frisket stencils with an X-Acto knife, using a #11 blade and working directly on the canvas so that each stencil will match perfectly. After a shape has been cut out, I peel off the piece of frisket and spray the acrylic paint, using as many colors and variations as the photograph indicates for that spot. I then cover that shape again with the piece of frisket and move on to another shape nearby. I never repaint an area.

Large areas of a picture can be painted without cutting a stencil. When doing those sections, I use a pistol-shaped Paasche AUF airbrush. The lightest color is sprayed first; then other values and colors are sprayed over it. To make colors appear more brilliant and varied, I sometimes hold the airbrush close and parallel to the surface of the paper or canvas. The paint collects on one side of the texture, giving a shimmering effect. The paint is sprayed with a sweeping arm motion, and I'm always afraid I will sweep in the wrong direction or make an area darker than it should be.

I never see the whole painting until it is finished; constantly removing and replacing frisket to see how the picture looks would take too much time. The day all the frisket is removed is a time of celebration. It's so exciting that I often invite friends over to watch the painting emerge!

Reprinted from *Watercolor 92* (Fall 1992), an American Artist publication.

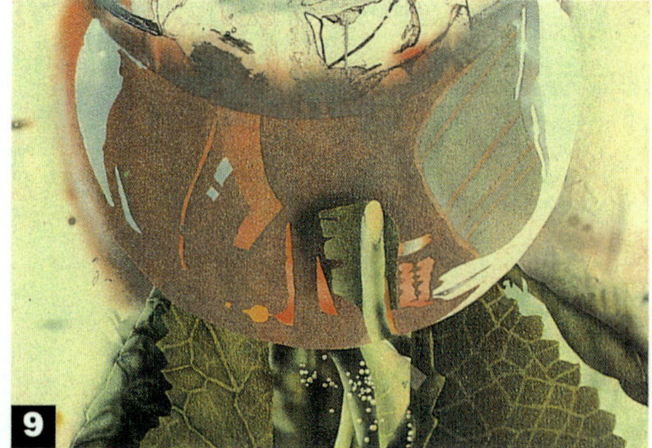

9 **At the bottom of the painting is a reflection of the flask and the galax leaf upside down in the mirror. I covered them while spraying the background. The photo shows the background still masked. I used inexpensive shelving paper for the areas of solid color.**

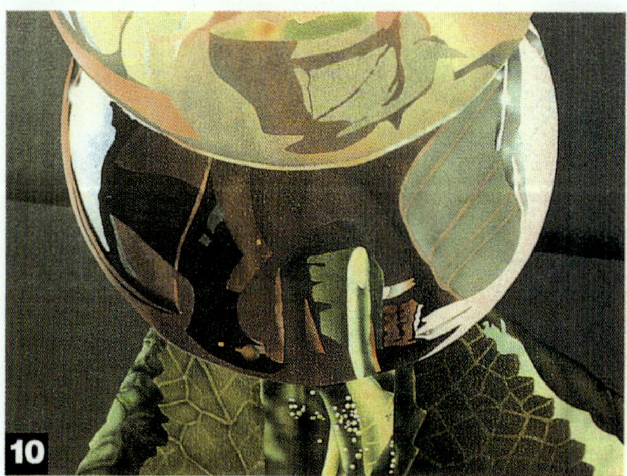

10 **The reflection and background were completed. Mirrors are exciting to paint, because they reveal surprising things. Their reflections show intriguing shapes that we otherwise would not see. Here, the mirror shows the bottom of the leaf stem.**

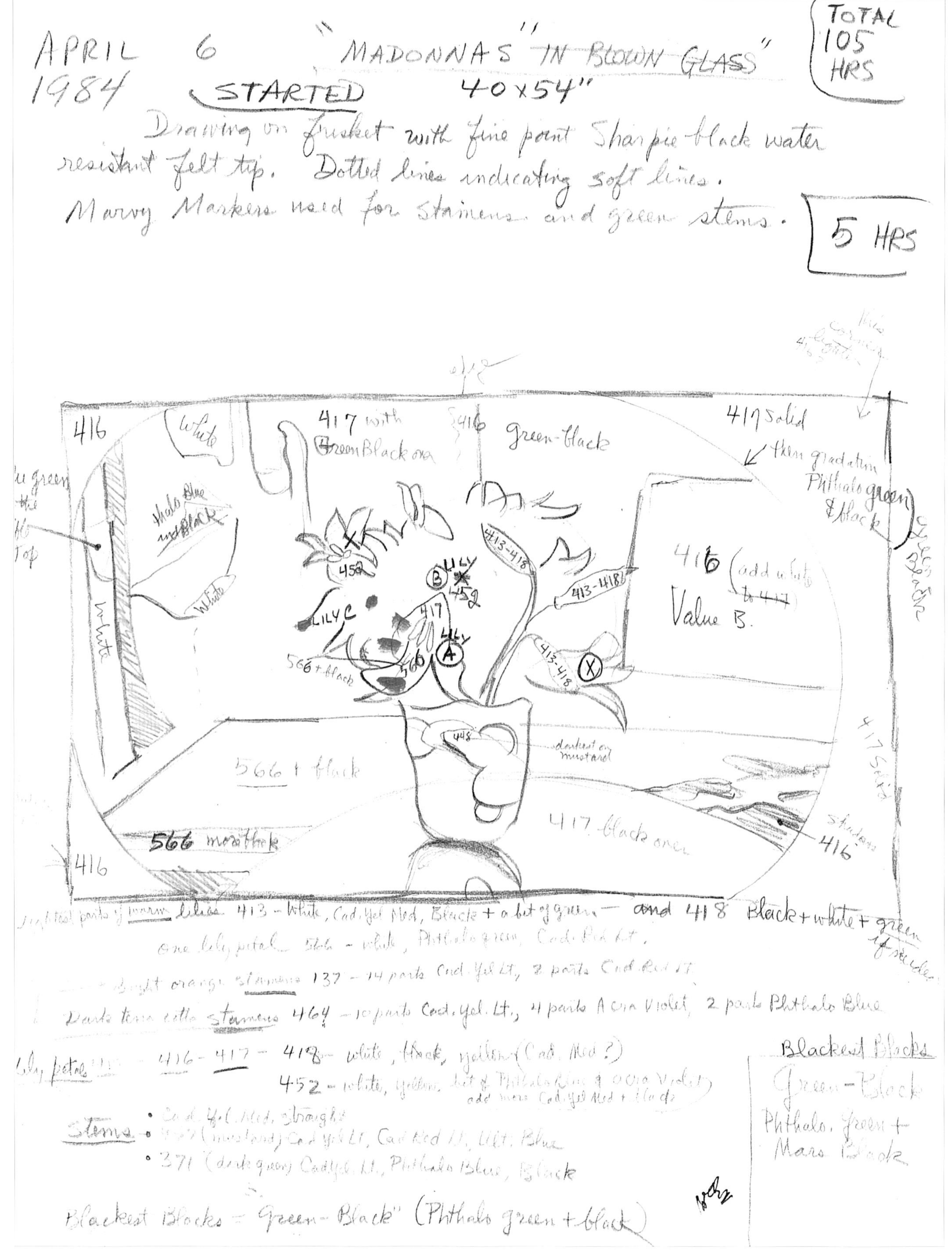
APRIL 6 "MADONNAS" "IN BLOWN GLASS"
1984
STARTED
40x54"
TOTAL 105 HRS
Drawing on frisket with fine point Sharpie black water resistant felt tip. Dotted lines indicating soft lines.
Marvy Markers used for stamens and green stems.
5 HRS
416
White
417 with Green Black ora
416
Green-black
417 solid
then gradation Phthalo green & black
416 (add white)
Value B.
413-418
452
LILY B
LILY C
LILY A
417
566
566 + black
413-418
X
448
darkest on mustard
566 + black
566 more black
417 black over
shadows 416
416
White
417 Solid
Blackest Blacks
Green-Black
Phthalo Green + Mars Black
Blackest Blacks = "Green-Black" (Phthalo green + black)

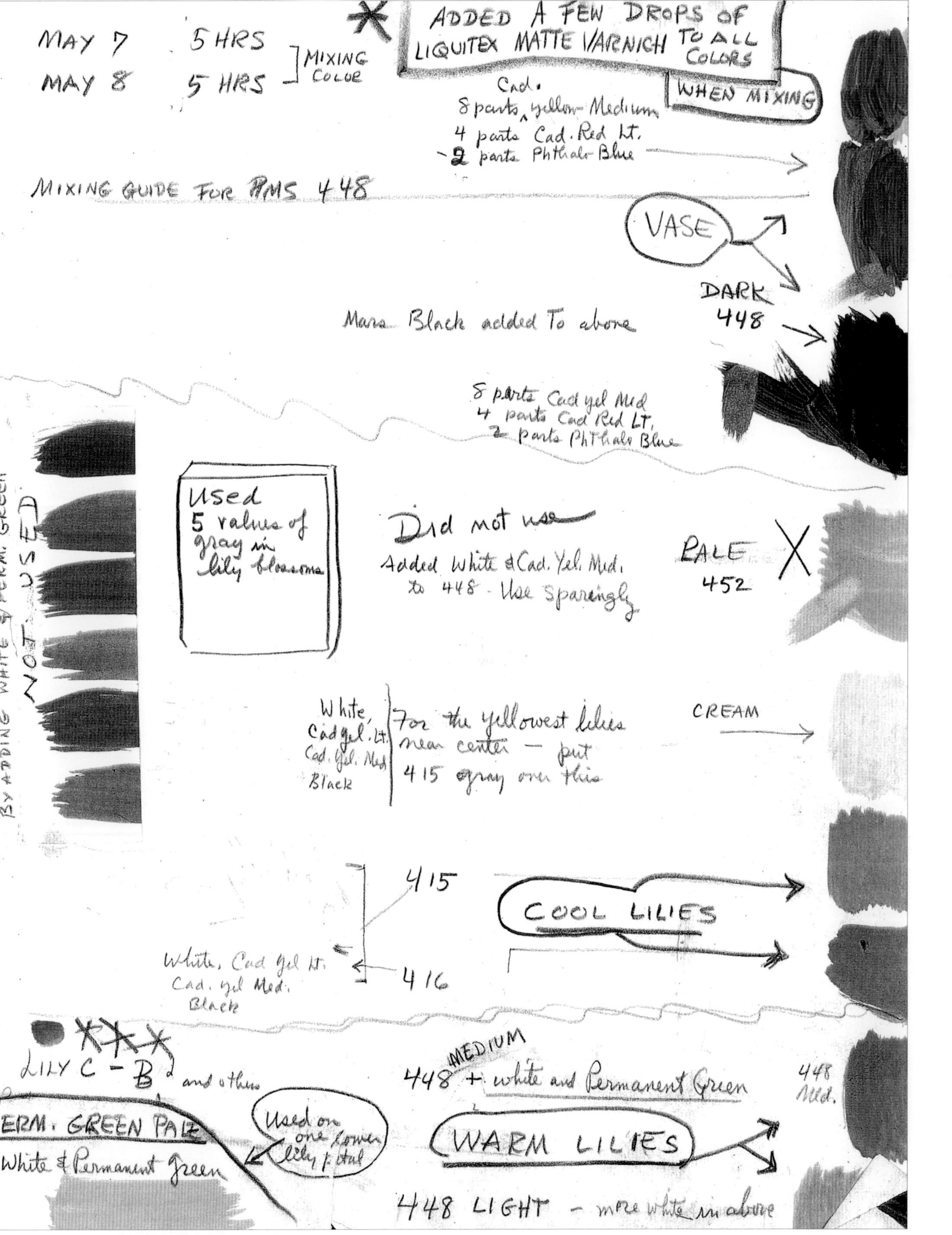

MAY 7 5 HRS
MAY 8 5 HRS
MIXING COLOR
ADDED A FEW DROPS OF LIQUITEX MATTE VARNICH TO ALL COLORS WHEN MIXING
8 parts Cad. yellow Medium
4 parts Cad. Red Lt.
2 parts Phthalo Blue
MIXING GUIDE FOR PMS 448
VASE
DARK 448
Mars Black added To above
8 parts Cad yel Med
4 parts Cad Red Lt.
2 parts Phthalo Blue
BY ADDING WHITE & PERM. GREEN
NOT USED
Used 5 values of gray in lily blossoms
Did not use
Added White & Cad. Yel. Med. to 448 - Use Sparingly
PALE 452
White, Cad yel. Lt. Cad. Yel. Med Black
For the yellowest lilies near center - put 415 gray over this
CREAM
415
COOL LILIES
White, Cad Yel Lt. Cad. Yel Med. Black
416
LILY C - B 2 and others
448 MEDIUM + white and Permanent Green
448 Med.
ERM. GREEN PALE
White & Permanent Green
Used on one lower lily petal
WARM LILIES
448 LIGHT - more white in above

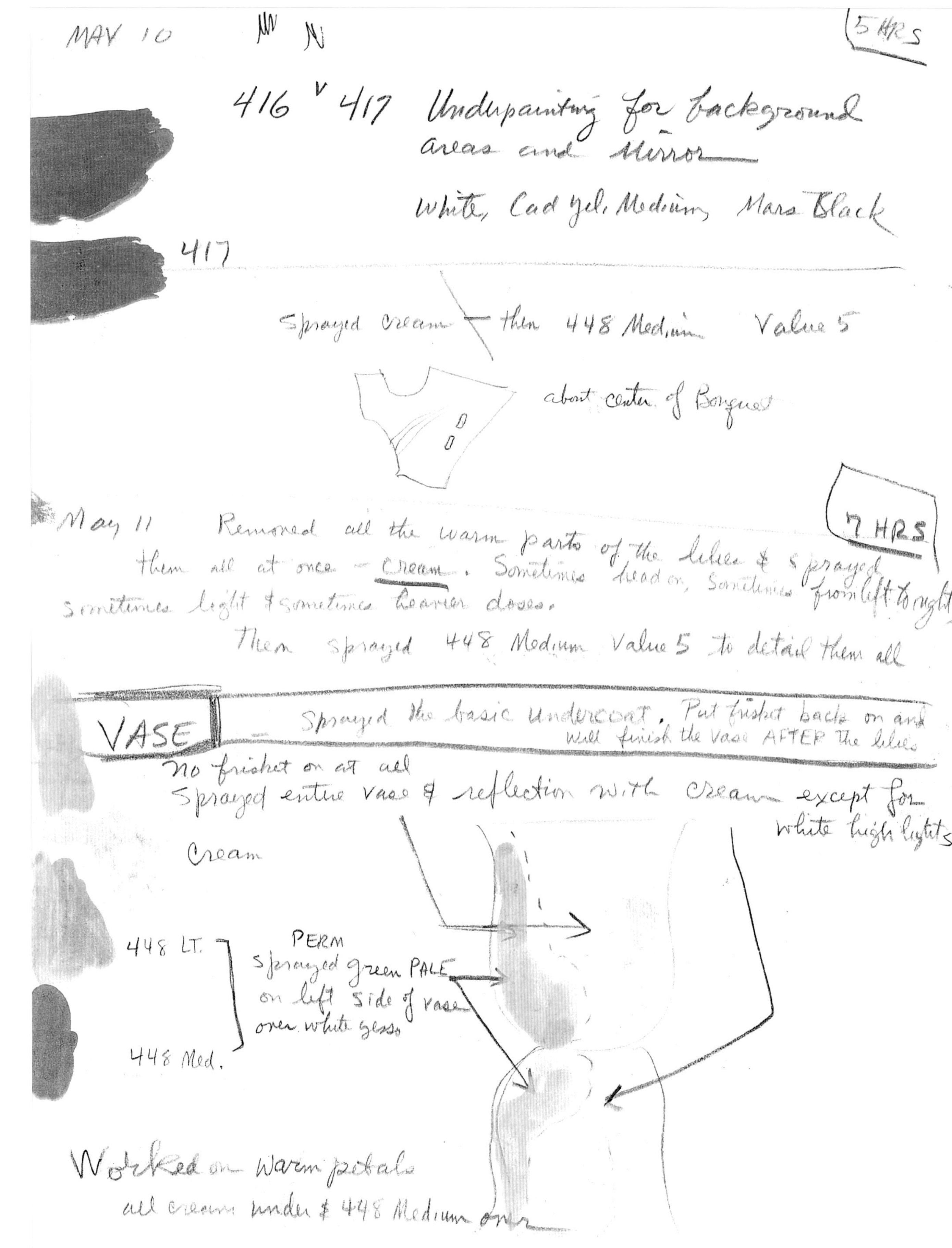

MAY 10 ⅢⅢ N — 5 HRS

416 & 417 Underpainting for background areas and Mirror

White, Cad Yel. Medium, Mars Black

417

Sprayed cream — then 448 Medium Value 5

about center of Bouquet

May 11 Removed all the warm parts of the lilies & sprayed them all at once — Cream. Sometimes head on, sometimes from left to right, sometimes light & sometimes heavier doses. — 7 HRS

Then sprayed 448 Medium Value 5 to detail them all

VASE — Sprayed the basic undercoat. Put frisket back on and will finish the Vase AFTER the lilies

No frisket on at all

Sprayed entire vase & reflection with cream except for white high lights

Cream

448 LT.

448 Med.

PERM

Sprayed green PALE on left side of vase over white gesso

Worked on warm petals

all cream under & 448 Medium over

8 HRS

Finished the bouquet

Indicated black background shapes in bouquet yet to be sponged

---

Having Compressor problems. The head plate gasket has trembled itself outside of the head and has a split in it. I called Van Wood of Small Corp. who got the compressor for me – and he advised my taking the 3 bolts out of the head and ~~coating~~ removing the head plate gasket coating the head with silicone (tube) and the plate with silicone, then setting the gasket back onto the head & placing the plate over it and tightening the 3 bolts back down.

This will hold me over until I get a gasket kit.

Let set 24 HRS. (2 nights)

The bolts ~~it~~ should be tightened with a tourque wrench which I don't have – but Van will do this for me later.

(NOTE: It is now JUNE 1985 and the gasket is still holding. It didn't need to be tightened more)

MAY 20 GESSOED 64 x 96 canvas

For "Goldenrod" – my ~~next~~ painting

linen sample used

Used Knap roller to apply Gesso.

Got stretchers & 3 cross bars from N. Y. Central Supply – also I'm using their Belgian linen – the heaviest I have ever used "T" 84" wide \# 21.55 per yard

and an electric staple gun from Sears Roebuck.

One coat (thinned) of Liquitex gesso – only went thru the weave very little

Used long handle on the medium Knap sheep skin roller.

MAY 21

Green-Black ↓

Sprayed black between flowers in Borquet. The same black as I used in "Late Shadow."

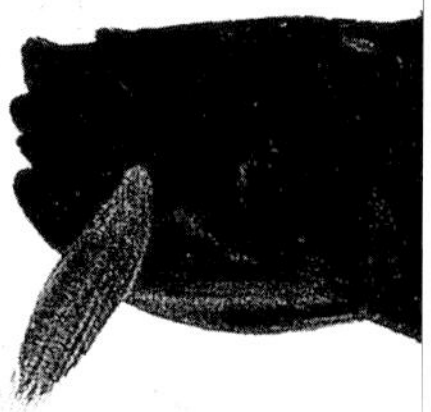

MARS BLACK + PHTHALO GREEN

added Liquitex Mat Varnish To this.. As I have, to all colors in this painting

146 I have a lot of this beautiful color left over.

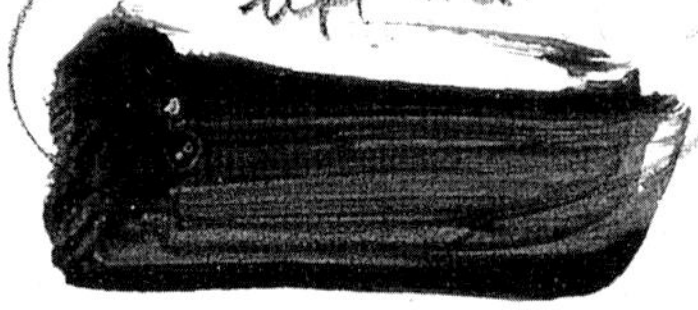

STAMENS

Cad. Yel. Lt. + acra violet

STAMENS IN MADONNA LILIES. SPRAYED ORANGE FIRST (CAD. ORANGE LT) ALL OVER – then the brown on dark side & Total brown ones

146

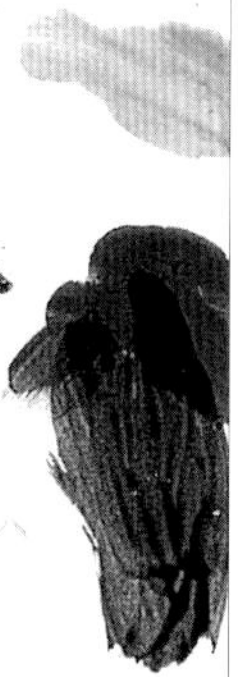

The upper left stamens are lighter in the Shadow so sprayed orange first then

made by putting RAW UMBER in above orange

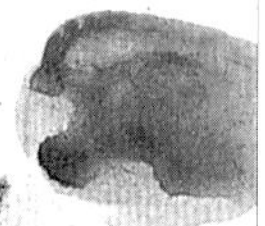

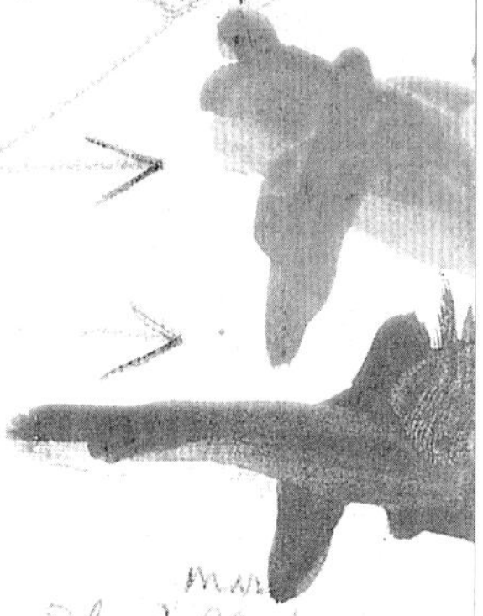

VASE

Second wack at it (see preceding page)

Sprayed 448 Light and 448 Medium left to right over the "pale green" and "Cream"

Phthalo Blue + Mars Black

shadow under Vase

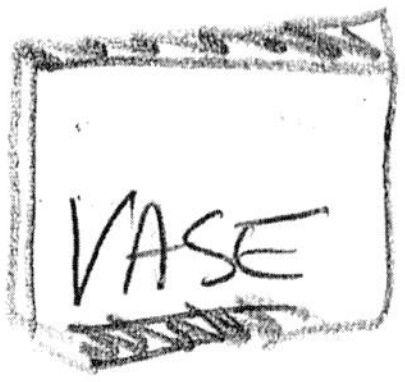

9 HRS

also used in upper part of vase Top right edge. With dark green over it

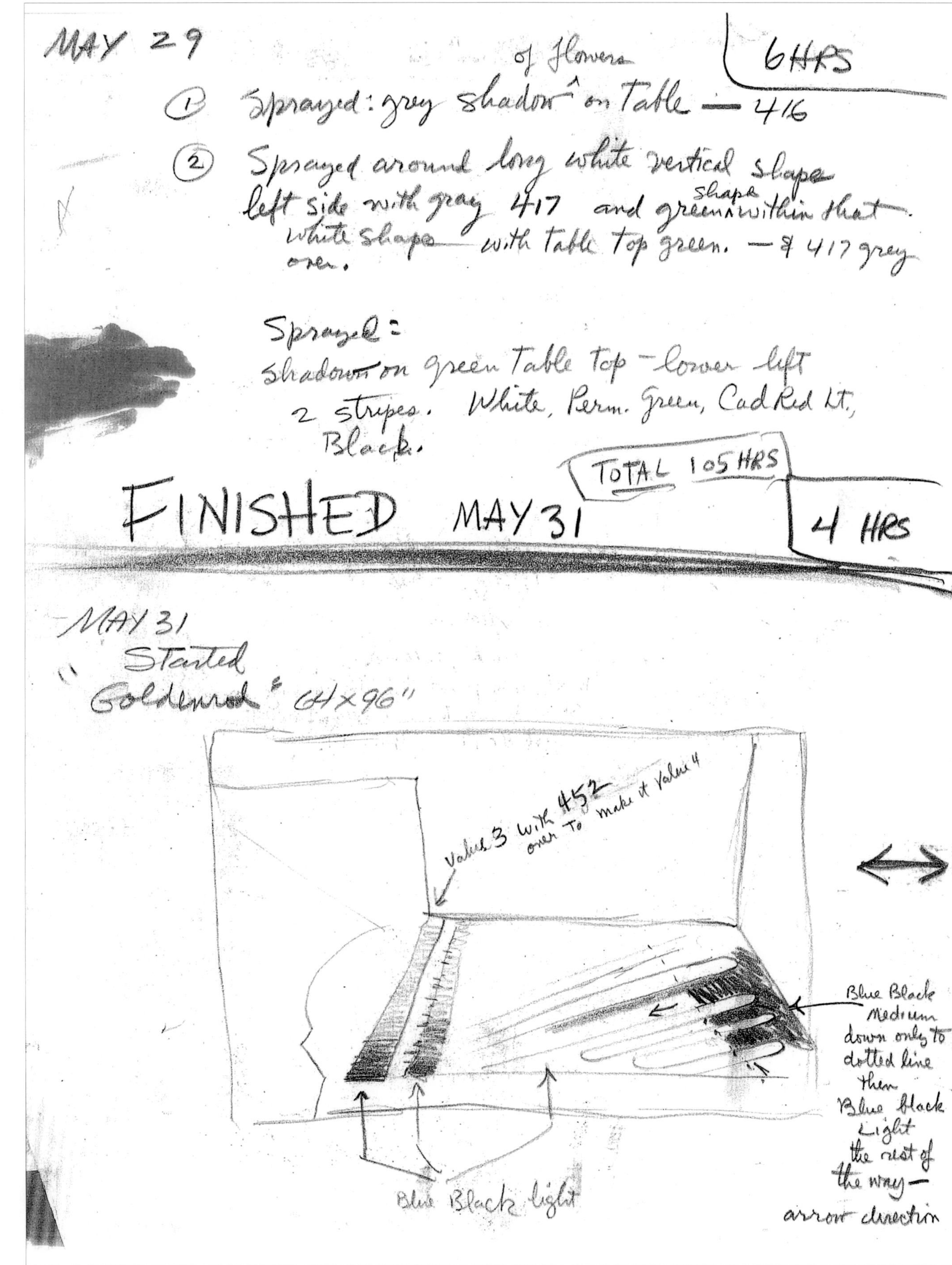

MAY 29
6 HRS
① Sprayed: grey shadow of flowers on Table — 416
② Sprayed around long white vertical shape
left side with gray 417 and green within that shape
white shape with table top green. — & 417 grey over.
Sprayed:
shadow on green Table top — lower left
2 stripes. White, Perm. Green, Cad Red Lt, Black.
TOTAL 105 HRS
FINISHED MAY 31
4 HRS
MAY 31
Started
"Goldenrod" 64×96"
Value 3 with 452 over To make it Value 4
Blue Black Medium down only to dotted line then Blue black Light the rest of the way — arrow direction
Blue Black light

BIBLIOGRAPHY:

"Beverly Hallam's Paintings," by Dorothy Adlow, *Christian Science Monitor*, June 28, 1954

"Beverly Hallam, Paintings, Drawings and Monotypes, 1956-1971" (catalogue preface), Addison Gallery of American Art, Andover, MA, Christopher C. Cook, director

"Two Artists Get $6000 Award under Blanche Colman Fund," *The Boston Globe*, July 15, 1960

"Art Along Newbury Street—Hallam Displays," by Dorothy Adlow, *Christian Science Monitor*, April 30, 1962

"Beverly Hallam Wins in Group and Solo," by Edgar J. Driscoll Jr., *The Boston Sunday Globe*, May 6, 1962

"Beverly Hallam to Hold One Man Show of Paintings," *Wells-Ogunquit Star*, Kennebunk, ME, May 3, 1962

"Maine and Her Artists," *Woman's Day*, August 1964

"Old-New Method of Print-Making Revived in Ogunquit" (feature article), *York County Coast Star*, June 25, 1969

"Five Women—They're Different" (feature article), *Maine Times*, November 5, 1971

"Art—Ogunquit's Indispensable Element" (feature article), by Robert Taylor, *The Boston Globe*, September 10, 1972

"Beverly Hallam at Hobe Sound Gallery," *Palm Beach Weekly Illustrated*, April 1, 1973

"16 Maine Artists," by Robert Taylor, *The Boston Globe*, January 30, 1974

"Maine in Painting and Sculpture," by Caron LeBrun Danikian, *Christian Science Monitor*, February 5, 1974

The Cove (Perkins Cove at Ogunquit, Maine), by Boyd, Ryan, Wills, Wills (see photograph credits), Lewiston, 1976

"76 Maine Artists" (catalogue), Maine State Museum, Augusta, 1976

"Beverly Finds a Roller Coaster" (feature article), by Lynn Franklin, *Maine Sunday Telegram*, Portland, February 27, 1977

"Archives of American Art Journal," *Smithsonian Institution*, vol. 18, no. 3, 1978

Creative Landscape Painting, by Edward Betts, Watson-Guptil Pub., 1978

"Beverly Hallam—A Talented York Woman Brings Interest to Her Methods As Well As Her Finished Art," *Maine Life*, Februar, 1980 (cover & article)

Creative Seascape Painting, by Edward Betts, Watson-Guptil, 1981

Curators' Choice, Northeastern edition by Babbette Brandt Fromme, Crown, 1981

"The History of the Ogunquit Art Colon," (group photo by Isabel Lewando), *York County Coast Star*, August 4, 1982

"Avant-Garde Takes a Turn to the Right," by Philip Isaacson, *Maine Sunday Telegram*, July 29, 1984

"Beverly Hallam—Her Canvases Shimmer," by Pati Wilson, *Art Gallery*, Aug./Sept. 1984

"Farnsworth Develops Flair for More Than Fashion" (feature article), by William David Barry, *Maine Sunday Telegram*, October 28, 1984

"Aspects of Reality," *Reflections by Beverly Hallam and Transformations by Abbott Pattiso*, (catalogue), Bartlett H. Hayes Jr., curator, William A. Farnsworth Art Museum and Library, 1984

"Faith & Form," Journal of The Interfaith Forum on Religion, Art and Architecture, Affiliate of the American Institute of Architects, vol. XVIII, spring 1985 (cover & feature article)

American Artist—An Illustrated Survey of Leading Contemporary Americans, by Les Krantz, The Krantz Co., 1985, Facts On File Publications, New York/Oxford

Washington Post, Sept. 29, 1985. Book review of above publication with photograph

"Contemporary Works from Maine," review of exhibition at University of Southern Maine Art Galleries, Gorham, ME, by William David Barry, *Portland Evening Express*, January 17, 1986, and *Art New England*, March 1986

"The Year Has Just Started, and This May Be Its Best Show," review of exhibition "Contemporary Works From Maine," at University of Maine, Gorham, by Edgar Allen Beem, *Maine Times*, January 24, 1986

"A Resurgence in Watercolor, But... (One Hundred Years of Watercolor)," New England Watercolor Society at Federal Reserve Bank of Boston, by Christine Temin, *The Boston Globe*, May 1986

"Beverly Hallam Makes Airbrush Magic" (feature article), by Robert Taylor, *The Boston Globe*, August 20, 1986

A Century of Color: Ogunquit, Maine's Art Colony 1886–1986, by Louise Tragard, Patricia E. Hart, W. L. Copithorne, Barn Gallery Associates Inc., 1987

New York Art Review (A Survey of the City's Museums, Galleries and Leading Artists), third edition, American References, 1988

Beverly Hallam, the Floral Image, Recent Paintings. Catalogue foreword by John Whitney Payson, an appreciation by Leslie D. Polk, journal notes by Hallam, Midtown Galleries, New York, NY, April 1988

"Hallam Exhibit Debuts at Midtown Galleries, Meet York Artist Beverly Hallam" (feature article), by Rose Safran, *The York Weekly*, York, ME, April 15, 1988

"York Artist in the Big Apple," review by Stuart Nudelman, *York County Coast Star*, May 25, 1988

"What's Hot: Art," review by Robert Taylor, *The Boston Sunday Globe*, June 5, 1988

"Happenings, Critic's Tip; Exhibits: Floral Magic" (featured review), by Robert Taylor, *The Boston Sunday Globe*, June 9, 1988

"Flower Power, Beverly Hallam's Floral Images Suggest the Eye Is Quicker Than the Hand" (feature article), by Edgar Allen Beem, *Maine Times*, June 24, 1988

"Beverly Hallam: The Floral Image," Hobe Sound Galleries North/Portland, review by William David Barry, *Art New England*, October 1988

"Art For Sale," *Florida Today*, October 8, 1988

"Voices of Maine," by Clark, Brosnan, Ward, and Crichlow. 35th anniversary issue, *Down East*, 1989

Maine Art Now, by Edgar Allen Beem, preface by Arthur Danto, The Dog Ear Press, Gardiner, ME, 1990

"Beverly Hallam: The Flower Paintings" (catalogue), text by John Whitney Payson, Evansville Museum of Arts & Science, Evansville, Indiana, 1990

"Floral Art Exhibit Blossoms," (feature article) by Sandra Knipe, The Evansville Press, Evansville, IN, April 20, 1990

"Airbrush Wizardry, Giant Floral Paintings to Add Touch of Color at Evansville Museum" (feature article), by Roger McBain, *The Sunday Courier*, Evansville, IN, April 22, 1990

"Airbrush Artistry, Mechanized Beauty, Maine Painter Brings Airbrush Canvases to Art Museum of Southeast Texas," by Shari Fey, *Beaumont Enterprise*, September 7, 1990

"Heavy Petals—Beverly Hallam's Art Stems from Flowers, Light, 'Horse Sense,' " by Arthur McCune, *The Ledger*, Lakeland, FL, February 7, 1991

"Beverly Hallam, The Flower Paintings," Polk Museum of Art Newsletter, January/April 1991

"Artist of the Week: Beverly Hallam, Seabury," by George Hosker Jr., York County *Focus*, August 28, 1991

"Museum in Bloom with Art and Flowers," by Bob Niss, *Portland Press Herald*, March 26, 1992

" 'Discovering' Women Artists: NMWA at Seville Expo," National Museum of Women in the Arts, Washington, DC, *Newsletter*, vol. IX, no. 4, winter 1992

"Museum in Bloom: Wall-to-Wall Arrangement Isn't Just for Show," by Greg Gadberry, *Maine Sunday Telegram*, March 22, 1992

Portland Museum of Art *Newsletter*, 1992 cover photograph

"Painting Acrylics with an Airbrush," by Beverly Hallam, *Watercolor 92*, an American Artist Publication, fall 1992

"American Artist Achievement Award/Airbrush," *American Artist Magazine*, June 1993

"On the Cutting Edge of Maine Art" (Portland Museum of Art), by Stuart Nudelman, *York County Coast Star*, March 3, 1993

"Mainescapes: Women Artists, 1900-1995," Ogunquit Museum of American Art, Sept. 5-30, 1995

"Different Beats: Maine Art in the 1950s," by Carl Little, *Down East*, January 1995

"The Importance of Thinking Abstractly," by Beverly Hallam, *Learning from Today's Art Masters*, an American Artist Publication, 1995

Women Artists, published by The National Museum of Women in the Arts, Washington, DC, 1995

Paintings of New England, by Carl Little; series editor Arnold Skolnick, Down East Books, Camden, Maine, 1996

"One Hundred Works from the 20th Century at the Colby College Museum of Art," by Lynn D. Marsden-Atlass, 1996

SOLO EXHIBITIONS:

1951 Boston Conservatory Auditorium, Boston Dance Theatre Associates presents "An Exhibition of Paintings by Beverly Hallam"

1952 Framingham State Teachers College, MA

1953 Wellesley College

Simmons College

Joe and Emily Lowe Art Center, Syracuse University "Paintings in Polyvinyl Acetate"

1954 DeCordova and Dana Museum, Lincoln, MA

Cambridge Art Association, MA

1955 Milton Academy, MA

1956 Institute of Contemporary Art, Boston

1957 20th Century Club, Boston, "Plants and Growing Things"

Shore Galleries, Boston (1959, 1962)

1962 Springfield Art Association, Springfield, IL

Shore Galleries, "Drawings and Paintings Done on Blanche E. Colman Award in Italy, France, and Spain"

1966 Nasson College, Springvale, ME, "Paintings in Acrylic Relief"

1968 Witte Memorial Museum, San Antonio, TX

Shore Galleries, "Monotypes"

1969 Lamont Gallery, The Phillips Exeter Academy, NH, "Monotypes"

University of Maine, Orono (Carnegie Hall) "Acrylic Paintings, Collage, and Reliefs"

Jewett Arts Center, Berwick Academy, ME, "Sea Change, A Collection of New Monotypes"

The Point Gallery, Kittery Point, ME, "Beverly Hallam's Window" (new monotypes)

1971 Addison Gallery of American Art, Phillips Academy, MA, "Retrospective Exhibition: Paintings, Drawings, and Monotypes, 1956–1971"

1972 Fitchburg Art Museum, MA "Paintings/Monotypes"

Fairweather Hardin Gallery, Chicago, "Recent Monotypes"

1973 Hobe Sound Galleries, Hobe Sound, FL, "Beverly Hallam/William Traber"

1975 Hildreth Gallery, Nasson College, Springvale, ME

"Beverly Hallam, A Decade of Monotypes"

1976 Westbrook College, ME, "A Selection of Monotypes"

1977 Institute of Contemporary Art (The Hermitage Restaurant), Boston, "Monotypes"

1979 Washington State College, Machias, ME, "Acrylic Castings and Paintings by Beverly Hallam"

1981 Ps Galleries, monotypes in silver, black and white, Ogunquit, ME (an exhibition with sculptor Harriett Matthews)

1984 Payson Weisberg Gallery, New York, "Recent Paintings"

William A. Farnsworth Library and Art Museum, Rockland, ME, "Aspects of Reality" (an exhibition with sculptor Abbott Pattison)

1988 Midtown Galleries, New York, "The Floral Image" (traveling exhibition)

Francesca Anderson Gallery, Boston

Hobe Sound Galleries North, Portland, ME

1990 Evansville Museum of Arts and Science, Evansville, IN, "Beverly Hallam: The Flower Paintings" (traveling exhibition)
Sheldon Swope Art Museum, Terre Haute, IN
Art Museum of Southeast Texas, Beaumont, TX
Bergen Museum of Art and Science, Paramus, NJ

1991 Polk Museum of Art, Lakeland, FL

1998 Farnsworth Art Museum, ME

GROUP EXHIBITIONS:

1944 Institute of Contemporary Art, Boston

1945 Institute of Contemporary Art, Boston

Stuart Art Gallery, Boston

1947 Boston Society of Independent Artists (1949–1954, 1956–1958)

1949 Ogunquit Art Association, Barn Gallery, Ogunquit, ME

1951 Symphony Hall, Boston (1952), subscribers exhibition

1952 Boston Arts Festival (1955, 1956, 1957, 1960, 1962, 1964)

The Silvermine Guild of Artists, New Canaan, CT (1955)

Massachusetts School of Art (faculty exhibition)

1953 Busch-Reisinger Museum, Harvard University, Cambridge Art Association (1954–1956, 1959, 1960)

1955 Boston Y.W.C.A.

1957 Boston University

1958 New England Watercolor Society (formerly, Boston Society of Water Color Painters) (1960–1965, 1967, 1986) Art Association of Nantucket, "Off Island Painters"

1959–1979
Shore Galleries, Newbury St., Boston/Provincetown, MA

1959 Portland Museum Art Festival, ME

1959–1960
Portland Museum of Art, "Ogunquit Art Association," December 8, 1959–January 8, 1960

1960 Institute of Contemporary Art, Boston, "View 1960," circulated through United States by Smithsonian Institution

1962 Pace Gallery, Boston

Stanhope Gallery, Boston

Auburndale Congregational Church, MA "Easter Festival of Religious Art"

1963 Radcliffe Graduate Center

DeCordova and Dana Museum, Lincoln, MA
"New England Art Part I—Drawings"
"New England Art Part II—Paintings"

Institute of Contemporary Art, Boston "Contributions—Exhibition Potlatch"

Fitchburg Art Museum, MA "Sixteen Massachusetts Women Painters"

Northeastern University, Boston
New England Contemporary Artists, Inc.
"New England Art Today," 1963
"New England Art Today," 1965

1964 DeCordova and Dana Museum "New England Art Part III—Paintings on Paper"

Ward-Nasse Gallery, Boston

Berwick Academy, ME "175th Anniversary Exhibition of Maine Art"

Ogunquit Museum of American Art (1970, 1971, 1978, 1979, 1980, 1984, 1989, 1991, 1995)

1965–1975 Fairweather Hardin Gallery, Chicago

1965 University of Connecticut

1966 Rhode Island Arts Festival

Institute of Contemporary Art and The Hague, Netherlands, "Art for U.S. Embassies," circulated by the State Department, Smithsonian Institution (1966–1970)

Prudential Center, Boston (1967)

1967 Carpenter Center for the Visual Arts, Harvard University

William A. Farnsworth Library and Art Museum, Rockland, ME

The American Watercolor Society, New York (traveling exhibition)

Chamberlayne Junior College, MA "Art Exhibition Preview"

Museum of Fine Arts, Springfield, MA "Eleventh Annual Eastern States Art Exhibition"

Barn Gallery, Ogunquit, ME "Art: Ogunquit" (national exhibition)

1968 Watercolor USA, Springfield, MO

DeCordova Museum

University of Maine, Orono, "Artists of Maine" (1969, 1970, 1972, 1973, 1976, 1978) (solo traveling exhibition of monotypes)

Horizon Gallery, Rockport, MA (1969, 1972)

1969 Berwick Academy, ME "Sea Change, A Collection of New Monotypes"

Priscilla Hartley Gallery, Kennebunkport, ME

Temple Beth El Art Festival, Portland, ME (1971)

Frost Gully Gallery, Freeport, ME

1970 DeCordova Museum, "Art Expo '70"

Boston City Hall

Down East Gallery, Washington, DC (1971, 1972)

University of Maine, Machias

1971 Barn Gallery, Ogunquit, ME "1971 Invitational Maine Artists' Exhibition"

DeCordova Museum, "Landscape II"

Art Festival of Tamworth New Hampshire

Bridgeton Arts Show, ME

The Maine Art Gallery, Wiscasset, ME "Five Women Artists"

"Ward-Nasse Gallery's SALON-71," SOHO, New York

1972 Old Sculpin Gallery, Martha's Vineyard Art Association, "Off Shore Artists" (invitational)

1974 Shore Galleries, Boston, "Sixteen Maine Artists"

Maine Coast Artists, Rockport, ME (1975–1977), (juried exhibitions) (1979, 1983)

1975 Lamont Gallery, The Phillips Exeter Academy, NH, "Artists from Maine"

The Talent Tree Gallery, Augusta, ME "Seven Selected Women Artists"

DeCordova Museum, "New England Women"

The Bowdoin College Museum of Art, Brunswick, ME, "Maine '75" (invitational art exhibition and sale)

Lamont Gallery, The Phillips Exeter Academy, Exeter, NH, "Artists from Maine" (a selection of painting and sculpture from the Frost Gully Gallery, Portland, ME)

1976 University of Maine, Orono, Carnegie Hall "Twenty-Five Women Artists"

Hobe Sound Galleries, Hobe Sound, FL "Expressions From Maine," traveling show: Pepperdine University, CA; Hamline University, MN; Headley Museum, KY; Agnes Scott College, GA

Maine State Museum, Augusta, "76 Maine Artists"

Hobe Sound Galleries, FL, "Fourth Annual Christmas Show Featuring Assemblages by Beverly Hallam"

1977 Institute of Contemporary Art, Boston "Collectors' Collect Contemporary"

1978 Talent Tree Gallery, Augusta, ME "Seven Selected Women Artists"

Colby College Museum of Art, Waterville, ME "Recent Acquisitions"

Ps Galleries, Ogunquit, ME

1980 The Joan Whitney Payson Gallery of Art, ME "Paperworks"

1981 Bowdoin College Museum of Art "Recent Acquisitions"

Ps Galleries, Ogunquit, ME, and Dallas, TX

1982 William A. Farnsworth Library and Art Museum "Selections from the Collection of the University of Maine, Orono"

University Art Galleries, NH, "New Friends: Recent Acquisitions to the Galleries"

Boston Symphony Hall, "Art in Support of Art" 1982 Musical Marathon

1983 Portland Museum of Art, ME "Works by Contemporary Maine Artists"

Maine Coast Artists, Rockport, ME "Painting and Sculpture" (invitational)

1984 Portland Museum of Art "Maine Drawing Biennial" (juried)

Bowdoin College Museum of Art "Inside/Outside" (Maine artists invitational)

Payson Weisberg Gallery, New York "Maine Streams" (Bellows, Buch, Cole, Etnier, Hallam, Hartley, Henri, Kuhn, Laurent, Marin, Sisson)

Robert Eric Moore Gallery, Rockport, ME

1985 Midtown Galleries, New York City "Seven New Members For Midtown" (Buch, Hallam, Laurent, Sisson, Iselin, Lyford, Estate of Langlais)

Midtown Galleries Inaugural Exhibition, New York City, "A New Era"

1986 University of Southern Maine, Gorham "Contemporary Works from Maine" (Clifford, Hallam, Laurent, Lynch, Nicoletti, Roberge, Ross, Ventimiglia)

New England Watercolor Society "100 Years of Watercolor 1886–1986" Federal Reserve Bank Gallery, Boston

1987 William A. Farnsworth Library and Art Museum "Invitational Featuring Artists from 11 Galleries"

1988 Francesca Anderson Gallery, Boston, MA "Almost Miniature: 7th Annual"

Art Expressions, Melbourne, FL "A Collaboration of Fine Art"

The Baxter Gallery, Portland School of Art, ME "Collectors: Contemporary Art from Maine Collections"

New England Center for Continuing Education, Durham, NH "Ogunquit Art Association" (1990)

The Ogunquit Art Center, "Ogunquit Art Association 60th Anniversary," Ogunquit, ME

Maine Nuclear Referendum Committee "Arts Auction II"

1989 Maine Coast Artists, Rockport, ME "From the Garden" (invitational)

Paul Creative Arts Center, University of New Hampshire "Highlights from the Permanent Collection"

Hobe Sound Galleries North, Premiere, Brunswick, ME "From the Twenties through the Present"

New England Center for Continuing Education, Durham, NH

Museum of Art of Ogunquit, "From the Collection of..."

1990 The Copley Society of Boston Exposition "Art Boston 1990," The Castle, Boston

Hobe Sound Galleries North, Brunswick, ME

Midtown Payson Galleries, New York "An Artist's Christmas" (holiday images by American artists 1880–1990)

1991 Hobe Sound Galleries, Hobe Sound, FL

Barn Gallery, Ogunquit, ME "Artists by Artists" (invitational)

Barn Gallery, Ogunquit, ME, "Four in Hand" (juried)

1992 Midtown Payson Galleries, New York "The Midtown Flower Show"

William A. Farnsworth Library and Art Museum, ME "Recent Acquisitions"

The National Museum of Women in the Arts, Washington, DC, World Expo '92, Seville, Spain

Bowdoin Art Museum, ME

Swan Coach House Gallery, Atlanta, GA

Portland Museum of Art, ME "The Flower Show" ("The Midtown Flower Show")

Maine Coast Artists, Rockport, ME "On the Edge: 40 Years of Maine Painting"

1993 The Barbara Scott Gallery, Bay Harbor Islands, FL, "Summer's Best"

Ogunquit Museum of American Art, 40th Anniversary, "Works from the Permanent Collection"

The Barbara Scott Gallery & Midtown Payson, New York, "An American Experience: Beverly Hallam, Walt Kuhn, Jack Levine, Hans Moller, Gregorio Prestopino"

Barn Gallery, Ogunquit, ME "Concerning Humor" (invitational)

1994 Ogunquit Art Association, ME, "Member's Choice" (Hallam's first-exhibited photographs)

1995 William A.Farnsworth Library and Art Museum, "Maine in the Late 20th Century" (Will Barnet, Dozier Bell, Brett Bigbee. Lois Dodd, Beverly Hallam, John Heliker, Alison Hildreth, Alex Katz, William Keinbusch, Alan Magee, Louise Nevelson, Fairfield Porter, Celeste Roberge, Karl Schrag, Neil Welliver, Jamie Wyeth)

Ogunquit Museum of American Art "Mainescapes: Women Artists, 1900–1995"

1996 Portland Museum of Art, ME "A Legacy for Maine: Selections from the Elizabeth B. Noyce Collection"

PUBLIC COLLECTIONS:

Addison Gallery of American Art, Andover, MA
The Art Gallery, University of New Hampshire
Bowdoin College Museum of Art
Colby College Museum of Art, Waterville, ME
The Corcoran Gallery of Art, Washington, DC
Currier Gallery of Art, Manchester, NH
DeCordova Museum, Lincoln, MA
Everson Museum, Syracuse, NY
Fitchburg Art Museum, MA
Fogg Art Museum (Harvard University Art Museums)
Lamont Gallery, The Phillips Exeter Academy, NH
McNay Art Museum, San Antonio, TX
Michigan State University, Kresge Art Center Gallery
National Museum of Women in the Arts, Washington, DC
Ogunquit Museum of American Art, ME
Portland Museum of Art, Portland, ME
Rose Art Museum, Brandeis University
University of Maine Museum of Art, Orono
University of Massachusetts
William A. Farnsworth Library and Art Museum, Rockland, ME
Witte Memorial Museum, San Antonio, TX
Worcester Art Museum, MA

CORPORATE COLLECTIONS:

Carnegie Corporation, New York
Central National Bank of Cleveland, OH
Ernst and Ernst, Chicago
First National Bank of Boston
Hine's Industry, Tulsa, OK
Isham, Lincoln & Beale, Chicago
The Kulicke Collection, New York
Marlennan Corporation, Chicago
Norman A. Coglin Associates, Chicago
Pierce, Atwood, Scriber, Allen & McKusick, Portland, ME
Ross, Hardies, O'Keefe, Babcock & Parsons, Chicago
Westinghouse Measurement Research Center, Iowa City

PRIVATE COLLECTIONS:

U.S.A., Canada, France, Belgium, Switzerland

AWARDS:

1955 Pearl Safir Award for Outstanding Painting by a Woman, The Silvermine Guild of Artists, New Canaan, CT

1956 Mina Pintner Memorial Award, Cambridge Art Association, Busch-Reisinger Museum, Harvard University

1957 Painting Prize (second), Boston Arts Festival

1958 First Prize, Cohasset Art Association, Cohasset, MA

1959 Popular Prize, Modern Group, Jordan Marsh Co., Boston

1960 First recipient: Blanche E. Colman Foundation Award $5,000.00 for Painting (Italy, France, Spain, Portugal)

First Prize, Cambridge Art Association, Busch-Reisinger Museum, Harvard University

1960 Hatfield Award, Boston Society of Watercolor Painters, Museum of Fine Arts, Boston

1962 First Prize, Edwin T. Webster Award, Boston Society of Watercolor Painters, Museum of Fine Arts, Boston

1964 Hatfield Award, Boston Society of Watercolor Painters, Museum of Fine Arts, Boston

1967 The A. H. Benoit Award in Graphics, "Art-Ogunquit," Barn Gallery, Ogunquit, ME

1973 1973 Medallion Award: "In recognition of having added distinction to the name of Lasell." Lasell Junior College, Auburndale, ME

1990 Deborah Morton Award, Deborah Morton Society Westbrook College, Portland, ME (selected Maine Women who have achieved distinction for their civic, humanitarian, or cultural leadership, or for their notable success in their profession)

1993 Artist Achievement Award/Airbrush, *American Artist*

VIDEO CASSETTE:

"Beverly Hallam: The Flower Paintings"
by Calvin Kimbrough, 1989, 15 minutes
Filmed in her studio, York, Maine
Evansville Museum of Arts and Science
411 Southeast Riverside Dr.
Evansville, IN 47713

REFERENCE MATERIAL:

Archives of American Art, Smithsonian Institution, Washington, DC

INDEX